Lecture Notes in Computer Science   8987

Commenced Publication in 1973
Founding and Former Series Editors:
Gerhard Goos, Juris Hartmanis, and Jan van Leeuwen

More information about this series at http://www.springer.com/series/7408

Bertrand Meyer · Martin Nordio (Eds.)

Software Engineering

International Summer Schools, LASER 2013–2014
Elba, Italy
Revised Tutorial Lectures

 Springer

Editors
Bertrand Meyer
ETH Zurich
Zürich
Switzerland

Martin Nordio
ETH Zurich
Zürich
Switzerland

ISSN 0302-9743   ISSN 1611-3349 (electronic)
Lecture Notes in Computer Science
ISBN 978-3-319-28405-7   ISBN 978-3-319-28406-4 (eBook)
DOI 10.1007/978-3-319-28406-4

Library of Congress Control Number: 2015958546

LNCS Sublibrary: SL2 – Programming and Software Engineering

Printed on acid-free paper

This Springer imprint is published by SpringerNature
The registered company is Springer International Publishing AG Switzerland

Preface

The LASER Summer School, organized by the Chair of Software Engineering at ETH Zurich, covers the concepts and practice of software engineering. Since its inception in 2004, the LASER Summer School has focused on an important software engineering topic each year. This volume contains selected lecture notes from the 10th LASER Summer School on Software Engineering: Software for the Cloud and Big Data, held during September 8–14, 2013, in Elba, Italy, and the 11th LASER Summer School on Software Engineering: Leading-Edge Software Engineering, held during September 7–13, 2014, in Elba, Italy.

This book contains contributions by Sebastian Proksch, Veronika Bauer, and Gail C. Murphy on building a recommendation system; Michael Jackson on behaviors as design components of cyber-physical systems; Carlo Ghezzi, Giovanni Paolo Gibilisco, Claudio Menghi, and Marco Miglierina on a control-theoretic approach to self-adaptive systems; Sebastian Burckhardt on consistency in distributed systems; Sven Amann, Stefanie Beyer, Katja Kevic, and Harald Gall on software mining studies; and Bertrand Meyer on a theory of programs.

We would like to thank the lecturers and their co-authors for contributing to this volume. We are grateful to Claudia Günthart, Nadia Polikarpova, Julian Tschannen, and the members of the ETH Chair of Software Engineering for assisting with the organization of the LASER Summer School. We thank Google, Microsoft, and ETH Zurich for their financial support.

September 2015

Bertrand Meyer
Martin Nordio

Contents

How to Build a Recommendation System for Software Engineering

Sebastian Proksch[1]([✉]), Veronika Bauer[2], and Gail C. Murphy[3]

[1] TU Darmstadt, Darmstadt, Germany
proksch@cs.tu-darmstadt.de
[2] TU München, Munich, Germany
bauerv@in.tum.de
[3] UBC, Vancouver, Canada
murphy@cs.ubc.ca

Abstract. Software developers must interact with large amounts of different types of information and perform many different activities to build a software system. To ease the finding of information and hone workflows, there has been growing interest in building recommenders that are intended to help software developers work more effectively. Building an effective recommender requires a deep understanding of the problem that is the target of a recommender, analysis of different aspects of the approach taken to perform the recommendations and design and evaluation of the mechanisms used to present recommendations to a developer. In this chapter, we outline the different steps that must be taken to develop an effective recommender system to aid software development.

1 Introduction

Software developers perform many different activities when building a software system: writing code, testing code, deploying to the cloud, coordinating via email and meetings, and many more [70]. Each of these activities requires finding and interacting with different kinds of information, using different tools and determining and preparing for the next activity to perform. For example, as part of writing code, a developer may inspect other code repositories to understand possible solutions, may browse web sites with relevant programming information, and may ask colleagues for information before programming a possible solution to the problem at hand and preparing to test the solution. For novice developers, performing these activities can be overwhelming. For expert developers, performing these activities near optimally is often impossible.

To ease the performance of activities and help hone workflow, recommender systems for software engineering have been introduced. Recommenders for software engineering are "software applications that provide information items estimated to be valuable for a software engineering task in a given context" [97]. Software developers are used to interacting with some recommenders that are directly related to coding activities. For example, in many integrated

© Springer International Publishing Switzerland 2015
B. Meyer and M. Nordio (Eds.): LASER 2013-2014, LNCS 8987, pp. 1–42, 2015.
DOI: 10.1007/978-3-319-28406-4_1

development environments, such as the Eclipse IDE[1], there are recommenders to overcome such problems as missing import statements in Java code. Recommenders for other activities and workflows have also been proposed, including recommenders for where code should be restructured [29], for which commands to learn next [76], and for requirements discovery [38], to name just a few. Recommenders for software engineering have been shown to provide productivity benefits; for example, the Eclipse Mylyn recommender, which provides individual recommendations of which source code is associated with a task, has been shown to improve developer productivity [53].

Given the wide range of activities a software developer performs, there are many untapped opportunities for improving software development with recommenders. In this chapter, we break the process of building a new recommender down into a series of steps:

- framing the problem (Sect. 2),
- determining the inputs (Sect. 3),
- building the recommender (Sect. 4),
- delivering the recommendations (Sect. 5), and
- evaluating the utility of the recommender (Sect. 6).

We describe each step using an example of a recommender to help a developer use an API of a library or framework with which they are unfamiliar. There are many ways in which such a recommender may be built and in how the recommender provides recommendations to a developer. As one example, the recommender could watch the code the developer is writing. If the developer becomes unsure of which type or method in an API of the framework to use, the developer can ask the recommender for suggestions. Based on the parts of the framework the developer is using, information collected about how other developers have used the framework and documentation and tutorial information gathered from web pages about the framework, the recommender could produce a list of suggested parts of the framework to use along with associated documentation.

Through this chapter, we use the following terminology. We use the terms *toolsmith* to refer to the individual or individuals designing and developing a software engineering recommender. We use the terms *user* and *developer* to refer to the individual making use of a software engineering recommender.

2 Framing the Problem

The first step in building a recommender is to determine what problem the recommender is intending to solve and to determine the assumption that a recommender can provide suggestions of value to a developer facing the problem. We refer to the many activities in this step as *framing* the problem.

---

[1] www.eclipse.org, verified 15/11/14.

The definition for a software engineering recommender we described in the introduction provides a basis on which to investigate the problem and solution targeted by a recommender. Specifically, when considering building a recommender, we must be clear about the *task* and *context* to which the recommender will apply. Additionally, we must consider for what kinds of developers, or *target users*, a recommender is intended.

The notion of a *task* targeted by a recommender refers to the particular goal of a developer at a given point in time, such as to implement an assigned feature in source code. Although a developer is always aware of the current task, the task may not be explicitly represented.

The notion of the *context* of a recommender refers to the information and tool environment in which the task is being performed, such as the source code and other artifacts available and the set of tools that can be used to perform the task. The context also captures the steps of a developer's activities for the given task.

The notion of *target users* for a recommender helps define when and what kinds of information a recommender might provide: novices typically have fundamentally different information need compared to expert users. Whilst the first group might find frequent proposals helpful, the latter often has a low tolerance for interruptions of their work that present already known facts.

> ### Example 1: Task, context, and target users
>
> For the recommender to help a developer use an API introduced in Sect. 1, the *task* is to find relevant types from the API to implement a specific piece of functionality by means of an unfamiliar library or framework.
>
> The *context* includes the source code on which the developer is working and web pages, including question and answer sites and open source repositories that provide examples of use of the parts of the framework of interest. The context may also include the actions a developer has taken recently in the development environment, such as recent searches for types or recent changes to the code.
>
> Our *target users* are experienced developers using a specific framework with which they are unfamiliar.
>
> In the absence of a recommender, developers may need to invest significant effort to manually search web pages and repositories. This may entail significant interruptions to their workflow, decreasing their productivity [71].

2.1 Understanding Task and Context

Obtaining a detailed understanding of the tasks that a recommender should support is critical for the success of the recommender. Without a detailed understanding, mismatches may occur between the perception of a task and the reality of a task that render recommendations invalid.

Assessing the Problem: A first activity to undertake is to assess the problem in terms of its generality, its frequency of occurrence and the impact of not

addressing the problem adequately. We use the term generality to refer to
the range of kinds of developers and range of different kinds of contexts—or
situations— across which the problem occurs. We use the term frequency to
refer to the number of times the problem occurs in a given context. We use the
term impact to refer to the severity of the problem, measured in such ways as the
perceived productivity gain or loss or the cost of recovering from the problem.

Example 2: Challenges

When using an API, the vocabulary problem [30] occurs frequently: a developer might correctly assume the presence of a specific functionality. However,
they might not guess the terminology or logical structure that the framework
designers used to capture the respective concepts [40]. As a result, they will
lose a significant amount of time before finding the required information.

Detailing the Problem: After establishing that a task is relevant enough to expend
effort to provide support, we need to understand the task in detail. This involves
understanding the scope of the task, the time at which it appears in different
workflows, and the different contexts that exist when the task manifests. Based
on this information, we need to pin down which aspects of a task we might
support with a recommender. Observational study of developer activities and
workflows is a rich method for obtaining a qualitative and detailed understanding of the task of interest. Furthermore, this study method can reveal useful
information about the context and the preferences of the target user group.
Other study methods can help to complete the picture; for instance, qualitative
and quantitative surveys and interviews can add requirements and clarifications
that may have been hidden during observation. We can distill the pieces of information retrieved from the qualitative studies into scenarios and use cases that
allow us to focus clearly on the specific situation we are going to support with
the recommender.

Example 3: Assessing the problem

Observation: During coding, a developer reaches a point at which the developer is no longer sure which method of a framework's API to use next.
The developer browses through the API by scrolling through the results
of the code completion offered by the IDE. The developer looks to see if
a more experienced colleagues is available. Last, the developer switches
to the browser and formulates tentative queries to find a solution. Once
a suitable solution has been found, the developer copies the solution into
their IDE and adapts it to their context.

Interview: In a follow-up interview, the developer states that she was expect-
ing a different logical organization of the framework. Furthermore, she
was reluctant to switch to the browser immediately because this inter-
rupts her train of thought. In the end, she realized that she had expected
different vocabulary for the given context.

Table 1. Methods that support framing activities based on [66].

Method	Scope	Types	Sources
AEIOU	Find components of problem domain	Qualitative, Exploratory	[116]
Contextual inquiry	Understand workflow, discover invisible work items	Qualitative, Exploratory	[9, 46]
Think aloud protocol	Capture reasoning guiding task execution	Qualitative, Exploratory, Evaluative	[28]
Observation	Collect sequence of interactions	Qualitative, Exploratory	[37, 55, 108, 120, 121]
Interviews	Collect judgement and impressions of target users	Qualitative, Exploratory, Generative, Evaluative	[55]
Laddering	Extract reasoning behind claims (e.g., during interviews)	Qualitative, Exploratory	[36, 39, 95, 99, 114]
Literature reviews	Understand current approaches including benefits and limitations	Qualitative, Exploratory	[11]
Concept mapping	Integrate multiple sources of information	Qualitative, Generative	[5, 6, 87, 88, 93]
Personas	Clearly define target user(s)	Qualitative, Generative	[17, 18, 25, 33]
Scenarios	Identify concrete situation(s) of interest	Qualitative, Generative	[15, 16, 33, 103]

Although we have presented these activities as first in a chain of activities to build a recommender, the activities may be interspersed with activities from other steps. In particular, choosing the aspects of a task to support partially involves considering available inputs (detailed in Sect. 3), investigating technical feasibility (see Sect. 4) and considering potential delivery mechanisms (see Sect. 5).

2.2 Supporting Methods and Techniques

There are many techniques available to help determine and assess the problem. Table 1 outlines specific methods that can be used for framing. We might need to begin with an *exploratory* technique to broadly understand the problem and the situation in which it occurs. When we need to better understand aspects of the problem in detail, a *qualitative* technique may be helpful. A *generative* technique helps suggest possible solutions based on how a user works. As we understand the problem in more detail, we might form hypotheses about the

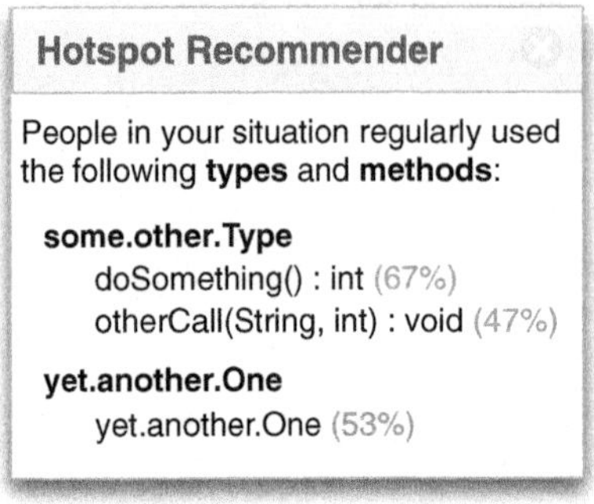

Hotspot Recommender

People in your situation regularly used
the following **types** and **methods**:

some.other.Type
    doSomething() : int (67%)
    otherCall(String, int) : void (47%)

yet.another.One
    yet.another.One (53%)

Fig. 1. Hotspot recommender

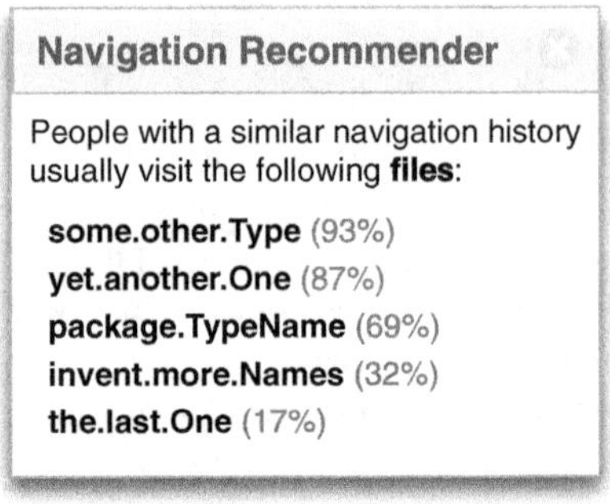

Navigation Recommender

People with a similar navigation history
usually visit the following **files**:

some.other.Type (93%)
yet.another.One (87%)
package.TypeName (69%)
invent.more.Names (32%)
the.last.One (17%)

Fig. 2. Navigation recommender

problem and potential solutions that an *evaluative* technique can help assess to further a toolsmith's understanding. As a toolsmith frames the problem, he or she will use multiple of these techniques. To further investigate a technique, the table indicates sources for further information.

2.3 Framing Results

The activities undertaken to frame the problem enable answer to the following questions:

– Who will be the *user* of the recommender?
– What *problem* is solved by the recommender?
   • In which contexts can the recommender be used?
   • When does the supported task start and end?
– Which *solution* is offered by the recommender?
– What is the *value proposition* of the recommender?

To provide concreteness to the outcome of framing, we answer these questions for four different aspects of the API usage problem that have been addressed by recommenders reported in the literature.

All examples assume that a developer works in an IDE and writes source code that uses a library or framework. The recommenders support common tasks like navigation in the code base, searching for examples, learning an API, and solving the task in case the developer is stuck.

Hotspot Recommender: For frameworks, it is often the case that some entities of the framework are supposed to be used in the context of others. In most user interface frameworks, for example, it is common to derive a super class that represents a `Pane` and to add widgets like `Button` or `TextField` to it. Another example is static methods that are used to access special entities of the framework.

User: Novice developers that are still unfamiliar with an API.

Problem: Writing source code in the editor of their IDE, novice developers are often not aware of classes relevant in their current context. They lose time, because they have to identify good terms first in order to find them or ask colleagues for help.

Recommender: The recommender suggests classes and methods that are regularly used in the current context.

Value: Time is saved when learning a new API. Even developers who know the API can benefit from convenient suggested access to relevant classes.

A sketch of a possible interface to a recommender that provides this kind of support is shown in Fig. 1. Working examples have been introduced in prior work, for example by Bruch et al. [13] and by Kersten [52].

Navigation Recommender: Object-oriented programming modularizes code into separate classes. Code must represent many different crosscutting concerns; the modularization can only capture a small number of concerns, leading to code for a concern being scattered across classes. To understand and change crosscutting code, developers have to navigate through many classes.

User: Developers working with existing code bases.

Problem: It is necessary to visit a number of different classes to understand or change all affected locations for a change of a crosscutting concern. Searching is not an efficient mechanism to use, because the locations are usually unknown and difficult to locate through search. As a result, developers spend significant time browsing the source code and may miss locations of interest.

Recommender: The developer is pointed to other locations in the code base that are related to the current task.

Value: Developers work more efficiently with lower cognitive overhead and the likelihood of missing a location is lower.

A sketch of a possible interface to a recommender that provides this kind of support is shown in Fig. 2. Working examples have been introduced in prior work, for example by DeLine et al. [22], Singer et al. [106], and Lee and Kang [57].

Snippet Recommender: To use frameworks and libraries efficiently, it is not uncommon that multiple classes of the framework have to be combined to work together. These classes have to be instantiated, configured, orchestrated, and executed as intended by the creators. In orchestrating this interaction, there are non-obvious pitfalls, such as implicit interaction protocols, necessary checks for corner cases, or simply incompatible configurations. Developers regularly search for working example code to understand how a specific API is used correctly.

User: Developers who work with frameworks or libraries.

Problem: Developers who lack experience with a particular API may find the API difficult to use. Sometimes, a single small piece of code is the difference between gaining the functionality desired from the framework or not. Finding examples of how to use a framework takes a lot of time and it can be challenging to find useful examples.

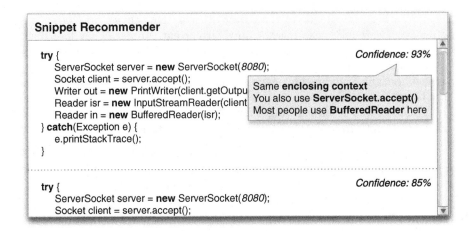

Fig. 3. Snippet recommender

Recommender: Related code snippets are provided that show how a specific API is used in released software.

Value: The most common rule in software engineering is *monkey see, monkey do.* Seeing how something is done correctly can significantly shorten the time to learn it.

A sketch of a possible interface to a recommender that provides this kind of support is shown in Fig. 3. Working examples have been introduced in prior work, for example by Holmes et al. [44], Nguyen et al. [80], and Sahavechaphan and Claypool [101].

Documentation Recommender: When learning a new API, the first step is often to read the documentation, the FAQs, and the tutorials provided by the creators of a framework. However, the resources are often outdated or do not exist at all. These resources may also not cover special cases as these cases were not anticipated by the creators of the framework. Sometimes, the framework simply does not meet the expectation and behaves differently. As a result, many developers use Q&A sites, such as StackOverflow[2] or other platforms, to find help or discuss their issues.

User: Developers that work with frameworks or libraries.

Problem: User-generated documentation is scattered across the internet, but it is hard to find for an individual developer. Most of the time the biggest challenge is finding the best search term to find the best document. Searches can require significant time and developers are likely to miss relevant information posted to an arbitrary platform.

Recommender: Related posts from various sources in the internet are aggregated and presented to the developer. They refer to the same context and discuss similar problems.

---

[2] stackoverflow.com, verified 18/02/15.

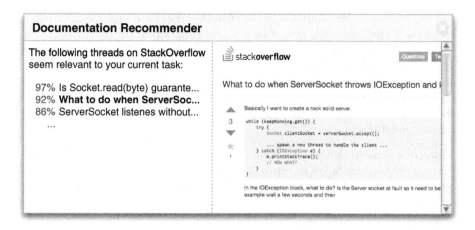

Fig. 4. StackOverflow recommender

Value: The time to find related documentation is significantly reduced.

A sketch of a possible interface to a recommender that provides this kind of support is shown in Fig. 4. Working examples have been introduced in prior work, for example by Henß et al. [42], Ponzanelli et al. [90], and Subramanian et al. [110].

3   Determining the Inputs

The toolsmith of a software engineering recommender must determine the inputs available to make a recommendation. The inputs available are dependent upon the context in which the intended recommender is to be used. If the recommender is to be used during programming in an IDE, there may be a number of inputs readily available including the source for the system and documentation for libraries being used. If the recommender is to suggest discussion threads in a forum, only information referred to in the forum may be available. When a toolsmith intends to make use of historical information as part of the possible inputs, the toolsmith must also determine how much of the historical information may be relevant to the recommendations. For instance, the past history of a source code file may not be relevant to a recommender suggesting how to overcome import statement problems in Java code, whereas the entire history of a forum may be relevant to determining to which discussions a current discussion pertains.

When designing the recommender, the toolsmith must consider the following questions:

– What kinds of information will the recommender require? For instance, will the recommender require source code, requirements, or information about a developer's activities?
– For each kind of information required, will the recommender require only the current state of the information or also historical information? For instance,

will the recommender require only the current state of a source file or previous revisions of the source file stored in a source code repository?

- If historical information is required, how far back in the history is the information relevant? For instance, are all issues in an issue repository relevant or only the past few months or years?
- If a desired source of information is not available in all instances, what are the alternatives? How will the lack of the information affect the quality of the recommendations?

To give a sense of the range of issues that must be considered by the toolsmith, we outline the range of types of input data that might be used and the preparation that might be required on those data types to be usable by the recommender.

3.1 Kinds of Input Data

There are multiple kinds of input data that could be used to drive a recommender. All input kinds come with advantages and drawbacks. There is no input class that is generally better than the rest, the toolsmith has to pick or combine inputs that are suitable for the recommender at hand.

Static Analysis. Input data may be generated by a *static analysis* of source code, either from the program on which the developer who will receive recommendations is working or from the large repositories of open source data that are accessible. The input data gained from static analysis is precise by definition because it follows the rules of the programming language. However, it can be challenging to ensure the source code of interest can be processed. For instance, all dependencies must be resolvable if the source code must be compiled. Additionally, toolsmiths may need to use a pre-processing or a screening step to ensure source code considered is of a suitable quality.

In addition to the information taken from the analyzed source code (e.g., involved types, invoked methods, etc.), further information about the editing process can be included as well (e.g., edit location, last change, etc.).

Example 4: Input from static analysis

To generate input for the *Hotspot Recommender*, a static analysis could extract all imports for each class to link all references between classes. For a more precise linking, the references could be extracted on method level, such that information about which other methods are called from within a specific method body is available.

User Feedback. A valuable kind of input data is feedback provided by developers that use the recommender, which may come via implicit feedback that is generated by transparently tracking interactions or explicit feedback provided by users. Unfortunately, this kind of input can be difficult to gather both due to ensuring appropriate consent is obtained and due to needing to motivate users to participate in providing feedback.

Tracked *user interactions* can be interpreted as *implicit feedback* [51]. For example, it is often possible to transparently capture all interactions of a developer while she is using an IDE. To achieve this, all existing tools have to be instrumented so that using the tools generates interaction events that can be stored. For example, to identify which features of an IDE are used, you could add a second listener to every button and menu item that logs every click in the IDE. Previous research has conducted such experiments [74].

While implicit feedback primarily contains information about the recommender that is used, it also provides feedback about the task at hand. Consider the case where a tool like the default code completion in Eclipse is instrumented to capture all interactions. The collected data can be used to analyze how developers typically use code completion, but it is also possible to use it as input to build a new recommender system for intelligent call completion [4].

Example 5: Generating navigation traces

Navigation traces could be tracked by monitoring the interaction of a developer to generate input for the *Navigation Recommender*. These traces describe how a developer navigated in the source code. Assuming that developers are not just randomly navigating all files, the order in which files were visited can be interpreted as implicit feedback about the relatedness of different files. It is expected to find patterns in such a data set taken from a large crowd of developers even though novice developers might visit irrelevant files regularly.

The tracking can happen on different levels: a simple approach could track the order in which files are opened or visited [106]. A more sophisticated approach could add more meta-data to those navigation steps to differentiate more, such as the navigation kind (e.g., the file was opened by browsing the source code or by explicitly searching for it), timing information (e.g., how long was the file visited), about the actions in the file (e.g., did the user scroll, were changes made), and so on.

Examples of *explicit feedback* are numerical ratings of recommendations, the reordering of proposals, or adding comments. A more traditional approach would be to use a questionnaire to learn about opinions and preferences of users. While the former can usually be incorporated when a recommender system is built, the later kind of feedback is hard to incorporate as input. However, it can serve as data for the evaluation of the system so its value should not be underestimated.

Example 6: Rating code snippets

Additional input for the *Snippet Recommender* could be generated by giving the developer the option to mark unrelated snippets. These rating can be used to further improve the data mining techniques or for evaluation purposes.

Whatever feedback is about to be collected –implicit or explicit– it is necessary to think about means of anonymization and to respect the privacy of the participants. Many people, especially developers, are very concerned about this and will not participate otherwise.

Unstructured Input. It is hard to use unstructured input to build a recommender, because at some point it needs to map to structured elements that are proposed to the developer. However, a plethora of unstructured information is available in the internet, which makes considering it as input worthwhile. Mapping structured and unstructured information works in both directions.

Destructuring: Source code is an example of a very structured form of input. However, it also contains substantial semantic information for the developer that is irrelevant for the compiler. Examples of the semantic information are identifiers in the source code like variable or method names and descriptions or explanations in comments. Noise can be reduced from this information by applying text mining techniques like *stemming* [64], by using automated spell correction to remove typos, or by identifying characteristic terms with a term frequency analysis [102].

Domain knowledge in software engineering can help to further improve the quality of the data. For example, it is common practice to split identifiers at the humps of the camel case notation [41]. Of course, there are also problems that cannot be tackled automatically, such as uncommon abbreviations or the simple fact that comments might be written in different languages.

Example 7: Destructuring of structured information

For the running example, we could tokenize the source code, split identifiers into words, and identify characteristic terms in comments. This converts a structured class file into a plain-text document that can be processed by established information retrieval techniques.

Structuring: Another source of input is the internet with reams of unstructured documentation and knowledge about software engineering tasks. Traditional sources are examples in books, tutorials, or lists of frequently asked questions. These traditional sources are often provided by the originators of the item of interest, such as a library or language, to demonstrate the use of the item. Newer examples of unstructured documentation are user-provided content in such form as blogs, forum posts, wiki pages, bug reports in issue repositories, or question and answer sites (e.g., StackOverflow).

Often, the unstructured content is labeled with structured elements; this labelling occurs in bug trackers, references to commit ids, ratings for postings, amongst others. The unstructured content may also contain semi-structured elements; that is, parts for which structure is expected but cannot be enforced as in example code snippets in postings and bug references in commit messages. If these semi-structured elements are preserved or if hidden structure can be recovered, they can help in mapping the content back to structured elements.

> **Example 8: Structuring of unstructured information**
>
> StackOverflow threads could be analyzed to generate input for the *Documentation Recommender*. For each thread, a vector of characteristic words could be created. Additionally, a dictionary could be created over all threads that contains the most characteristic words for StackOverflow discussions. The latter is used to locally identify characteristic words in a source file. After that, related threads could be identified.
>
> Another example that extracts information from StackOverflow was given by Subramanian et al. [110]. They created a tool called *Baker* that can recover code snippets from postings, add code elements to make them compile, and resolve all contained types. This type information is very valuable for the mapping of a source file under edit to relevant documentation on StackOverflow.

3.2 Preparing the Input Data

Once the input necessary to build the recommender is determined and an appropriate source for this data is identified, the input data has to be collected and transformed into a format that is processable by a machine.

Collection: A toolchain is necessary that automatically extracts the input data from the data sources. In addition to providing an import tool that extracts information from the input source, it is also necessary to think about a data management strategy. The extracted data need to be systematically stored on the hard-drive to make it easy to maintain it. This is true for all steps of the building process and all generated intermediate artifacts.

Clean-Up: Automatically extracted input data is usually very noisy: the data points can be incomplete, erroneous, or duplicated. The data needs to be cleaned before it is used in further steps and checked for validity. If a data point is identified as incorrect, it should be corrected—if possible—or discarded otherwise. It is important that this filtering is done very carefully and that the amount of filtered data points is analyzed. If the ratio of filtered data is too big, it might be necessary to provide a more robust implementation of the data collector instead.

Preprocessing: The collected data is usually not directly processable, because it is optimized for space efficiency, ease of collection, or for any other reason. A preprocessing step has to be applied to the raw data to transform it into a format that is processable by the following steps. Several collected data points might be aggregated into a single data point or the information might be enriched from other sources.

4 Building the Recommender

Once the inputs are determined, the toolsmith must choose one or more mechanisms for taking the inputs and transforming those inputs into a set of recommendations. This set may be empty, may have just one recommendation or may have a number of, possibly ranked, recommendations.

There are a variety of mechanisms that can be used to build a recommender system. Felfernig and colleagues break the mechanisms into collaborative filtering, content-based filtering and knowledge-based recommendation [50]. In this chapter, we briefly describe a broader set of mechanisms: static information, heuristic, data mining and machine learning, and collaborative filtering. We do not try to provide a comprehensive description of each mechanism category but instead describe how each mechanism might be applied to provide the example recommender we have been considering in this chapter. Our intent is to demonstrate that no one mechanism dominates, but instead the choice of mechanism must be made in concert with the quality of the recommendations to be produced.

4.1   Static Information

Perhaps the easiest approach to creating a recommender is to build upon the syntax or the static type system of a programming language. All necessary information is taken from the editing environment and the programming language. Examples of such a system are the Eclipse code completion[3] or Visual Studios IntelliSense.[4] Another example is a syntax recommender that completes language constructs like loops, conditions, etc.

Naturally, a recommender of this type typically performs well in terms of the speed of providing recommendations because few computations are necessary that are not already being performed. On the other hand, recommendations only reflect *syntactically correct* and *type safe* completions. The recommendations are not sensitive to the task at hand and are not based on any rationale so many proposals may be meaningless. As a result, a lot of recommendations may be presented to a developer and the expected precision of the recommendations is low. A recommender like this might be used by novice developers to explore available options or by seasoned project members to understand an existing code base during maintenance tasks.

An example of a more sophisticated approach that leverages type information is *Baker*, a tool that resolves types in code snippets from StackOverflow [110]. After the resolution is done, it is possible to bidirectionally link the example snippets and the corresponding API documentation. A link to the API is very convenient when browsing StackOverflow, and a list of usage examples of an API element is helpful to understand correct usage when reading the API documentation.

Example 9: Static information

A simple approach to build the *Navigation Recommender* aggregates all types used in the class currently under edit. The aggregation is presented in a list to provide an overview of frequently used items and to provide short cuts for the navigation. A drawback of this simple approach is that it cannot link new items, which are not yet included in the code. For further improvement, a ranking could be introduced to the listing by ordering the items according to the occurrence count.

---

[3] http://www.eclipse.org/jdt/overview.php#JDT_Text, verified 02/14/15.
[4] http://msdn.microsoft.com/en-us/library/hcw1s69b.aspx, verified 02/14/15.

4.2 Heuristics

A heuristic approach provides solutions for a problem that are based on experience or intuitions. No perfect proposals are expected from such systems, quality is usually traded in for execution time, memory consumption, or implementation effort. Sometimes these approaches are also called "recommendation systems in-the-small" [49].

There are three ways to come up with such heuristics. The straightforward approach is to leverage the experience of an expert in that domain. The heuristic reflects the intuition of the expert about the problem. However, it is also possible to identify heuristics in a more systematic manner. Data mining techniques can be applied to an available data set, to identify the heuristic and optimize or validate it for this dataset. Alternatively, by instrumenting the recommender tool and logging interaction with it, machine-learning techniques can be used to learn and refine the heuristic for the recommender on-the-fly.

Using heuristics for a recommender system has several advantages. They are comparably easy to implement, because they are usually not built with a sophisticated data mining technique. Therefore, it is not necessary to provide a complex infrastructure or big datasets as input to create a model for the recommender. Additionally, proposals can usually be computed very fast because the computation is only based on local data.

However, there are also some drawbacks. A heuristic does not produce *optimal* solutions, the precision and recall of the proposals is usually lower than for more sophisticated approaches. Additionally, substantial experience is typically necessary to identify valid and helpful heuristics and even then, it is still possible that the intuition of the expert is wrong.

There are many examples where heuristics are used to create recommender systems in software engineering. *Suade* identifies related groups of program elements and links them together [96]. *Strathcona* recommends source code examples similar to the current coding context, which are matched with simple heuristics [45]. *Quick Fix Scout* ranks quick fix[5] proposals by the reduction of compilation errors that a selection results in [78].

Example 10: Heuristic recommender

A trivial heuristic for the *documentation recommender* example is to use the current location in the source code to extract a search query for StackOverflow. For example, a search query could be generated that just contains the unqualified names of all implemented interfaces of the current class or the name of method that encloses the current coding location. The search query could be passed to StackOverflow and all resulting threads are just listed in the browsing window of the recommender.

---

[5] *QuickFix* is an Eclipse tool that can be triggered to get context sensitive support.

4.3   Data Mining and Machine Learning

Applying data mining or machine learning techniques to explore large amounts of data can also create recommender systems. The availability of increasing amounts of open source software and corresponding artifacts (e.g., bug reports) makes it more feasible to build recommenders in this way. The goal is to find re-occurring relationships or to detect patterns in the data that present valuable information about the inner workings of software.

Data mining and machine learning are rapidly changing areas, the techniques in these areas most related to recommendation systems in software engineering are:

Pattern detection: Often, the amount of available data makes it necessary to reduce information before it can be used to create recommendations. Many techniques exist that solve this by reducing the data to identified patterns, such as *frequent items mining, association rule mining,* or *clustering.* Applying these techniques is very common in the area of recommendation systems for software engineering [2,13,57,61,63,65,72,112].

Classification: Often it is necessary to classify new data points and to assign labels in an automatic way. A simple application of this approach is a *junk detector* for a mailbox, but it is also relevant for software engineering. An example application is the detection of outliers or anomalies [91,117]. It is also relevant in many recommender systems for the identification of the proposal that is most similar to a given context.

Information retrieval: and *text mining* Large amounts of data are available in the internet. However, most of it is stored in an unstructured form. There are many approaches that extract or recover knowledge from unstructured sources [40,43,64,90,102,110].

Online learning: In many cases, the data to be mined is not available when a recommender is build. Many approaches suffer from this *cold start problem*[6]. Online learning solves this issue with incremental learning [4]. The mining of increments, instead of complete datasets, also improves scalability.

Feature learning: It is hard to identify relevant features that best describe the current context. Previous work presented automated approaches that support this step [10,81].

In the area of recommendation systems in software engineering, these topics are usually intertwined and are not mutually exclusive. For example, after applying clustering techniques to build a model from data, classification techniques are used to find the best cluster in case of a request to the recommender. Another example is the application of information retrieval techniques to various sources to extract data. This data is analyzed afterwards with data mining techniques.

If a new recommender is to be built, there is not the one optimal technique that every recommender should use. The best solution always depends on the concrete recommendation problem. Exploring and developing possible solutions

---

[6] Also called the *ramp-up problem* [97].

is usually an iterative approach that requires the toolsmith to analyze intermediate results and improve the learning stepwise by fine-tuning configuration
options. Usually many configuration options exist and have to be evaluated to
find the best combinations. To give a sense of the ways in which data mining
and machine learning can be used, we cover several techniques that apply to the
recommenders we introduced in Sect. 2.3.

Frequent Itemset Mining. Can be applied to databases of items $I =$
$\{i_0, i_1, ..., i_n\}$ to detect set of items that frequently occur together. The *apriori* algorithm is the standard way to detect frequent itemsets [3]. The core idea
of the algorithm is to calculate the *support* of all items, i.e., their count in the
database. Afterwards, the items are combined to sets of items. A set is discarded
if its support is lower than a defined threshold.

This kind of data-mining has been successfully applied to create recommendation systems for software engineering. Nguyen et al. created the mining tool
GrouMiner that extracts code snippets from a large corpus of example source
code [83]. Li et al. base their inference of violation rules for their tool *PR-Miner*
on frequent itemsets that are mined from source code [59].

Example 11: Frequent itemset mining

To come up with a *snippet recommender*, the structural context can be used.
All programming constructs (e.g., loops, conditions, statements, etc.) are
broken down into smaller pieces. Similar to *GrouMiner*, these pieces are
iteratively combined to identify frequent snippets. If a recommendation is
requested, the structural context of the current edit location is used to find
and rank related snippets. The snippets are then presented to the developer
in an ordered list.

Association Rule Mining. Can be applied to databases of items $I =$
$\{i_0, i_1, ..., i_n\}$ to detect relations between items [2]. The mining algorithm identifies rules for reoccurring item combinations of the form $A \Rightarrow B$, where $A, B \subseteq I$.
A is called the *antecedent* or *body*, B is called the *consequent* or *head*. Each rule
also has values for *confidence* and *support*. The confidence value denotes how
likely it is to observe B if A is given, the support denotes how likely it is to
observe A. The *apriori* algorithm first mines frequent item sets in the database
and uses those sets to infer the association rules [3].

Based on a given set of mined rules, proposals are generated by finding
matching rules with unfulfilled implications. For example, assume that a rule
$i_x \rightarrow i_y, i_z$ was learned. Assume further that the recommender is triggered in a
context where i_x can be extracted from the context, but i_y or i_z are not present.
In such a case, both could be recommended. Instead of creating boolean proposals, the recommender could be further refined by calculating a probability for
each proposal by taking confidence and support of affected rules into account.

Association rule mining was successfully applied in the area of recommendation system in software engineering, for example in [13,61,65,72].

Example 12: Create a hotspot recommender

To create the *hotspot recommender* based on association rules, the available input information is restricted to the structural context information of the current enclosing method of the code that is edited (context c_i) and all fully-qualified method names m_j that can be observed in that context. It is easy to bootstrap a database consisting of the items $I = \{c_1, .., c_i, m_1, ...m_j\}$ by analyzing a source code repository.

The association rules are mined in the database, in which each data point consists of a single context c and multiple method invocations m_j. The same information is extracted from source code being edited by the developer and used to calculate proposals, whenever a recommendation is requested.

Clustering. Is usually applied to identify patterns and to group similar items. Using the same input as for association rules, one could use clustering algorithms like Canopy [68], K-means [62], or Expectation Maximization [23] to group similar items in the data into a cluster. All items in a cluster can be reduced to a representative value; for example, by averaging over all items in a cluster to calculate its *centroid* or by selecting the most representative item that is closest to the centroid. Huge amounts of input data are reduced to a smaller number of clusters, this leads to smaller models, better scaling approaches, and removes noise from the data.

After the input is clustered, a separate strategy is necessary to create proposals. In case of a request to the recommender system, a query is generated from the context of the developer. The query is then classified according to the clusters to come up with proposals. You can use the best match or a combination of the most similar examples to the query and combine them for the recommendation [12]. An alternative is to use probabilistic approaches like naive Bayes to assign a probability instead of assigning a single class and propose a list.

Clustering was successfully applied in the area of recommendation system in software engineering, for example in [57,63,112].

Example 13: Clustering

The approach to create a *hotspot recommender* by means of clustering is very similar to the previous example. The algorithm uses the same database I, detects similar items and groups them together in a cluster. In case of a recommendation request, a list of proposals can be generated from the cluster that is most similar to the context in which the recommender was triggered.

Event-Stream Mining: Frequent episode discovery can be applied to detect frequently reoccurring patterns in streams [1,56], these patterns are often called *sequences* or *episodes*. A stream s consists of events $e_1, e_2, ..., e_n$. Approaches that mine event streams often assume that the events build a Markov chain, a special case of a hidden Markov model [82]. These chains have the property, that the probability of any event e_n is only influenced by the previous i events $e_{n-i}, e_{n-i+1}, ..., e_n$. Restricting the event stream like this is often called a *sliding window* approach [31].

To apply these concepts to create recommendation systems for software engineering, the problem at hand either has to have event-based input or needs to be mapped to an event stream. There are examples were this was successfully applied. Wasylkowski et al. mapped source code to an event stream and mined temporal properties [117], this approach could be easily adapted to mining of navigation traces. Singer et al. mine the navigation histories of developers to identify related files [106]. Pradel et al. mined event streams taken from execution traces to capture usage protocols in automata [92]. Gabel et al. created an approach that learns and enforces temporal properties in method call sequences [31].

Example 14: Navigation-event stream

The navigation steps of developer form a stream of navigation events. A *navigation recommender* could be built by mining this stream to identify reoccurring navigation sequences. Whenever recommendations are requested, the navigation history of a developer is then used to propose likely next navigation steps to related files.

Text Mining: Prior work has shown that source code is natural and that it is possible to build a language model that captures the regularities [43]. Therefore, it is possible to apply established techniques from text mining to extract knowledge, as already discussed in Sect. 3.1.

Prior work introduced different ways to bridge the gap between unstructured information and the structured world of source code in which the developer is supported. Heinemann et al. tokenized source code and included variable names to better capture the intention of a developer [40]. Ponzanelli et al. identified important terms in source code [90]. They used these terms for a textual search on StackOverflow and ranked the results. Subramanian et al. recovered hidden source code structures from StackOverflow posts [110]. They introduced *deductive linking* to resolve missing typing information and bidirectionally link API documentation and examples on StackOverflow.

Example 15: Text mining

Text mining can be applied to create a *documentation recommender*. In a first step, all postings of StackOverflow are analyzed and characteristic terms are identified for all threads. If a recommendation is requested by a developer, the current source file is analyzed in a similar fashion: the source file is tokenized and characteristic terms are extracted for it. Proposals are created by finding the threads that are most similar to the current development context.

4.4   Collaborative Filtering

With collaborative filtering, a large dataset can be filtered for information [32, 111]. Observing the interactions of multiple *users* with *items* of a system generates the dataset. Examples of these interactions could be "buying a book", "reading an article", or "rating a post". The interactions can be positive indicators (e.g., a specific interaction was observed), boolean ratings (e.g., like or dislike), or continuous ratings (e.g., five-star rating).

There are two different approaches to use this data for recommendations. A *user-based* approach interprets the interactions as preferences of a user that describe opinions or personal taste. To generate recommendations for a user, similar users are identified based on shared preferences. Preferences of these similar users that are still unknown to the user in question are then proposed by the system. While this works well, the approach does not scale in practice. A newer approach is an *item-based* calculation. An *item-to-item* matrix is created that contains pairwise similarities of all items i_n. The similarity $sim(i_a, i_b)$ is calculated based on the ratings of all users that rated both items, usually the cosine similarity is used for that. Existing ratings of a user u for items similar to p are used to calculated the expected rating $r(u, p)$, i.e., an item p that is still unrated by user u. The drawback of this approach is that recommendations are not only based on a user but also on an item. To come up with the best recommendation, a recommender would need to iterate over all items and calculate the expected rating.

Collaborative filtering can be applied in different domains by mapping the concept of users and items accordingly. In the area of software engineering, a user could be a class definition and items could be method invocation. If a method invocation m exists in class c, it represents an interaction of c with m [69,118].

Example 16: Collaborative navigation recommendations

A recommender for the *navigation recommender* example could be created with collaborative filtering: assume that the navigation history between different contexts c is tracked for a developer with tuples of the form (c_{from}, c_{to}) where each tuple represents one navigation step. The rating of each navigation step is determined by its *usefulness* for the developer. This rating could be decided based on a threshold, such as higher rating is assigned if a developers stays in the target context long enough, if changes are performed there, or if the developer does not return to the original context. These tuples are used to build a large *context to context* matrix that contains the similarity of all contexts. This matrix is used to recommend the next navigation step to a developer by identifying users with similar navigation preferences.

Developers navigate all the time and they work on very different tasks each day. Simply aggregating the traces *by user* mixes up navigation histories for different tasks and is of little help to identify similar navigations. To make the navigation traces more precise, they should be generated *by coding session* or - if possible - even *by task*, to make it easier to find *similar navigation histories*.

5 Delivering the Recommendations

Even if a recommender can provide perfect recommendations, the recommender is not helpful unless it is designed to deliver the recommendations such that the recipient can act upon the information in a timely manner without interrupting or distracting more important parts of a task. Although there are many ways to deliver a recommendation, careful design is necessary to meet the constraints of providing recommendations. Even though a developer might need the information, it should be presented at a suitable point in time, at which the developer is not interrupted (e.g., after a specific time of inactivity or after a save action).

The following examples discusses trade-offs for the delivery of different recommenders that were introduced in Sect. 2.3.

Example 17: User requirements delivery

Considering the *snippet recommender*, the recommender might be capable of auto-completing the proposed source code snippets in the editor. Depending on the scope of the recommended snippets, user feedback may be required for the auto-completion, such as selecting or creating missing types. A developer that is using this recommender may expect an immediate response time and a clear presentation of available options. The developer may also want to see an explicit presentation of the differences between available recommendations.

Considering the *documentation recommender* that proposes related web pages, the recommendation might happen at a different time, even after the developer has integrated a recommendation into their code. When presenting ranked articles from the web, developers may be willing to wait longer for presentation of the information than for an auto-complete mechanism, as long as this delay does not block their workflow. Information that is not provided immediately should be presented in a separate window.

5.1 Delivery Quality Factors

Murphy-Hill and Murphy propose five quality characteristics that must be considered when delivering recommendations, namely *understandability, transparency, assessability, trust, and timing* [77]. These quality characteristics follow the natural flow of activities and decisions a developer using a software engineering recommender must make. If the flow is smooth between a developer's actions, the willingness of developers to rely on the recommender may rise. Frictions in this workflow risk interrupting the train of thoughts of developers using a recommender, who, subsequently, will perceive the recommender as a burden to their work.

Example 18: Delivery quality, user and toolsmith perspectives

In designing the delivery mechanism for our API usage recommender, we must consider the following questions.

Understandability: *What does the recommender suggest?*

The API usage recommender will present the user with snippets of framework code implementing a specific functionality, suggesting to include the code at the currently active point in a source code editor. From a toolsmith perspective, it is necessary to understand the exact steps of the delivery, e.g., which options are presented to the developer to select and insert the recommended code.

Transparency: *Why is the recommendation provided in this context?*

To justify the recommendations, our recommender would present reasoning based on which the recommendations were derived, such as: "in similar contexts, other developers have used the following functions". The toolsmith should consider the amount of detail needed by the developer to comprehend the reasoning behind the recommendation.

Assessability: *Is this recommendation relevant to my task?*

Our recommender complements the recommendations on the code level with information from the web, presenting the user with natural language descriptions of the recognized issues. This "summary" might increase the speed in which the user can assess the relevance to their current task.

Trust: *Will the recommender integrate the proposed change in a good way?*

When proposing changes to the code that exceed the scope of a few lines, the front end needs to provide the user with the possibility to interact with the insertion process. Possibilities could be guided stepwise execution of code changes, or a preview mechanisms.

Timing: *When is the recommendation most useful?*

There are several scenarios that can be supported with the example recommenders. In one scenario, the recommendation might be useful when the developer is stuck with their current task. In this case, we could wait for them to invoke the recommender manually. In another scenario, we could make the developer aware that there is a better way to solve their current task as soon as the recommender is sufficiently confident that the proposed solution is beneficial over what the developer is currently doing. For each scenario, toolsmiths should consider the exact workflow to find out natural points for providing the information to the developer.

Toolsmiths aiming for a smooth delivery need a very detailed understanding of the task, context, and user group they want to support (see Sect. 2). If these have been carefully framed initially, we can fall back on rich sources of information when designing the delivery mechanism. It is important to note that, whilst framing greatly increases the chances to get the user interface right, we still need to plan for several iterations to validate and improve our delivery mechanism (for UI evaluation methods see Sect. 6).

When selecting options for delivery, toolsmiths need to make choices in two important domains: interaction and presentation.

5.2   Interaction

Depending on the nature of the information presented by the recommender, toolsmiths need to choose between *proactive* or *reactive* paradigms to bring the results to the attention of the developer [77]. In the former, the recommender provides the user with results proactively whilst in the latter, the user explicitly prompts the recommender. Triggers for proactive recommending could be specific actions executed by the user, such as navigation and browsing patterns, or the specific current work context. Whilst a proactive interaction ensures that users do not miss potentially useful recommendations, it risks distracting users when it does not exactly fit their current needs. Thus, proactive interaction should be used only when the timing of the recommendation is critical (i.e. the recommendation is only useful right now and not at a later point) and the relevance can be assessed quickly.

For more extensive information with a longer validity, the user's attention can be attracted proactively; however, this should occur in a non-invasive way that allows the user to defer the reaction to a later point in time.

Example 19: Interaction choices

According to our framing, we want to support developers that are in the process of implementing a given functionality with an unfamiliar framework. This task requires them to build a clear mental model of what they are trying to achieve. Our recommender provides two kinds of information to support this task: on the one hand, it proposes functions of the framework by means of code in the style of the *snippet* or *hotspot recommenders*. On the other hand, it provides usage guidance from established websites, as proposed by the *documentation recommender* (for details on the recommenders, see Sect. 2.3).

Our recommender could support developers by means of a combination of proactive and reactive interaction, depending on their preferences and usage scenarios: we can assume a scenario in which developers will invoke the recommender whenever they do not know how to continue. We can, therefore, choose a reactive paradigm for the code recommendation, minimizing the interruptions to the user's workflow. To ease the assessability of the recommendations, we could proactively display the matching web resources for each recommendation the developers assess. In another scenario, we might provide the code recommendations proactively, and present additional information only when the developer prompts for it. In this scenario, the timing for drawing the developers attention to the recommendations is critical to avoid distraction.

Since both scenarios provide benefit to developers, we could consider offering both interaction modes and allow users to pick which they consider more suitable for their current task.

To make a decision for either of the paradigms, toolsmiths need to consider when information is required and how long it will be valid. These factors weigh against the cost of interruptions and context switches. In addition, studying the paradigms with which the developer usually performs similar tasks provides cues on how to craft a smooth integration into their workflow. The less friction the developers perceive, the higher they will estimate their productivity [71] and the value provided to them by the recommender.

5.3 Presentation

Three questions need to be answered with respect to the quality criteria introduced in the last section.

First, what kind of information must be shown to the user? If the recommendation involves information that is close, in terms of cognitive distance, to the user's current task, it might be sufficient to show the user the suggestions proposed by the recommender, possibly enhanced by pretty printing highlighting key words or concepts. Users need to establish a complex mental model to understand and assess the recommendations. Therefore, the toolsmith needs to provide background information and possibly provide additional information to surface why a recommendation is being made. It is important to consider the type of information that our recommender delivers. Does it communicate structure, locations in code, natural language, and key concepts? How many elements or information chunks does the recommender need to convey? Different ways exist to visualize software related information, the section depends on these characteristics (e.g., [24]).

Second, how will we make the information in a recommendation accessible? Our initial framing of the problem (Sect. 2) could help here in deciding whether to provide a separate tool or to integrate the recommender into an existing toolchain and interface. The integration of a recommender into a toolchain has to consider the interactions that make sense when no recommendations are available or when supplementary material, such as retrieved from a website, is unavailable due to being offline or on a slow connection.

Third, how should we capture the user's attention when recommendations are available? Many options are available, ranging from visual cues, such as annotations in editors, to popup windows [77]. Again, the results of framing may provide us with cues as to which kind of notification might be acceptable for the given situation.

Example 20: Visualization choices

According to our framing, we want to support developers that are implementing a given functionality. The required framework is unfamiliar to them. We aim to support them with suitable code propositions as well as background information on how to solve the given problem within the framework. This means that they will be focused on working within their IDE. To minimize the friction of using the recommender, it might be a good option to integrate the recommendations in their given development environment.

UI Representation Options. The UI choices are influenced by the nature of the information, as well as by the chosen representation: One approach is to piggyback our recommendations onto existing UI concepts. For instance, code recommenders often hook into already existing auto-complete functionality, which is usually triggered by keyboard shortcuts, thus integrating seamlessly into a developer's workflow. Using known graphical expressions, such as annotations and icons, is another way to tap into a conceptual vocabulary that is known to

Fig. 5. A potential API usage recommender - In this example, *navigation, snippet, and documentation recommenders* (see Sect. 2.3) are integrated into separate windows of an IDE. We build on the Prompter system that automatically suggests StackOverflow question and answers that may be relevant to the code being written (two views on right of screen) [90]. The recommender also shows classes used commonly by developers as part of using this API, building on ideas presented in Team Tracks for sharing navigation information, and an example of the API in use (bottom left of the screen), building on ideas from the Strathcona system for recommending examples [45].

our users. This way of reusing proven concepts has the benefits of being intuitive to our target group. However, this way of presenting recommendations carries the significant risk to overload the work environment. Current IDEs feature 500+ keyboard shortcuts[7] (involving up to four keys) which makes finding a suitable

---

[7] Counted from an eclipse cheat-sheet at http://de.scribd.com/doc/60629986/ Eclipse-Keyboard-Shortcuts.

command very challenging. As a result, we need to study carefully how to integrate and provide the recommendations even in already highly functionality rich environments.

Another approach is to develop new UI concepts that are tailored to the recommendations. For instance, in the API usage example, a navigable ontology of related framework functionality could be presented to users, enabling them to surf a specific part of the problem space. Or, new visual cues could be introduced to create user awareness of available recommendations with additional information encoded into the cues. An example of such tailored cues is the petal visualization for code smells [75]. An advantage of tailored UI concepts is that we can fit them perfectly to our kind of information. However, they require users to get acquainted with and learn how to read the visualizations. As a consequence, we cannot rely on proven strategies; we need to address the burden of validating the usefulness of the representation ourselves. This can incur a significant effort in evaluating the front-end iteratively with user studies.

In the following, we assume that the recommender will be integrated into an IDE[8]. Whilst this decision removes some presentation options, we still need to decide on how to present the recommendations to the user. Table 2 presents methods and techniques that can help when designing the user interface.

Integrating a Recommender in a Given Toolset. When integrating a recommender into an existing toolset, we need to consider a highly diverse range of topics starting from consistent interaction paradigms, to competition for screen real estate. Figure 5 displays a screenshot of such a possible recommender. The following paragraphs highlight several critical points of integration.

One detail that impacts the smoothness of integration is the adoption of the established interaction paradigms and conceptual vocabulary. We can reduce friction of use if we study carefully the characteristics of the host environment and make sure that we follow its conventions as much as possible. Aspects to consider include the predominance of reactive over proactive interaction, the logic of concept names or the conventions behind visual cues in the form of icons. Consistency in this respect supports users in intuitively understanding the suggestions of the recommender.

The number of recommendations can exceed the space available to represent them. In these cases, toolsmiths need ways to structure the content in a meaningful way. In the software engineering code recommender tradition, this situation is addressed either by delivering a small subsets of the results (such as the top five proposals [40]) or by presenting the results ranked by confidence [13].

Depending on the flexibility of the host environment, users might expect configuration options with respect to window arrangements, commands, and notifications. One important rule is that the user should remain in command. As a consequence, they should be able to determine which information to see.

---

[8] Following the argument that too many context switches between the use of different tools can significantly impact the productivity of a developer [73].

Table 2. Methods that support UI development activities based on [66].

Method	Scope	Types	Sources
Card sorting	Find out how users would categorize the information	Quantitative, Qualitative, Exploratory, Generative, Observational	[8,19,84,86, 109]
Contextual inquiry	Determine when, where, and how to display information	Qualitative, Innovative, Exploratory, Observational	[9,46]
Critical incident technique	Obtain feedback on when and how users get blocked or supported	Quantitative, Qualitative, Exploratory	[27,100,104, 105,113]
Prototyping	Validate technical feasibility and workflow support of design	Qualitative, Generative	[47,60,115]
Scenarios	Determine which information is valuable when	Qualitative, Exploratory, Generative, Evaluative	[15,16,33,103]
Task analysis	Find a natural point to provide the information	Qualitative, Exploratory, Observational	[20,37,54,55]
Wizard of Oz	Evaluate current UI choices	Quantitative, Qualitative, Generative, Evaluative, Observational	[14,26,34,89]

Furthermore, they must have the option to deactivate every proactive interaction mechanism the recommender offers.

Whatever innovative or conventional representation we choose, we need to validate it by collecting feedback from our users in an iterative process.

6   Evaluation

Each recommender consists of two parts, the proposal presentation and the recommender engine that creates the proposals. The quality of recommendations produced by different algorithms and in different situations may need to be evaluated to determine the overall best algorithm to embed in the recommender. However, even the best recommender is meaningless if its presentation of the recommendations is not understandable or the meaning of the proposals are hard to grasp so the presentation part needs to be evaluated as well. Unfortunately, evaluation is one of the hardest steps in building a useful recommender. There is no golden approach to achieve a perfect evaluation, it always depends on the problem and approach. The two main aspects of evaluation, accuracy and presentation, are intertwined.

In this section, we provide an overview of considerations in evaluation and provide references to other works that consider aspects of evaluation in more detail. The scientific community has a natural interest in creating reproducible, repeatable results, and reusable datasets. Therefore, this section also includes a discussion of good practices that every toolsmith should consider if a scientific publication of an approach is planned.

6.1   Recommender Engine

The evaluation of the underlying recommender engine should allow a comparison of different recommender approaches. The goal is to show that one approach is better than another. All recommender systems might be based on different models internally, but they are designed to provide the same kind of recommendations in the end. You cannot compare different types of recommenders.

Previous work stressed that it is necessary to use standardized datasets and common evaluation metrics in evaluations and that significance tests should support the findings [58]. Different options exist to evaluate a recommender system and all of them are valid alternatives. However, they present different advantages and drawbacks and a careful decision is necessary [94].

Evaluation Strategies. There are two ways to conduct an evaluation: empirical *user studies* and automated *experiments*. The selection depends on the aspects of the recommender that should be validated.

User Studies. Test the integrated recommender system with users. Developers may be observed as they use the recommender and such aspects as task completion can be measured. The assessment of the recommender may then involve comparisons of measurements with and without the recommender. User studies provide a very good insight in the impact of a recommender system on developers. However, major effort is necessary to conduct such an evaluation. Additionally, there are different biases: (1) The results are always intertwined with the presentation. It is not possible to evaluate an approach in separation, you can only measure the difference between two approaches within the same recommender type. (2) The results depend on the developers. Running study with novice developers and repeating it with experts may lead to different results.

It is important to consider both the *evaluation environment* and the *evaluation task* for a user studies, because they represent large differences in the setup. The two most contrary cases of user studies are *controlled experiments* and *field studies*.

A *controlled experiment* is conducted, if the evaluation should prove a strong implication. A controlled experiment takes place in an environment, in which external variables that influence the experiment are controlled or their influence on the results of the experiment is eliminated [107]. To conduct the experiment, the participants are grouped and different tasks are assigned to the groups. The tasks are manually designed and reflect a specific problem that is solved by the recommender system. Each group solves its task while having access to only one specific version of the recommender system. The performance is measured for all groups and the results of the different groups are analyzed to compare different approaches. The drawback of this approach is that it is hard to find participants, most of the time they have to be paid, so funding is necessary.

The focus of a *field study* is more to show causal effects. It is conducted in the work environment of the participants and better reflects a real scenario. The participants work on their day-to-day tasks, so it is necessary to think about means for a performance assessment, perhaps by observing and assessing them personally. Sometimes it is also possible to track participant behavior and to automatically assess the behaviors. Often, this kind of evaluation is conducted in collaboration with companies, who provide access to the developers. The involvement of companies may introduce additional overhead and there might be limitations to which kinds of results can be reported upon.

There are many nuances of evaluation styles in between controlled experiments and field studies. One example is a *case study*, which is similar to a controlled experiment. The main difference is that the environment in which the participants work is not controlled and that the participants usually work unsupervised [7]. While this results in more realistic results, it is usually a lot harder to assess the performance of the participants. A meaningful metric for the performance needs to be identified to create comparable results.

Example 21: Field study

To evaluate the *navigation recommender* in a user study, we would conduct a field study. We instrument both the IDE of the developers and their browsers. We collect the context in which a user is working and detect visited Stack-Overflow threads in the browser history. The combination of this information can be used to automatically evaluate, whether the recommender system is capable of proposing the visited threads, given the working context.

There is no clear answer which evaluation style to choose. The choice mainly depends on the question to answer and the available resources.

Automated Experiments. Present an alternative, in which the evaluation does not involve users. There are two styles in which an experimental evaluation can be conducted: *case-study* style and *cross-folding* style.

In *case study* style experiments, the toolsmith usually picks several corner cases and checks the proposed solutions from the tool with the expected outcome that is known a priori. The test scenarios are explicitly selected and the validation is correct. However, a high manual overhead is necessary to select the cases and, therefore, the number of scenarios is usually very limited. The evaluation might underline the strong scenarios of the approach, if only few scenarios are used and might miss scenarios in which the approach does not work well.

Example 22: Case-study-style experiments

To evaluate all kinds of recommenders introduced before, the toolsmith could pick examples from tutorials, books, guidelines, etc. that relate several classes or link to external documentation. It is also possible to manually craft examples; for example, by coming up with a problem and manually selecting related StackOverflow posts. The automated evaluation then analyzes if the external information is proposed by the recommender system, when queried in the specific scenario.

In *cross folding* style, observed examples are used as ground truth, evaluated through *cross validation*, a general technique used to evaluate the quality of a recommender system. The available dataset is split into n different buckets. One bucket is used as validation set and the remaining $n - 1$ buckets as the training set. This *cross folding* over the buckets ensures that no data point is used for training and validation at the same time, which would result in a over-fitting to the data. It is possible to use all available input for validation by rotating the validation bucket. Instead of creating the buckets by a random split over all available data, the toolsmith should ensure that all data extracted from a single project is assigned to the same bucket to avoid a bias introduced by inner-project relation (e.g., special coding or naming conventions).

Example 23: Cross-folding-style experiments

An n-fold cross validation could be used to evaluate the *hotspot recommender*. The input data is combinations of contexts (i.e., enclosing methods) and contained method calls. By removing some contained method calls, *incomplete* observations are created that can be given as queries to the recommender system. The removed method calls represent the expected outcome. The accuracy is determined by comparing the actual proposals and the expectation.

Evaluation Metrics. Regardless of the strategy that is used for the evaluation, it is necessary to represent the accuracy of an approach in a number that can be compared between the different approaches. There are a number of standard evaluation metrics that can be used for this purpose.

Recommender systems in software engineering usually propose either a single item or a group of items. To evaluate these proposals, they are compared to an expected outcome, such as a single item or a group of items. The proposals can be classified into *true positives* (i.e., relevant proposals), *false positives* (i.e., irrelevant proposals), and *false negatives* (i.e., missing proposals). If it is possible to enumerate all items that should not be proposed, then it is also possible to take *true negatives* into account (i.e., proposals that are left out correctly). These numbers are the same for all metrics, which metric to choose depends on the concrete recommender.

Most of the time evaluations consider input that was collected before so the categorization is easy (e.g., related files for the navigation recommender). However, sometimes there is no oracle that can identify true positives or true negative. Considering our StackOverflow recommender, we do not have a classification for all existing threads so it is hard to automatically decide about the relatedness of a given recommendation to the problem at hand without manual classification. Additionally, automated evaluation techniques have to show that

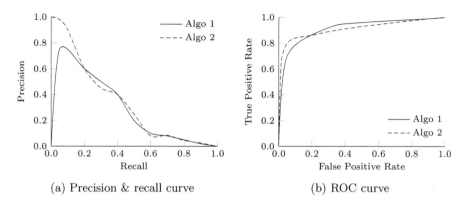

(a) Precision & recall curve   (b) ROC curve

Fig. 6. Different curves types

their automatic categorization reflects the human intuition. Many evaluations simply assume that without ever analyzing this assumption.

Precision and *Recall* are two common metrics used to assess the quality of recommender systems that propose a set of recommendations. While precision measures the ratio of correctly proposed items, recall measures the ratio of how many of the missing items are actually proposed.

$$precision = \frac{\#TP}{\#TP + \#FP} \qquad recall = \frac{\#TP}{\#TP + \#FN}$$

Both numbers can be visualized in a plot as shown in Fig. 6a. The optimal point is $(1,1)$, which means that all missing and no irrelevant items were proposed. However, real experiments usually show curves as shown. The precision is initially high, but decreases constantly with an increasing recall. An alternative visualization is a *receiver operating characteristic* (ROC) curve as shown in Fig. 6b. Here, the *true positive* and *false positive* rates are plotted. The optimal point in a ROC curve is $(0,1)$. Here the *true positive* rate is very high with few *false positives*. The closer the curve gets to the imaginary diagonal, the worse is the prediction quality. The diagonal itself would be the result of a random guessing approach and represents the worst case possible. Previous work has already proved that both the precision and recall curve and the ROC curve are related [21].

While these visualizations are helpful for the toolsmith in the tuning phase, they cannot be used in experiments, because it is hard to programmatically decide which plot is better. This is illustrated in Fig. 6b: while *Algo 1* provides better values in the left part of the plot, *Algo 2* is better in the right part. The solution is to calculate the *area under curve* (*AUC*) for both plots, this creates a comparable number for both approaches and the better one can be selected.

The same problem exists for *precision* and *recall*. Here, calculating the F_n *measure* combines both values into a single value that is comparable. The parameter n controls the weight of both values and can be used to emphasize the

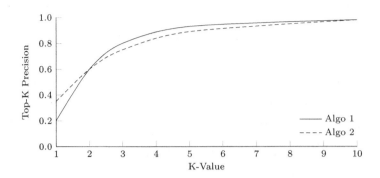

Fig. 7. Top-K precision curve

effect of one value. Usually F_1 is calculated, which represents the geometric mean of both values.

$$F_n = (1 + n^2) \cdot \frac{precision \cdot recall}{n^2 \cdot precision + recall}$$

An alternative measure for the quality of the proposals is *accuracy*. In addition to the positive proposals, it also takes the negative proposals into account. Therefore, all items that should not be proposed need to be enumerable.

$$accuracy = \frac{\#TP + \#TN}{\#TP + \#FP + \#TN + \#FN}$$

Recommender system that present a list of ranked proposals to find one missing item, are usually evaluated with *top-k precision*. Only the top k proposals are considered for the evaluation, if the missing item is included, it is considered a *hit*, otherwise a *miss*. The result of the evaluation lists the average top-k precision over all queries to the recommender system. The question is how many proposals should be presented to the user? Of course, less is preferable, because it is easier for the user, but the correct proposals should also be included in the list as many times as possible. To answer this, different k values are usually compared in a plot like the one shown in Fig. 7. The curve make it easy to decide how much an increase of k pays off in terms of quality. However, picking the right k is always a trade-off between achieved quality and ease of use.

Example 24: Evaluation metrics

To evaluate the *navigation recommender*, we could use collected navigation traces and remove the last step. By feeding the previous steps to the recommender, the next step is guessed in form of a list of candidate files. The previously removed step is searched in this list and its position is used to assess the quality.

The performance of different numbers of presented candidates could be compared in a top-k precision plot. This visualization is useful to fine-tune the number of files that should be proposed by the recommender. Usually, the top-k precision saturates with an increasing k. The challenge is to select a reasonably small k that is as close to the saturation point as possible.

The easiest way to evaluate the *documentation recommender*, is to conduct a user study. It is very time-consuming to automatically evaluate the quality of proposed StackOverflow threads. However, this can be done after collecting the data. Every time a developer triggers the recommender, the current working context and the proposed threads are stored. Afterwards, the relatedness is manually categorized for all proposals and the precision is calculated.

6.2   Presentation of Recommendations

Apart from the learning algorithm, the presentation of the recommendations needs to be evaluated as well to ensure that the recommender is useful to developers. Creating a recommender system is a two-step iterative process of designing the proposal presentation and evaluating its usefulness. Section 5 already presented techniques for designing, the focus of this section is on the evaluation.

The *proposal presentation* and the underlying *recommendation engine* are strongly intertwined in an evaluation. The perceived usefulness of the proposals is biased when bad recommendations are made, however, both are usually developed in parallel and it is impossible to expect good recommendations from an early version of the recommendation engine. To avoid a bias in these early stages, different techniques need to be used to evaluate the presentation that reflect the maturity of the recommender engine.

According to Murphy-Hill et al., the toolsmith should select an evaluation strategy for the evaluation that has the same level of commitment as the design approach [77]. We base the ideas in this section on their work and introduce evaluation strategies for three different stages in the creation process of a recommender system.

Up-Front UI Evaluation: When building a new recommender system for software engineering, you should evaluate your idea as soon as possible to validate that the recommender solves a real problem, provides value for developers, and that the presentation mechanism actually helps to access and use the recommendations. This is even necessary in the case when an established presentation concept is reused, because even though the recommender representation by itself is clear and clean-cut, it might interfere with other elements in the developer's work area or lead to an increased cognitive effort. It is not necessary to provide any working implementation in order to conduct an *up-front evaluation*. Instead, we can use sketches of a *mock-up* created in the early design stages and a clear vision of the recommender to explain its value to others.

A *heuristic evaluation* can be achieved by presenting the mock-up to users to get early feedback on the idea and the concept. As, in our case, developers are the target user group, they serve as a panel of experts that evaluate the usefulness of the new approach compared to established usability practices [85].

An alternative approach is to conduct an *cognitive walkthrough* as proposed by Wharton et al. [119]. In a first step, the toolsmiths can exercise this by themselves, but eventually users are walked through the interactions step-by-step. This is useful to validate that the recommender provides value to them without disturbing their workflow. In addition, walkthroughs make it possible to detect and remove inconsistent, disturbing, or incomplete concepts early on and to fine-tune the interaction with the recommender system.

Example 25: Up-front evaluation

The mock-ups that are shown in Sect. 2.3 could be used to discuss the concepts with developers. By illustrating all possible clicks in the mock-up, they can also be used in a cognitive walkthrough.

Early UI Evaluation: In order to evaluate a working tool as soon as possible, the first part of the recommender that should be implemented is the presentation. There is no need for the recommendation engine to be implemented; it can be replaced with a fake recommender that simulates the recommendation process. This can be done by either operating it manually in the background or by hardcoding specific answers into the fake recommender. This approach is called "Wizard of Oz" experiment [67].

The advantage of this evaluation approach is that the recommendations are perfect and, therefore, their quality does not influence the evaluation of the presentation. However, depending on the way the fake recommendations are created, either the production of recommendations has a high latency or the evaluated system supports only a limited number of working cases. In the later case, the manual effort of providing the examples is also very high.

Example 26: Early evaluation

Conduct a user study in which developers work on a specific task that is supported by the recommender system. A basic evaluation could use a questionnaire to formally capture opinions of the developers. More sophisticated evaluations have been introduced in Table 1. For example, the toolsmith could interview the participants [55], use think-aloud programming techniques [28], or establish basic measurements of the performance.

Integrated Evaluation: As soon as both the proposal presentation and the recommender engine are implemented, the whole system can be evaluated in an integrated evaluation by conducting a user study.

Example 27: Integrated evaluation

A user study can be conducted to evaluate the example recommenders. The main challenge is to find a way to measure the performance of the developer. This could be achieved via measurement of the average duration it takes a participant to finish a specific task or via calculation of the ratio of tasks that are correctly implemented by the study participants.

Evaluating the presentation of a recommender is a very time-consuming task. Many papers stop at one kind of evaluation and very few involve users. There is a chance for future evaluation to improve this situation.

6.3   Considerations for Good Scientific Practice

If a publication of the recommender system is intended, the toolsmith should follow good scientific practices. It is the focus of this section to introduce several practices that should be considered by the toolsmith.

An extensive evaluation of the approach is mandatory. It is expected that it shows that the approach generalizes to a large number of scenarios. Therefore, it is necessary that a diverse set of input scenarios is used and that this set is representative for the common case [79].

It is necessary not only that the findings are published, but that all necessary information is provided to allow other researchers to reproduce the results. Many publications do not meet this requirement [98]. The toolsmith needs to publish all tools used for the evaluation. Additionally, it is necessary to carefully describe the environment of the evaluation, especially if standard software is used that needs to be configured for the concrete use case. The exact configuration options need to be provided.

In addition to the evaluation tools, a reusable data set should be provided as well [48]. Both the raw input data and the preprocessed dataset should be published as artifacts. This is necessary to reproduce the results of the work, but it also encourages other researchers to solve the same recommendation task with different approaches. If external data is used (e.g., results from search engines or posts on Q&A sites), it is advisable to not reference the website directly, but to publish a local snapshot of the data (e.g., [35]). This snapshot serves as a stable base for a comparable evaluation, even though that evaluation might be run years after the original publication.

The published artifacts should support future extensions of the work. It should be easy for other researchers to try new ideas and to compare their results with the published work. A detailed description of implementation details helps other researchers to understand design decisions and supports an adaptation of the work.

7   Summary

Recommenders can help a developer perform the myriad of activities that must occur to build and deploy a successful and useful software system. However, it is far easier to hypothesize potentially useful recommenders than it is to construct a recommender and show that the recommender actually does provide value to a developer. In this chapter, we have outlined the questions that must be asked and the steps taken by a toolsmith to go from an idea of a recommender to focusing work on building that recommender and showing its value proposition. Through the use of examples and pointers to the literature, we have shown the variety of choices a toolsmith must make in the iterative process of recommender development.

Acknowledgements. We thank the organizers of the Laser 2014 Summer School for an invigorating week of discussion, which has carried through the writing of this chapter. We also thank the anonymous reviewer for the valuable comments and suggestions to improve the quality of the paper.

The work presented in this paper was partially funded by NSERC and by the German Federal Ministry of Education and Research (BMBF) within the Software Campus projects *KaVE* (grant no. 01IS12054), and *IndRe* (grant no. 01IS12057).

References

1. Achar, A., Laxman, S., Viswanathan, R., Sastry, P.: Discovering injective episodes with general partial orders. Data Min. Knowl. Discov. **25**(1), 67–108 (2012)
2. Agrawal, R., Imieliński, T., Swami, A.: Mining association rules between sets of items in large databases. In: SIGMOD Record, vol. 22, pp. 207–216. ACM (1993)
3. Agrawal, R., Srikant, R., et al.: Fast algorithms for mining association rules. Proc. of VLDB **1215**, 487–499 (1994)
4. Amann, S., Proksch, S., Mezini, M.: Method-call recommendations from implicit developer feedback. In: Proceedings of the International Workshop on Crowd-Sourcing in Software Engineering, pp. 5–6. ACM (2014)
5. Ausubel, D.P.: The Psychology of Meaningful Verbal Learning. Grune and Stratton, New York (1963)
6. Ausubel, D.P., Novak, J.D., Hanesian, H., et al.: Educational Psychology: A Cognitive View. Holt, Rinehart and Winston, New York (1968)
7. Baxter, P., Jack, S.: Qualitative case study methodology: study design and implementation for novice researchers. Qual. Rep. **13**(4), 544–559 (2008)
8. Berg, E.A.: A simple objective technique for measuring flexibility in thinking. J. Gen. Psychol. **39**(1), 15–22 (1948)
9. Beyer, H., Holtzblatt, K.: Contextual Design: A Customer-Centered Approach to Systems Designs. Morgan Kaufmann, San Fransisco (1997)
10. Blum, A.L., Langley, P.: Selection of relevant features and examples in machine learning. Artif. Intell. **97**(1), 245–271 (1997)
11. Booth, W.C., Colomb, G.G., Williams, J.M.: The Craft of Research. University of Chicago Press, Chicago (2003)
12. Bruch, M., Monperrus, M., Mezini, M.: Learning from examples to improve code completion systems. In: Proceedings of ESEC/FSE, pp. 213–222. ACM (2009)
13. Bruch, M., Schäfer, T., Mezini, M.: FrUiT: IDE support for framework understanding. In: Proceedings of the 2006 OOPSLA Workshop on Eclipse Technology eXchange, pp. 55–59. ACM (2006)
14. Buxton, B.: Sketching User Experiences: Getting the Design Right and the Right Design. Morgan Kaufmann, Amsterdam (2010)
15. Carroll, J.M.: Scenario-based Design: Envisioning Work and Technology in System Development. Wiley, New York (1995)
16. Carroll, J.M.: Making Use: Scenario-Based Design of Human-Computer Interactions. MIT Press, Cambridge (2000)
17. Cooper, A.: The Inmates are Running the Asylum: Why High-Tech Products Drive Us Crazy and How to Restore the Sanity, vol. 261. Sams Indianapolis, Indianapolis (1999)
18. Cooper, A.: The origin of personas. Innovation **23**(1), 26–29 (2004)
19. Coxon, A.P.M.: Sorting Data: Collection and Analysis, vol. 127. Sage Publications, USA (1999)

20. Crystal, A., Ellington, B.: Task analysis and human-computer interaction: approaches, techniques, and levels of analysis. In: Proceedings of AMCIS, p. 391 (2004)
21. Davis, J., Goadrich, M.: The relationship between precision-recall and ROC curves. In: Proceedings of the International Conference on Machine Learning, pp. 233–240. ACM (2006)
22. DeLine, R., Czerwinski, M., Robertson, G.: Easing program comprehension by sharing navigation data. In: IEEE Symposium on Visual Languages and Human-Centric Computing, pp. 241–248. IEEE (2005)
23. Dempster, A.P., Laird, N.M., Rubin, D.B.: Maximum likelihood from incomplete data via the EM algorithm. J. R. Stat. Soc. Ser. B (Methodol.) **39**, 1–38 (1977)
24. Diehl, S.: Software Visualization: Visualizing the Structure, Behaviour, and Evolution of Software. Springer, Heidelberg (2007)
25. Djajadiningrat, J.P., Gaver, W.W., Fres, J.: Interaction relabelling and extreme characters: methods for exploring aesthetic interactions. In: Proceedings of the Conference on Designing Interactive Systems: Processes, Practices, Methods, and Techniques, pp. 66–71. ACM (2000)
26. Dow, S., MacIntyre, B., Lee, J., Oezbek, C., Bolter, J.D., Gandy, M.: Wizard of Oz support throughout an iterative design process. IEEE Pervasive Comput. **4**(4), 18–26 (2005)
27. Flanagan, J.C.: The critical incident technique. Psychol. Bull. **51**(4), 327 (1954)
28. Fonteyn, M.E., Kuipers, B., Grobe, S.J.: A description of think aloud method and protocol analysis. Qual. Health Res. **3**(4), 430–441 (1993)
29. Foster, S.R., Griswold, W.G., Lerner, S.: WitchDoctor: IDE support for real-time auto-completion of refactorings. In: Proceedings of the International Conference on Software Engineering, ICSE 2012, pp. 222–232. IEEE Press, Piscataway (2012)
30. Furnas, G., Landauer, T., Gomez, L., Dumais, S.: The vocabulary problem in human-system communication. Commun. ACM **30**(11), 964–971 (1987)
31. Gabel, M., Su, Z.: Online inference and enforcement of temporal properties. In: Proceedings of the International Conference on Software Engineering, pp. 15–24. ACM (2010)
32. Goldberg, D., Nichols, D., Oki, B.M., Terry, D.: Using collaborative filtering to weave an information tapestry. Commun. ACM **35**(12), 61–70 (1992)
33. Goodwin, K.: Designing for the Digital Age: How to Create Human-Centered Products and Services. Wiley, New York (2011)
34. Gould, J.D., Conti, J., Hovanyecz, T.: Composing letters with a simulated listening typewriter. Commun. ACM **26**(4), 295–308 (1983)
35. Gousios, G.: The GHTorrent dataset and tool suite. In: Proceedings of the 10th Working Conference on Mining Software Repositories, pp. 233–236 (2013)
36. Gutman, J.: A means-end chain model based on consumer categorization processes. J. Mark. **46**, 60–72 (1982)
37. Hackos, J.T., Redish, J.: User and Task Analysis for Interface Design. Wiley, New York (1998)
38. Hariri, N., Castro-Herrer, C., Cleland-Huang, J., Mobasher, B.: Recommendation systems in requirements discovery. In: Robillard, M.P., Walker, R.J., Zimmermann, T. (eds.) Recommendation Systems in Software Engineering, Chap. 17, pp. 455–476. Springer, Heidelberg (2014)
39. Hawley, M.: Laddering: A Research Interview Technique for Uncovering Core Values. UX Matters (2009)

40. Heinemann, L., Bauer, V., Herrmannsdoerfer, M., Hummel, B.: Identifier-based context-dependent API method recommendation. In: Proceedings of CSMR (2012)

41. Heinemann, L., Hummel, B.: Recommending API methods based on identifier contexts. In: Proceedings of the International Workshop on Search-Driven Development: Users, Infrastructure, Tools, and Evaluation, pp. 1–4. ACM (2011)

42. Henß, S., Monperrus, M., Mezini, M.: Semi-automatically extracting FAQs to improve accessibility of software development knowledge. In: Proceedings of the International Conference on Software Engineering, ICSE 2012, pp. 793–803. IEEE Press, Piscataway (2012)

43. Hindle, A., Barr, E.T., Su, Z., Gabel, M., Devanbu, P.: On the naturalness of software. In: Proceedings of the International Conference on Software Engineering, pp. 837–847. IEEE (2012)

44. Holmes, R., Murphy, G.C.: Using structural context to recommend source code examples. In: Proceedings of the International Conference on Software Engineering, pp. 117–125. ACM (2005)

45. Holmes, R., Walker, R.J., Murphy, G.C.: Strathcona example recommendation tool. In: Proceedings of ESEC/FSE, pp. 237–240. ACM, New York (2005)

46. Holtzblatt, K., Wendell, J.B., Wood, S.: Rapid Contextual Design: A How-to Guide to Key Techniques for User-Centered Design. Elsevier, San Francisco (2004)

47. Houde, S., Hill, C.: What do prototypes prototype. Handb. Hum.-Comput. Interact. 2, 367–381 (1997)

48. Hummel, O.: Facilitating the comparison of software retrieval systems through a reference reuse collection. In: Proceedings of the ICSE Workshop on Search-Driven Development: Users, Infrastructure, Tools and Evaluation, pp. 17–20. ACM (2010)

49. Inozemtseva, L., Holmes, R., Walker, R.J.: Recommendation systems in-the-small. In: Robillard, M.P., Maalej, W., Walker, R.J., Zimmermann, T. (eds.) Recommendation Systems in Software Engineering, Chap. 4, pp. 77–92. Springer, Heidelberg (2014)

50. Jannach, D., Zanker, M., Felfernig, A., Friedrich, G.: Recommender Systems: An Introduction. Cambridge University Press, Cambridge (2010)

51. Kelly, D., Belkin, N.J.: Reading time, scrolling and interaction: exploring implicit sources of user preferences for relevance feedback. In: Proceedings of the SIGIR Conference on Research and Development in Information Retrieval, pp. 408–409. ACM (2001)

52. Kersten, M.: Focusing knowledge work with task context. Ph.D. thesis, University of British Columbia (2007)

53. Kersten, M., Murphy, G.C.: Using task context to improve programmer productivity. In: Young, M., Devanbu, P.T. (eds.) Proceedings of FSE, pp. 1–11. ACM (2006)

54. Kirwan, B., Ainsworth, L.K.: A Guide to Task Analysis: The Task Analysis Working Group. CRC Press, Boca Raton (1992)

55. Kuniavsky, M.: Observing the User Experience: A Practitioner's Guide to User Research. Morgan Kaufmann, Boston (2003)

56. Laxman, S., Sastry, P., Unnikrishnan, K.: Discovering frequent episodes and learning hidden markov models: a formal connection. IEEE Trans. Knowl. Data Eng. 17(11), 1505–1517 (2005)

57. Lee, S., Kang, S.: Clustering navigation sequences to create contexts for guiding code navigation. J. Syst. Softw. 86(8), 2154–2165 (2013)

58. Lessmann, S., Baesens, B., Mues, C., Pietsch, S.: Benchmarking classification models for software defect prediction: a proposed framework and novel findings. Trans. Softw. Eng. **34**(4), 485–496 (2008)

59. Li, Z., Zhou, Y.: Pr-miner: automatically extracting implicit programming rules and detecting violations in large software code. In: ACM SIGSOFT Software Engineering Notes, vol. 30, pp. 306–315. ACM (2005)

60. Lidwell, W., Holden, K., Butler, J.: Universal Principles of Design, Revised and Updated: 125 Ways to Enhance Usability, Influence Perception, Increase Appeal, Make Better Design Decisions, and Teach Through Design. Rockport Publishers, Rockport (2010)

61. Livshits, B., Zimmermann, T.: Dynamine: finding common error patterns by mining software revision histories. In: ACM SIGSOFT Software Engineering Notes, vol. 30, pp. 296–305. ACM (2005)

62. Lloyd, S.: Least squares quantization in PCM. IEEE Trans. Inf. Theor. **28**(2), 129–137 (1982)

63. Lo, D., Khoo, S.C.: Quark: empirical assessment of automaton-based specification miners. In: Proceedings of Working Conference on Reverse Engineering, pp. 51–60. IEEE (2006)

64. Lovins, J.B.: Development of a Stemming Algorithm. MIT Information Processing Group, Electronic Systems Laboratory, Cambridge (1968)

65. Lozano, A., Kellens, A., Mens, K., Arevalo, G., et al.: Mentor: mining entities to rules. In: Proceedings of the Belgian-Netherlands Evolution Workshop (2010)

66. Martin, B., Hanington, B., Hanington, B.M.: Universal Methods of Design: 100 Ways to Research Complex Problems, Develop Innovative Ideas, and Design Effective Solutions. Rockport Publishers, Rockport (2012)

67. Maulsby, D., Greenberg, S., Mander, R.: Prototyping an intelligent agent through wizard of Oz. In: Proceedings of the INTERACT 1993 and CHI 1993 Conference on Human Factors in Computing Systems, pp. 277–284. ACM (1993)

68. McCallum, A., Nigam, K., Ungar, L.H.: Efficient clustering of high-dimensional data sets with application to reference matching. In: Proceedings of the Sixth ACM SIGKDD International Conference on Knowledge Discovery and Data Mining, pp. 169–178. ACM (2000)

69. McCarey, F., Cinnéide, M.O., Kushmerick, N.: A case study on recommending reusable software components using collaborative filtering. In: Proceedings of the MSR, pp. 117–121. IET (2004)

70. Meyer, A., Fritz, T., Murphy, G., Zimmermann, T.: Software developers' perceptions of productivity. In: Proceedings of the ACM SIGSOFT Foundations of Software Engineering, pp. 19–29 (2014)

71. Meyer, A.N., Fritz, T., Murphy, G.C., Zimmermann, T.: Software developers' perceptions of productivity. In: Proceedings of SIGSOFT International Symposium on Foundations of Software Engineering (2014)

72. Michail, A.: Data mining library reuse patterns using generalized association rules. In: Proceedings of the International Conference on Software Engineering, pp. 167–176. ACM (2000)

73. Monsell, S.: Task switching. Elsevier TRENDS Cogn. Sci. **7**(3), 134–140 (2003)

74. Murphy, G.C., Kersten, M., Findlater, L.: How are java software developers using the elipse IDE? IEEE Softw. **23**(4), 76–83 (2006)

75. Murphy-Hill, E., Black, A.: An interactive ambient visualization for code smells (2010)

76. Murphy-Hill, E., Jiresal, R., Murphy, G.C.: Improving software developers' fluency by recommending development environment commands. In: Proceedings of the ACM SIGSOFT 20th International Symposium on the Foundations of Software Engineering, FSE 2012, pp. 42:1–42:11. ACM (2012). http://doi.acm.org/10.1145/2393596.2393645

77. Murphy-Hill, E., Murphy, G.C.: Recommendation delivery. In: Robillard, M.P., Maalej, W., Walker, R.J., Zimmermann, T. (eds.) Recommendation Systems in Software Engineering, Chap. 9, pp. 223–242. Springer, Heidelberg (2014)

78. Muşlu, K., Brun, Y., Holmes, R., Ernst, M.D., Notkin, D.: Speculative analysis of integrated development environment recommendations. ACM SIGPLAN Not. **47**(10), 669–682 (2012)

79. Nagappan, M., Zimmermann, T., Bird, C.: Diversity in software engineering research. In: Proceedings of ESEC/FSE, pp. 466–476. ACM (2013)

80. Nguyen, A.T., Nguyen, T.T., Nguyen, H.A., Tamrawi, A., Nguyen, H.V., Al-Kofahi, J., Nguyen, T.N.: Graph-based pattern-oriented, context-sensitive source code completion. In: Proceedings of the International Conference on Software Engineering, pp. 69–79. IEEE Press (2012)

81. Nguyen, H.A., Nguyen, T.T., Pham, N.H., Al-Kofahi, J.M., Nguyen, T.N.: Accurate and efficient structural characteristic feature extraction for clone detection. In: Chechik, M., Wirsing, M. (eds.) FASE 2009. LNCS, vol. 5503, pp. 440–455. Springer, Heidelberg (2009)

82. Nguyen, T.T., Nguyen, A.T., Nguyen, H.A., Nguyen, T.N.: A statistical semantic language model for source code. In: Proceedings of the 2013 9th Joint Meeting on Foundations of Software Engineering, pp. 532–542. ACM (2013)

83. Nguyen, T.T., Nguyen, H.A., Pham, N.H., Al-Kofahi, J.M., Nguyen, T.N.: Graph-based mining of multiple object usage patterns. In: Proceedings of ESEC/FSE, pp. 383–392. ACM (2009)

84. Nielsen, J.: Card Sorting: How Many Users to Test. Jakob Nielsen's Alertbox (2004)

85. Nielsen, J., Molich, R.: Heuristic evaluation of user interfaces. In: Proceedings of the SIGCHI Conference on Human Factors in Computing Systems, pp. 249–256. ACM (1990)

86. Nielsen, J., Sano, D.: Design of sunweb-sun microsystems' intranet. Useit.com (1994)

87. Novak, J.D.: Learning How to Learn. Cambridge University Press, Cambridge (1984)

88. Novak, J.D., Cañas, A.J.: The theory underlying concept maps and how to construct and use them. Technical report HMC CmapTools 2006–01, Institute for Human and Machine Computation (2008)

89. Patel, S., Bosley, W., Culyba, D., Haskell, S.A., Hosmer, A., Jackson, T., Liesegang, S.J., Stepniewicz, P., Valenti, J., Zayat, S., et al.: A guided performance interface for augmenting social experiences with an interactive animatronic character. In: AIIDE, pp. 72–79 (2006)

90. Ponzanelli, L., Bavota, G., Di Penta, M., Oliveto, R., Lanza, M.: Mining Stack-Overflow to turn the IDE into a self-confident programming prompter. In: Proceedings of the 11th Working Conference on Mining Software Repositories, MSR 2014, pp. 102–111. ACM (2014)

91. Pradel, M., Gross, T.R.: Leveraging test generation and specification mining for automated bug detection without false positives. In: International Conference on Software Engineering, pp. 288–298. IEEE (2012)

92. Pradel, M., Jaspan, C., Aldrich, J., Gross, T.R.: Statically checking API protocol conformance with mined multi-object specifications. In: Proceedings of the International Conference on Software Engineering, pp. 925–935. IEEE Press (2012)

93. Preszler, R.: Cooperative concept mapping: improving performance in undergraduate biology. J. Coll. Sci. Teach. **33**(6), 30–35 (2004)

94. Proksch, S., Amann, S., Mezini, M.: Towards standardized evaluation of developer-assistance tools. In: Proceedings of the 4th International Workshop on Recommendation Systems for Software Engineering, pp. 14–18. ACM (2014)

95. Reynolds, T.J., Gutman, J.: Laddering theory, method, analysis, and interpretation. J. Advertising Res. **28**(1), 11–31 (1988)

96. Robillard, M.P.: Topology analysis of software dependencies. ACM Trans. Softw. Eng. Methodol. **17**(4), 18 (2008)

97. Robillard, M., Walker, R., Zimmermann, T.: Recommendation systems for software engineering. Software **27**(4), 80–86 (2010)

98. Robles, G.: Replicating MSR: a study of the potential replicability of papers published in the mining software repositories proceedings. In: Proceedings of Mining Software Repositories, pp. 171–180. IEEE (2010)

99. Rosenberg, M.J.: Cognitive structure and attitudinal affect. J. Abnorm. Soc. Psychol. **53**(3), 367 (1956)

100. Ryan, G.W., Bernard, H.R.: Data Management and Analysis Methods. Handbook of Qualitative Research (2000)

101. Sahavechaphan, N., Claypool, K.: Xsnippet: mining for sample code. ACM Sigplan Not. **41**(10), 413–430 (2006)

102. Salton, G., Wong, A., Yang, C.S.: A vector space model for automatic indexing. Commun. ACM **18**(11), 613–620 (1975)

103. Schwarz, P.: The Art of the Long View–Planning for the Future in an Uncertain World. Currency Doubleday, New York (1991)

104. Serenko, A.: The use of interface agents for email notification in critical incidents. Int. J. Hum.-Comput. Stud. **64**(11), 1084–1098 (2006)

105. Serenko, A., Stach, A.: The impact of expectation disconfirmation on customer loyalty and recommendation behavior: investigating online travel and tourism services. J. Inf. Technol. Manag. **20**(3), 26–41 (2009)

106. Singer, J., Elves, R., Storey, M.A.: Navtracks: supporting navigation in software maintenance. In: Proceedings of the IEEE International Conference on Software Maintenance, ICSM 2005, pp. 325–334. IEEE Computer Society, Washington, DC, USA (2005)

107. Sjøberg, D.I., Hannay, J.E., Hansen, O., Kampenes, V.B., Karahasanovic, A., Liborg, N.K., Rekdal, A.C.: A survey of controlled experiments in software engineering. Trans. Softw. Eng. **31**(9), 733–753 (2005)

108. Sommer, B., Sommer, R.: A Practical Guide to Behavioral Research: Tools and Techniques. Oxford University Press, Oxford (1991)

109. Spencer, D.: Card Sorting: Designing Usable Categories. Rosenfeld Media, New York (2009)

110. Subramanian, S., Inozemtseva, L., Holmes, R.: Live API documentation. In: Proceedings of the International Conference on Software Engineering, ICSE 2014, pp. 643–652. ACM (2014)

111. Terveen, L., Hill, W.: Beyond recommender systems: helping people help each other. HCI New Millennium **1**, 487–509 (2001)

112. Thummalapenta, S., Xie, T.: Parseweb: a programmer assistant for reusing open source code on the web. In: Proceedings of the International Conference on Automated Software Engineering, pp. 204–213. ACM (2007)

113. Urquhart, C., Light, A., Thomas, R., Barker, A., Yeoman, A., Cooper, J., Armstrong, C., Fenton, R., Lonsdale, R., Spink, S.: Critical incident technique and explicitation interviewing in studies of information behavior. Libr. Inf. Sci. Res. **25**(1), 63–88 (2003)

114. Wansink, B.: Using laddering to understand and leverage a brand's equity. Qual. Mark. Res.: Int. J. **6**(2), 111–118 (2003)

115. Warfel, T.Z.: Prototyping: A Practitioner's Guide. Rosenfeld Media, New York (2009)

116. Wasson, C.: Ethnography in the field of design. Hum. Organ. **59**(4), 377–388 (2000)

117. Wasylkowski, A., Zeller, A., Lindig, C.: Detecting object usage anomalies. In: Proceedings of ESEC/FSE, pp. 35–44. ACM, New York (2007)

118. Weimer, M., Karatzoglou, A., Bruch, M.: Maximum margin code recommendation. In: Proceedings of the Conference on Recommender Systems (2009)

119. Wharton, C., Rieman, J., Lewis, C., Polson, P.: The cognitive walkthrough method: a practitioner's guide. In: Usability Inspection Methods, pp. 105–140. Wiley Inc. (1994)

120. Zeisel, J.: Inquiry by Design: Tools for Environment-Behaviour Research. CUP Archive (1984)

121. Zeisel, J.: Inquiry by Design: Environment/Behavior/Neuroscience in Architecture, Interiors, Landscape, and Planning. WW Norton and Co, York (2006)

Behaviours as Design Components of Cyber-Physical Systems

Michael Jackson[(✉)]

The Open University,
Milton Keynes MK7 6AA, UK
jacksonma@acm.org

Abstract. System behaviour is proposed as the core object of software development. The system comprises both the software machine and the problem world. The behaviour of the problem world is ensured by the combination of its given properties and the interacting behaviour of the machine. The fundamental requirements do not mandate specific system behaviour but demand that the behaviour exhibit certain desirable properties and achieve certain effects. These fundamental requirements therefore include usability, safety, reliability and others commonly regarded as 'non-functional'. A view of behaviour content and structure is presented, based on the Problem Frames approach, leading to a specification in terms of concurrent behaviour instances created and controlled within a tree structure. Development method is not addressed in this short paper; nor is software architecture. For brevity, and clearer visibility of the thread of the paper's theme, much incidental, explanatory, illustrative and detailed material is relegated to end notes. A final section summarises the claimed value of the approach in addressing the characteristic challenges of cyber-physical systems.

1 Introductory Remarks

In a cyber-physical system the software controls a part of the physical and human world. The system comprises both the computing equipment and the parts of the physical world it governs. Examples are vending machines, radio-therapy machines, cars, aircraft, trains, lifts, cranes, heart pacemakers, automatic lathes, ATMs, and countless others.

© Springer International Publishing Switzerland 2015
B. Meyer and M. Nordio (Eds.): LASER 2013-2014, LNCS 8987, pp. 43–62, 2015.
DOI: 10.1007/978-3-319-28406-4_2

This paper aims to explain and justify an improved version of the *Problem Frame* approach [1] to the development of such systems. The approach deals with the pre-formal[1] work that creates a bridge from the stakeholders' purposes and desires[2], leading to a detailed software specification, emphasising the centrality of the system behaviour. The main text of the paper is itself no more than an outline: some illustrations, clarifications and additional details are presented in notes, along with appeals to some eminent authorities.

The process of creating the bridge must start from the stakeholders' purposes and desires—that is, from the system requirements. But the satisfaction of those requirements by the running system in operation starts from the other end. The *machine*—the system's computing equipment executing the system's software—interacts with the physical *problem world* to monitor and control what happens there: it is the resulting *system behaviour*[3] that must satisfy the requirements. The system behaviour is the essential product of software development.

The requirements[4] are desired properties of the system behaviour; but they are distinct from it. The development problem, therefore, is to design a behaviour that satisfies the requirements, with an accompanying software specification that can be

---

[1] The work described is *pre-formal* because its desired product is a documented understanding of the system, sufficiently sound and well-structured to justify and guide the subsequent deployment of formal techniques. As von Neumann and Morgenstern wrote [3]:

"There is no point in using exact methods where there is no clarity in the concepts and issues to which they are to be applied. Consequently the initial task is to clarify the knowledge of the matter by further careful descriptive work."

In addition to careful description, software development demands exploration, invention and design. These activities must be open to unexpected discoveries, and should therefore not be constrained by *a priori* commitment to the tightly restricted semantics of a formal language. This does not mean that pre-formal work is condemned to gratuitous vagueness. It means only that for describing each particular topic and aspect that will be encountered the appropriate semantics and appropriate scope and level of abstraction cannot be exactly determined in advance. The freedom to make these choices in an incremental, opportunistic and emergent fashion should not be hampered by premature choice of a formal language.

[2] The stakeholders of a system are those people and organisations who have a legitimate claim to influence the design of the system behaviour. Some stakeholders—for example, the driver of a car or the wearer of a cardiac pacemaker—are themselves participants in the system behaviour. Others—for example, the representative of a regulatory body or of the company paying for the system—are not. Stakeholder purposes and desires may be formally or informally satisfiable, and may be observable in the problem world or outside it.

[3] The word *system* is often used to denote only the machine executing the software. Here, instead, we always use it to denote the machine and the physical problem world together. For a cyber-physical system the execution of the software is merely a means to obtain a desired behaviour in the physical world outside the machine, and has no significance except in that role. We use the word *behaviour* to denote either an assemblage of processes with multiple participants or an instance of the execution of the assemblage; which is meant should be clear from the context in each case.

[4] There are many kinds and forms of requirements. Some are constraints on budgets and delivery dates, on the composition and organisation of the development team, and other such matters of economic or social importance. Here we are concerned only with those requirements whose satisfaction is to be judged solely by the behaviours and effects of the system in operation.

shown to ensure that behaviour. Evaluating whether a proposed behaviour design is satisfactory must be a co-operative task for developers and stakeholders together[5]; producing and validating the accompanying software specification is primarily the developers' responsibility.

2   The World and the Machine

The problem world is, in general, a heterogeneous[6] assemblage of identifiable distinct parts of the material and human world that are of interest to the stakeholders. These parts are called *problem domains*: a vital task in development is investigating and analysing their *given properties* and behaviours on which the design will rely[7]. These properties are given, in the sense that they are independent of the machine[8]; but in combination with the domains' acceptance of the constraints imposed by the machine[9] they will determine the system behaviour[10].

---

[5] A stakeholder criterion of requirement satisfaction may lie far outside the problem world: for example, the system may be required to attract a large number of new, as yet unidentified, customers in new markets. A requirement may be insufficiently exact to allow rigorous validation: for example, that the behaviour of a car should never surprise its driver. Satisfaction of such requirements must be carefully considered by the stakeholders and developers during the design work; but cannot be formally demonstrated and can be convincingly evaluated only by experience with the installed system.

[6] The problem world of an avionics system, for example, includes the airframe, its control surfaces and undercarriage, the engines, the earth's atmosphere, the airport runways, the aviation fuel, the pilots and other crew, the passengers, the gates for embarkation and disembarkation, other aircraft, the air traffic control system, and so on.

[7] We regard the problem domains as given in the sense that the task of software engineering, *per se*, is not to develop or redesign physical artifacts, but to create software that will monitor and control their behaviour. In practice, of course, some projects may demand a degree of co-design of physical and software artifacts, and software engineers will have a central contribution to make to that work.

[8] The given properties and behaviours of a physical problem domain are constrained by the laws of physics, by its designed or otherwise constituted form, and also by its external environment. A domain is potentially capable of exhibiting varying behaviours according to the contexts in which it may be placed.

[9] Constraints on a domain's potential behaviour are applied by its context. In a cyber-physical system the immediate context comprises its physical neighbours—the machine and other domains with which it interacts. A domain that does not interact directly with the machine may be constrained by causal chains involving other domains.

[10] The system behaviour is not to be conceived or expressed as a set of stimulus-response pairs or in any other similarly fragmented form. It extends over time, and is to be understood as a whole. As Poincaré asked [4]:

"Would a naturalist imagine that he had an adequate knowledge of the elephant if he had never studied the animal except through a microscope?"
"It is the same in mathematics. When the logician has resolved each demonstration into a host of elementary operations, all of them correct, he will not yet be in possession of the whole reality; that indefinable something that constitutes the unity of the demonstration will still escape him completely."

The disadvantages of a fragmented view of behaviour are made explicit in another paper elsewhere [5].

The problem world must not exclude human domains. People participate in systems in many different roles—for example: as a casual user of a vending machine, as a plant operator, as the driver of a car or train or the pilot of an aircraft, as a passenger, as the patient in a surgical operation or a radiotherapy system, as the recipient of medication dispensed by an infusion pump, as the wearer of a cardiac pacemaker, as a source of problem world data that is otherwise inaccessible[11] to the machine. In various ways and to various extents the physical and behavioural properties of a human participant contribute to the system behaviour[12]. The development must investigate and understand them in all their relevant aspects.

We speak of the machine in the singular: a development problem has multiple problem domains, but only one machine. This is, of course, a conceptual simplification: the computing equipment of a realistic system may be distributed, and even shared with another system. The simplification is appropriate in an initial view of the problem: while the physical structure of the problem world is largely given, and offers clear enough distinctions among problem domains, the structure of the machine[13], which we must develop, has not yet been designed[14].

3   Challenges of Cyber-Physical Systems

Each system presents its own particular challenges to the developers; but some important challenges are common to all cyber-physical systems that are to any degree critical. Among the most salient are two intertwined challenges: formal description of the ineluctably physical problem world, and dependable design of the complex system behaviour. If the system behaviour resulting from its interactions with the designed software is to be the subject of fully convincing reasoning, the problem world must be

---

[11] For example, to describe the precise layout of a road junction for a traffic control system, and the positions within it of the lights, vehicle sensors and pedestrian crossing request buttons.

[12] For example, the physiology of a recipient of a cardiac pacemaker is crucial to the system design. So too is the physical size of a machine press operator whose safety depends on the limited arm span which prevents the operator from pressing the start button with one hand while the other hand is in the danger area.

[13] The machine specification produced by the development approach presented here is simultaneously physical—being explicitly described in terms of its interfaces to the physical world—and abstract—because it need not necessarily correspond to a software or hardware module of the eventual implementation.

[14] The problem world naturally presents itself to us as populated by distinct entities or domains, whereas the machine does not. The design process, briefly presented in later sections, allows decomposition of what was initially postulated to be one machine into two or more smaller machines.

formally described. But the problem world is not a formal universe[15]: any formalisation is an approximation, at best barely adequate to its particular purpose, context and use. The system behaviour of any realistic system is inevitably complex, and the non-formal nature of the problem world adds greatly to this complexity.

The response to the physicality challenge must itself be twofold. First: it must embody the practice of a sound modelling discipline[16] to minimise uncertainty in the mapping between each description and its physical subject. This is a requirement for any development method, and we will not discuss it further here.

Second: a dependable structuring of the system behaviour must address both the inherent complexity of the system's function and purpose, and the added complexity due to the non-formal physical problem world. Inherent complexity arises from the multiplicity of system functions, features, modes and phases of any realistic system. Further, design of a critical system is likely to demand a wide operating envelope, encompassing a very wide variety of conditions in which the system must behave dependably. This inherent complexity cannot be mastered by *ad hoc* variations within one monolithic behaviour. Instead, multiple behaviours must be specifically designed for specific conditions and functions and activated as conditions and needs demand.

The complexity added by the physicality of the problem world springs from reality's deviations from any one formal model, manifested as equipment failures, unexpected behaviour due to neglected physical effects, operator errors, and other exceptional contingencies. These deviations must be accommodated while maintaining safe and dependable—though possibly degraded—operation. This complexity may require a variety of formalisations of the same physical domains[17], which in turn requires a variety of behaviours that depend on those domains.

---

[15] In an unjustly neglected response [16] to Fred Brooks's acclaimed talk *No Silver Bullet*, Wlad Turski wrote:

"There are two fundamental difficulties involved in dealing with non-formal domains also known as 'the real world':

(1) Properties they enjoy are not necessarily expressible in any single linguistic system.
(2) The notion of mathematical (logical) proof does not apply to them."

This is the salient challenge that physicality presents to dependable system design. It is absent from abstract mathematical problem worlds, such as the world of integers and the problems of finding and dealing with large primes.

[16] Such a discipline would contribute to solving the problem characterised in an illuminating paper [17] by Brian Cantwell Smith as the relationship between the model and the world: "In the end, any adequate theory of action, and, consequently, any adequate theory of correctness, will have to take the model-world relationship into account". A discipline of description should constitute a major topic of research in its own right, but the need has been largely ignored by the software engineering community. Some aspects are touched on informally in a 1992 paper [18] and a 1995 book [19]. Further work is in progress but is not discussed in the present paper.

[17] For example, tolerating faults in physical equipment may demand at least two formalisations. In one, the equipment is assumed faultless, and the associated behaviour relies on that faultless functionality. In the other, the potentiality for fault is acknowledged, and the associated behaviour relies only on residual domain properties that allow faults to be detected, diagnosed, and mitigated. The two behaviours may be concurrently active, and the two—even potentially conflicting—formalisations are relied on simultaneously.

4   Dependability and the Problem World Boundary

The general form of a development problem is shown in Fig. 1.

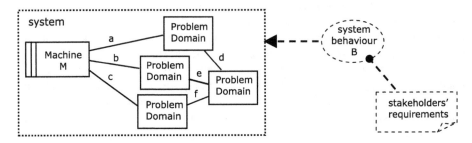

Fig. 1. Problem diagram

The single striped box represents the machine; the plain boxes represent problem domains; the solid lines (labelled *a,b,.. f*) represent interfaces of physical *shared phenomena* such as events and states[18]. Together, the machine, the problem domains, and their mutual interfaces constitute the *system*; the *system boundary* is represented by the dotted box. The ellipse represents the system behaviour[19] resulting from the interaction of the machine with the problem world. The document symbol represents the *requirements*.

Let us suppose that the developers have calculated or otherwise determined that the desired system behaviour is to be B; and that their designed behaviour of the machine at its problem world interfaces *a,b,c* is M[20]. Then, if the given behaviours of the problem domains are $\{Wi\}$, it is necessary for system dependability to demonstrate convincingly the *fundamental entailment*, that

---

[18] Phenomena are shared in the CSP [6] sense that more than one domain participates in the same event, or can observe the same element of a domain state. A shared event or shared mutable state is controlled by exactly one participating domain and observed by the other participants.

[19] In the problem diagram a symbol with a dashed outline represents a symbolic, possibly informal, description. The behaviour ellipse represents a behavioural description of the system. The requirements symbol represents a description of stakeholder desires and purposes. The level of abstraction at which the subject matter is described will, of course, vary according to the context and purpose of the description.

[20] The relationship between machine, problem world properties and system behaviour is complex. It should not be assumed that the machine design can be derived formally, or even systematically, from the other two. In particular, there may be more than one machine that can achieve a chosen behaviour in a given problem world.

$$M, \{Wi\} \,| = B.$$

That is: the designed machine M installed as shown in the problem world whose given domain properties are $\{Wi\}$, will ensure the behaviour B[21]. For a critical system this demonstration should be formal[22], to provide the strongest possible assurance of the system behaviour. The domain properties $\{Wi\}$—and the machine specification M—must therefore be captured in an adequate formalisation that is sufficiently faithful[23] to the physical realities it approximates.

---

[21] As Harel and Pnueli rightly observe [7]:

"While the design of the system and then its construction are no doubt of paramount importance (they are in fact the only things that ultimately count) they cannot be carried out without a clear understanding of the system's intended behavior. This assertion is not one which can be easily contested, and anyone who has ever had anything to do with a complex system has felt its seriousness. A natural, comprehensive, and understandable description of the behavioral aspects of a system is a must in all stages of the system's development cycle, and, for that matter, after it is completed too."

[22] The intrusion of non-formal concepts and concerns vitiates a formal demonstration. The system boundary is therefore related in its aim, though not in its realisation, to Dijkstra's notion of program specification as a firewall. He wrote [8]:

"The choice of functional specifications—and of the notation to write them down in—may be far from obvious, but their role is clear: it is to act as a logical 'firewall' between two different concerns. The one is the 'pleasantness problem,' i.e. the question of whether an engine meeting the specification is the engine we would like to have; the other one is the 'correctness problem,' i.e. the question of how to design an engine meeting the specification.... the two problems are most effectively tackled by... psychology and experimentation for the pleasantness problem and symbol manipulation for the correctness problem."

Dijkstra's aim was to achieve complete formality in program specification and construction. Our aim here is to preserve a sufficient degree of formality within the system boundary to achieve dependability of system behaviour. The firewall ensures—*pace* Dijkstra's dismissive characterisation of the 'pleasantness problem'—only that what is inside is sufficiently formal: not that everything outside is informal. Some requirements are formal: for example, the requirement in an electronic purse system that money is conserved in every transaction even if the transaction fails.

[23] All formalisation of the physical world, at the granularity relevant to most software engineering (though not, perhaps, to the engineering of experiments in particle physics) is conscious abstraction. Because the physical world, at this granularity, is not a formal system, a formal model can be only an approximation to the reality. In a formal world, after the instruction sequence

$$\text{"}x := P; y := x; x := y\text{"}$$

the condition "$x = P$" will certainly hold. But in a robotic system, after the sequence

$$\text{"}x := P; \ Arm.moveTo(x); x := Arm.currentPosition\text{"}$$

the condition "$x = P$" may not hold. Moving the arm and sensing its position both involve state phenomena of the physical world. Movement of the arm may fail, and will certainly be imprecise; and the resulting position will be imprecisely sensed and further approximated in the machine by a floating-point number.

Unreliability and approximation limit the dependability of any cyber-physical system [9] and the confidence that can be legitimately placed in formal demonstration. A crucial concern in the design of a critical system is achieving acceptable dependability within these limits.

Furthermore, the problem world and machine must be regarded as a closed system: the demonstration of the fundamental entailment must not rely on any assertion that cannot be inferred from the physical laws of nature and the explicitly stated properties[24] of the problem domains[25]. These constraints on the problem world necessitate the distinction[26] shown in Fig. 1 between the system behaviour and the stakeholders' requirements—which are often informal, and often related to parts of the world outside the system boundary.

5 Complexity of System Behaviour

Satisfying the system requirements may demand great behavioural complexity. Some of this complexity springs from normal system operation, which may comprise many necessary functions and features structured in multiple phases and modes[27]. Interaction among these functions (especially when they operate concurrently, but also when they are consecutive, or nested, or alternating) is a source of further complexity[28]. Some complexity is due to the need to detect and mitigate equipment faults, operator errors or other exceptional events. Some springs from the need to coordinate normal operation

---

[24] The given properties of each problem domain must be investigated and explicitly described: together, they provide the $\{Wi\}$ in the entailment $M,\{Wi\} \models B$. It is a mistake to elide these descriptions into a single description encompassing both the machine and the problem domains. A separate description of a domain's given properties clearly distinguishes what the machine relies on from what it must achieve, and allows those potential properties and behaviours to be made explicit that the machine, by its behaviour, suppresses, avoids or neglects.

[25] The system can be closed in the necessary sense by *internalising* external impacts on the problem domains. Suppose, for example, that domains A and B are both vulnerable to failure of a common electrical power supply P. If P is not included as a problem domain, electrical power failure in A must be formalised as a spontaneous and unpredictable internal event of A, and similarly for B. It is then impermissible to assert that power failures of A and B are coordinated, since there is no problem domain to which this co-ordination can be ascribed. Similarly, in an automotive system the driver must be included as a problem domain if the driver's physical capabilities and expected behaviours are relied on to prove the entailment $M,\{Wi\} \models B$.

[26] Unfortunately, in many development projects this distinction is elided, and requirements are stated as explicit direct descriptions—albeit often fragmented descriptions—of system behaviour. This is a mistake, exactly parallel to the classic mistake of specifying a program by giving a procedural description of its behaviour in execution.

[27] For example, an avionics system must support the normal sequence of flight phases: gate departure, taxiing, take-off, climbing, cruising, and so on. A radiotherapy system must support the normal prescription and treatment protocols: prescription specification and checking, patient positioning, position adjustment, beam focusing, dose delivery, beam shutoff, and so on.

[28] In telephone systems of the late 20th century such features as call forwarding, call blocking and voicemail proliferated. The complexity resulting from their interactions caused ever-increasing difficulty in the development of those systems, and often produced inconvenient and disagreeable surprises for users. This *feature interaction* problem [10, 11] became widely known: it was soon recognised as a serious problem in most realistic systems.

with equipment maintenance and repair. Some is due to the need to maintain safe operation even in extreme adverse conditions.

In general, dependable system behaviour means behaviour that varies in a comprehensibly dependable[29] way, according to what is possible and desirable in different circumstances. Fault tolerance, for example, does not demand that normal functional behaviour continue in the presence of a major fault, but permits it to be replaced by a different behaviour, functionally degraded but dependable and preserving safety[30]. Complex system behaviour is understood as a combination of simpler *constituent behaviours*. A constituent behaviour has the same structure and pattern as the complete system behaviour pictured in Fig. 1: it has a machine, an assemblage of problem domains, and a number of relevant requirements. The development problem, both for the complete behaviour and for each constituent behaviour, has two interrelated aspects: to design a behaviour to satisfy the requirements; and to specify an associated machine that will ensure that behaviour[31].

An ill-chosen constituent can complicate the task of developing the whole to which it belongs—either by itself presenting excessive difficulty in its own development, or by leaving a misshapen residual complement[32]. Identifying suitable constituent behaviours is the primary task in structuring the system behaviour. An essential guide in this

---

[29] 'Comprehensibly dependable' does not imply 'predictable'. A realistic system has problem domains— notably its human participants—that exhibit non-deterministic behaviour. In general, therefore, prediction of system behaviour is always contingent. What matters is that neither the developers nor the human participants should be surprised by unexpected occurrences of anomalous behaviour.

[30] For example, if the main power supply fails in a passenger lift system the car is to be moved, under auxiliary power, to the nearest floor for the passengers to disembark. If the hoist cable breaks a more radical solution is necessary: the lift car is locked in the shaft to prevent free fall, and the passengers must then wait to be rescued by an engineering crew.

[31] The development problem for a constituent behaviour is spoken of as a *subproblem*. Initially the constituent behaviour is considered in isolation from other behaviours, ignoring both its interactions at common problem domains and its interaction with its controlling behaviour. (Behaviour control is discussed in Sect. 8.)

[32] The second of Descartes's famous rules of thought [12] was:

"Divide each problem that you examine into as many parts as you can and as you need to solve them more easily."

Leibniz rightly observed in response [13]:

"This rule of Descartes is of little use as long as the art of dividing remains unexplained… By dividing his problem into unsuitable parts, the inexperienced problem-solver may increase his difficulty."

Any discipline that aims to master complexity by decomposition must identify and apply criteria of component simplicity.

task is a set of explicit criteria of behavioural simplicity. These criteria include: regularity of the machine's software structure[33]; constancy of given domain properties during the behaviour[34]; a clear and tersely explicable purpose for the behaviour[35]; and simplicity of the causal pattern by which the machine ensures the behaviour in the problem world[36].

6 Large Behaviour Structure: Principles

This structuring of complex system behaviour, in terms of constituent behaviours, aims above all at producing an understandable and verifiable[37] specification of system behaviour. It is not the immediate aim of this structuring to produce a modular software structure capable of translation into efficient executable code. If a specification is executable, that is an advantage. But the primary aim is intelligibility of the system behaviour, demanding a correspondence between constituent behaviours and functional purposes that can be understood and evaluated by the stakeholders[38].

A constituent behaviour should initially be analysed in a simplified form in which its possible interactions with other behaviours are ignored: consideration of those

---

[33] A machine's software structure is regular if there is no *structure clash* [14]. That is: the dynamic structure of the software clearly composes the dynamic structures at its interfaces to problem domains.

[34] Reasoning about the relationship between the machine and the system behaviour is greatly complicated if the given domain properties are not constant. For example, they may vary with environmental conditions or with varying loads imposed by varying requirements on the system behaviour.

[35] Both top-down and bottom-up design of the system behaviour are used as necessary. If—as is the case for any realistic system—no tersely explicable purpose of the whole system behaviour can be identified, bottom-up design must be used: the purpose of the whole will then emerge from the designed combination of the constituents.

[36] The causal pattern by which the machine ensures the problem world behaviour is what Polanyi [15] calls the *operational principle* of a *contrivance*—and a system is a contrivance in his sense. Simplicity of this causal pattern is one important characteristic of a simple behaviour.

[37] Formal verification of a specification proves the entailment M, $\{Wi\} \models B$. Some additional formal and informal verification is needed to demonstrate the quasi-entailment $\{Wi\}, B \mid\sim R$—that is, that the requirements are satisfied. Demonstrating that the formalisation of the given problem world is sufficiently faithful to the physical reality is an entirely distinct task: it is inherently non-formal, and is typically both the hardest and the most vital.

[38] For example, an automotive feature such as Cruise Control or Stop-Start must correspond to an identifiable part or projection of the system behaviour specification, not to a collection of stimulus-response pairs distributed among many parts of the whole specification.

interactions and the complexities they introduce should be postponed until a later point at which the behaviours are to be combined[39]. The same strategy—an incremental approach to inescapable complexity[40]—can be applied to other complexities due to exceptional conditions that can arise within the behaviour itself.

Initially considering constituent behaviours—more exactly, *candidate* constituent behaviours[41]—in isolation encourages an important separation of concerns. To the greatest extent possible, the functional content of each behaviour should be separated from the control of its initiation and, in certain circumstances, of its termination. Since the concept of a constituent behaviour rests on a relationship of inclusion of an instance of one behaviour in an instance of another, this separation cannot be complete. But its aim remains valid: to maintain modularity in the explicit structure of the behaviour specification[42]. This modularity supports the understanding of each constituent behaviour as an independent unit of system functionality: it must be allowed to persist as long and as fully as possible, throughout the development and use of the specification[43].

---

[39] It makes obvious sense to understand the components before addressing the task of their composition. Neglect of this principle is the Achilles heel of top-down decomposition and of its cousin stepwise refinement.

[40] The third of Descartes's famous rules of thought [12] was:

"... to conduct my thoughts in such order that, by commencing with objects the simplest and easiest to know, I might ascend by little and little, and, as it were, step by step, to the knowledge of the more complex; assigning in thought a certain order even to those objects which in their own nature do not stand in a relation of antecedence and sequence."

[41] Candidate constituent behaviours arise both in *top-down decomposition*, as briefly illustrated in Sect. 7, and in *bottom-up development*, in which candidate constituents are identified piecemeal. In both cases each candidate constituent must be analysed, and its simplicity evaluated, before it can be definitely accepted as a component in the system behaviour design.

[42] Traditional block-structured programming establishes frame conditions for modules based on scope rules. In a cyber-physical system such frame conditions are frustrated by the connectedness of the physical problem world: behaviours interact unavoidably at physical domains that are common—directly or indirectly—to their problem worlds.

[43] Eagerness to rush to design a software architecture is usually misplaced. One freedom that software—unlike hardware—allows to its developers is the freedom of malleability of their material. Many structural transformations are possible that can preserve chosen specification properties of the source while endowing the target with a completely new property suited to efficient implementation for program code construction and execution. Knowing that such transformations are available, developers should resist the temptation to cast behaviour specifications in the form of an architecture of software modules. The machine associated with the behaviour in each subproblem should be regarded as a projection, not a component, of the complete software.

7 Large Behaviour Structure: Designed Domains

Large behaviour structure is defined in terms of a designed structure of the machines that ensure the constituent behaviours[44]. One—but not the only—design motivation for structuring is decomposition[45]: a behaviour which is proving less simple than originally expected, is restructured with two or more constituent behaviours.

Figure 2 shows, in general terms, a trivial case. In behaviour B0, machine MB0 monitors Domain X and controls Domain Y so that its behaviour is kept in some required relationship with Domain X. The Stop Switch allows behaviour B0 to be terminated on command. On analysis, we are supposing, the tasks of monitoring X and controlling Y prove too complex to be combined in a single undecomposed behaviour B0[46]: so B0 is decomposed into B0' and two constituent behaviours BX and BY.

In B0, the information obtained from Domain X and needed for proper control of Domain Y would be represented and maintained in a data structure in the local store of machine MB0. In B0' this data structure has been 'promoted' from a machine local variable to a problem domain, X-to-Y, common to the two constituent behaviours BX and BY. A problem domain originated in this way is represented by a box with a single stripe: it is a *designed domain* because it is a design artifact of the software development, not a given part of the physical problem world of the original undecomposed problem[47].

In general, the function of a designed domain is to communicate information across time and space between parts of the system behaviour which we want—or are compelled—to separate. The X-to-Y domain allows the constituent behaviours BX and BY to be separated for reasons of behaviour simplicity, while allowing each to conform to

---

[44] Associated with each machine, from its expression as a problem in the pattern of Fig. 1, are the documented descriptions: M of the machine; {Wi} of the problem domains' given properties and behaviours; and B of the system behaviour. The machine is also associated with the relevant requirements {Rj}. It is this assemblage of descriptions that define the behaviour: the machine is the designed means of realising each of its necessary instances.

[45] This is *top-down* structuring. It starts from a firm conception of the function of the whole behaviour to be developed, and, level by level, identifies constituent parts that for any reason should be regarded as separate components. In a realistic cyber-physical system the proliferation of functions and features demands extensive use of *bottom-up* structuring, in which initially there is no firm conception of the whole behaviour: it emerges only gradually from the piecemeal identification and combination of constituents. Bottom-up structuring is briefly discussed later, in Sect. 8.

[46] For example, because there is a structure clash [14]: the process structures of BX and BY are incompatible, and the simplicity criterion that stipulates regular process structure cannot be satisfied in a single undecomposed behaviour B0.

[47] It may seem paradoxical—or, at least, inconsistent—to promote a designed domain, which was merely a local data structure in the software of a machine, as a legitimate problem domain on all fours with the physical domains Domain X and Domain Y. But of course the unpromoted local variable was physically realised in the store of the machine MB0. Its promotion merely makes visible and explicit what was previously hidden and implicit. From the point of view of MBX and MBY it is a problem domain, external to those machines, to be respectively controlled and monitored.

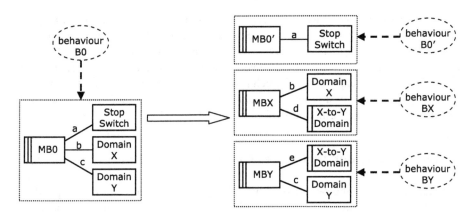

Fig. 2. Decomposition of a simple behaviour

the general pattern and structure of a development problem as shown in Fig. 1, and to benefit from the attendant advantages. The concept of a designed domain is very versatile: its ubiquitous utility reflects the ubiquitous utility of program variables. Some examples of designed domains are: a database in a bank accounts system; a data structure in a road traffic control system, representing the road layout and the positions of traffic light units, pedestrian buttons and vehicle sensors; a train operating timetable; the seat configuration data maintained for each driver by the software of a luxury car; the content and format of a document in an editing and presentation system; and countless others[48].

---

[48] A designed domain, once identified in a proposed or existing system, raises many important questions about its purpose, use and realisation. Between which behaviours does the domain provide communication? Of which behaviour's machine is the domain a local variable? Can the domain be instantiated more than once? How long does each instance persist? By which behaviours are the values of the domain state initialised and mutated? The reader may wish to ponder these questions for the examples mentioned in the text. Consider, for instance, the road layout domain in the traffic system. It is a designed domain for the traffic control behaviour. In which other behaviour is it a designed domain? Of which machine is it a local variable? Considering these questions can identify important large-scale concerns in system design. For example: a database associated with the operating parameters and constraints of a chemical process plant or a power station can be regarded as a designed domain. Safety demands that update access to this database must be explicitly controlled by the machine of which it is a promoted local variable. Apparent absence of such a machine from the behaviour specification indicates a severe safety exposure.

In some of these examples the designed domain is clearly an *analogical model* of the problem world—dynamic in the accounts system, and static in the traffic system[49]. In other examples it is less obviously a model of the physical problem world. In the editing system, for example, it would be very contrived to regard the document domain as a model of the editing events by which it was created. But in all cases the purpose of a designed domain, as of a program variable, is to communicate information between separate behaviours performed or evoked by the machine[50].

8 Large Behaviour Structure: Control Mechanism

The original machine of a decomposed behaviour controls the machines corresponding to its immediate constituent behaviours. This control relationship induces a rooted tree whose nodes are machines and designed domains, represented in a *behaviour control diagram* as shown in Fig. 3:

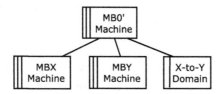

Fig. 3. Behaviour control diagram: controlling and controlled machines and a designed domain

---

[49] A *model* is an artifact providing information about its *subject*. We may distinguish *analogic* from *symbolic* models. A symbolic model—for example, a set of equations or a state transition diagram—is entirely abstract. The notational expression of a symbolic model itself carries no information about the subject: essentially, the model is simply a description that allows formal reasoning in the hope of revealing or proving some implied property or behaviour of its subject. An analogic model—for example, a system of water pipes demonstrating the flow of electricity in a circuit—is a physical object whose physical characteristics are analogues of those of the subject: water flow is analogous to electric current, pipe cross-section to the inverse of electrical resistance, a tank to a battery, and so on.

Often, a software model such as a database or an assemblage of objects is an analogic model of its subject. Each subject entity is analogous to a certain type of record or object; relationships between entities are analogous to pointers or record keys, and so on. The motivation for an analogic model is clear: the model is a surrogate, immediately available to the software, for historical or current aspects of the subject that are not readily accessible to direct inspection.

The danger of an analogic model is, of course, confusion of properties peculiar to the model with those belonging also—albeit by analogy—to the subject. Breaking a water pipe causes water to spill out; but breaking a wire in an electric circuit causes no analogous effect. A well-known example of such confusion in software engineering is the common uncertainty about the meaning of a *null* value in a cell of a relational database table.

[50] In the word processing system, for example, the document designed domain communicates information between the editing behaviour and other behaviours—storage, printing, transformation, and others—in which the document participates.

A machine node can be either a leaf or the root of the tree or of a subtree; a designed domain node can only be a leaf. A machine node represents possible instantiations of the machine: each instantiation starts the machine's execution and hence starts the corresponding problem world behaviour. The machine root node of the tree represents an instantiation of the whole system by an external agent; in any other case a machine is instantiated by its immediately controlling machine[51]. Machine execution instances may be specialised by arguments bound to instances of problem domains[52].

Temporal relationships among machine instances, including concurrency, are determined by the controlling machine[53]. For example, the execution pattern in Fig. 3 may be:

```
begin
instantiate X-to-Y;
instantiate MBX; instantiate MBY;
terminate MBX; terminate MBY
end.
```

in which MBX and MBY execute concurrently.

Machine execution may be terminated in several ways. First: a terminating behaviour may come to an autonomous *designed halt*—that is, a halt corresponding to a particular final outcome foreseen in the design of the machine[54]. Second, although the instantiating agent of a machine is responsible for ensuring that the relevant assumed conditions are present at instantiation, changing environment conditions and other vicissitudes may require *pre-emptive abortion* of the instantiated behaviour by the instantiating agent[55]. Third: it may be necessary in the ordinary course of system execution to bring a non-terminating behaviour, or a terminating behaviour that has not yet reached a designed halt, to an *orderly stop*—for example to cease operation of a vending machine when next there is no customer interacting with the machine. This, too, must be commanded by the instantiating agent.

---

[51] The behaviour control diagram shows only the parent-child relationship. The dynamic rules and patterns of instantiations are not shown in the diagram but only in the specification or program text of the controlling machine. Although designed domains appear in a behaviour control diagram, their associations with individual behaviours by membership of their problem worlds are not represented.

[52] Where a problem domain is populated by multiple individual entities there will be behaviours whose instantiations must be specialised in this way. In a library system, for example, a *loan* behaviour must be specialised to the borrowed book and the borrowing member.

[53] Instances of distinct behaviours, and distinct instances of the same behaviour, suitably specialised, may be temporally related by concurrency or in any other way governed by the controlling behaviour.

[54] A designed *halt* may occur when the goal of the behaviour been attained or has become unattainable. The associated failure condition is within the envisaged results of execution, and must be clearly distinguished from a failure of the assumed environment conditions—which, by definition, is not addressed within the behaviour's own design.

[55] Pre-emptive abortion is typically needed only in emergency conditions. In a lift system, for example, the normal lift service behaviour must be pre-emptively aborted if the hoist cable breaks; in an automotive system, the cruise control behaviour must be aborted if a crash impact is detected. Abortion is, of course, not represented as a behaviour state in Fig. 4. Pre-emptive abortion destroys the behaviour instance, which therefore no longer has any state.

Where two constituent behaviours fulfil closely related functions, their controlling behaviour becomes responsible for orderly termination of the whole. For example, in a system to control paid admissions to a zoo, there may be two constituent behaviours: one to manage payments, the other to manage admissions. On terminating the system behaviour when the zoo closes it is necessary for the controlling behaviour to command an orderly stop of the payments, followed by an orderly stop of admissions when the payments received have been exhausted—or, perhaps when it is clear that there are no more visitors to be admitted.

The controlled states of a machine are shown in Fig. 4.

On instantiation the machine enters its initialising state. If initialisation completes successfully the machine enters its running state; alternatively, it may first reach a *designed halt*, or receive a *stop* command from its controller. A *stop* command causes the machine to halt at the next occurrence of a stable problem world state satisfying a defined condition: for example, orderly termination of a lift behaviour might require the lift car to be stationary at a floor with the doors open[56]. While stopping, the machine may reach a state [*term*] in which it is designed to terminate unconditionally, or it may first reach a stable [*non-term*] state at which termination is not unconditional.

The controller can observe—but not modify—the states of the controlled behaviour shown in Fig. 4, along with more specific state details explicitly exported by the controlled behaviour. For example, the *Halted* state may be accompanied by an indication *failed* or *OK*.

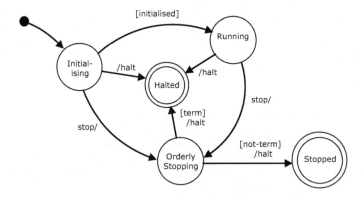

Fig. 4. Standard interface for behaviour control

---

[56] An orderly stop of lift service might take two forms. The fast form brings the lift car to the nearest floor to allow passengers to disembark because the normal power supply has failed and the lift is moving under emergency power; the slower form brings the car to the ground floor under normal power to allow lift service to be suspended without inconveniencing users.

9 Bottom-up Structuring of Large Behaviour

The starting point for the problem depicted in Fig. 2 was a broad, somewhat abstract, understanding of the functional goal of B0: maintaining a certain stated relationship between domains X and Y, constraining Y but not X. Understanding of this *abstract goal behaviour* B0 led to the problem diagram on the left in Fig. 2. On closer examination of the problem, simplicity criteria demanded the decomposition to behaviours B0', BX and BY. Understanding of the desired abstract goal behaviour B0, and the analysis which revealed its complexity, anchored the decomposition and provided a first view of the constituent behaviours BX and BY. B0 might even be imagined as the initial step in a refinement process of which the decomposition, and the design of the three behaviours and the designed domain X-to-Y, are the product of imagined subsequent steps. The end effect of these refinement steps is that the original causal chain $X \rightarrow MB0 \rightarrow Y$ has been refined to $X \rightarrow MBX \rightarrow X\text{-to-}Y \rightarrow MBY \rightarrow Y$[57].

For a complete system of realistic size and complexity no abstract goal behaviour can be identified that captures the overall behaviour as a whole[58]. Instead, the many modes, features, functions, phases, fault mitigations and exception handlers present an almost chaotic population of foreseeable constituent behaviours. Some candidates may be motivated by apparently discrete features or by particular requirements. Others may be hard to identify clearly or even to think of. The eventual interactions and temporal relationships among these candidate behaviours are largely unknown when development is begun. Study and design of these interactions and relationships cannot begin until the constituent behaviours have themselves been brought under some degree of intellectual control by identifying and analysing the subproblems that will define them.

When some candidate constituent behaviours have been identified and analysed in their simplest forms, it becomes possible to consider their relationships and interactions. The whole behavioural structure of the system is progressively[59] built up as a behaviour control tree of accepted candidates. Some constituent behaviours are identified from needs arising only in the process of constructing the tree. Some constituent

---

[57] This refinement process is imaginary because formal refinement cannot be a reliable technique in a non-formal world: the more concrete models may vitiate unacceptable or impractical simplifications in their more abstract predecessors. For example, in Fig. 2 the interposition of the designed domain may introduce sources of latency or error that were implicitly excluded in behaviour B0. When development has been completed it may be possible to retrofit the complexities of the concrete reality to an elaborated abstraction; but this exercise would belong to *ex post facto* rationalisation and formal verification, not to development method.

[58] In the absence of an identified and broadly understood abstract goal behaviour that comprehensibly includes all its constituent behaviours, the overall behaviour must emerge eventually from work on the constituent behaviours at lower levels. No starting point for a refinement process can be identified, because nothing definitive can be said of the overall behaviour while it has not yet emerged.

[59] The bottom-up construction of the behaviour tree is progressive only in the sense that constituent behaviours are gradually pieced together as their individual designs and interactions become progressively clearer. In general, the intermediate products of the construction process will constitute a forest rather than a tree. It is too optimistic to conceive of this forest as an ordered structure, similar to a layered hierarchy to be built up in successive layers from the bottom upwards.

behaviours and designed domains are introduced by local applications of top-down design. Very often these designed domains will be analogic models of parts of the system. Behaviour control may be exerted to terminate one behaviour in order to allow another, incompatible, behaviour to be initiated.

10   From Behaviour Specification to Software Execution

The distinction between the problem and subproblem view, as sketched in Figs. 1 and 2, and the behaviour control diagram, as exemplified in Fig. 3, is essentially the distinction between a set of system behaviour views and a unified software view[60].

The software specification, in terms of machine executions, resulting from the approach described here can be regarded as a large concurrent program, in which each instantiated machine execution corresponds to a process execution. (We note, however, that if two concurrent behaviours produce identical machine responses to the same instance of a problem world event or state change, duplication of the response may be assumed to be harmful. It is then necessary to ensure that the response occurs only once in the problem world for each occurrence of the stimulus.)

If the problem world descriptions {Wi} are expressed in a suitable form they may form the basis for a simulation of the physical problem world, as is normal practice for some systems (an avionics example is presented by O'Halloran [2]). Alternatively, if actual instances of the problem world are conveniently, cheaply and safely available, they may provide a test environment for the software.

Finally, for some purposes—including formal verification of pre-formal reasoning— it may prove expedient to fragment the machine behaviour specification into a set of stimulus-response pairs. In this transformation the structure and dynamic state of the behaviour control tree, the designed domains, and the text pointers of the machine instances must all be faithfully represented.

11   System Behaviour and the Salient Challenges

This paper has sketched an approach to development whose central theme and constant concern is the structuring and design of the system behaviour. The system behaviour is the visible intended effect of software execution, and is therefore the true end product of software development. The identification of the stakeholders' role as stating and validating desired properties of the system behaviour—rather than mandating beha- vioural details—is entirely appropriate: responsibility for designing a feasible beha- viour that exhibits those properties must lie with the developers.

---

[60] An obvious possible extension is a third view. The problem diagrams show the relationships between machines and problem domains at the level of each constituent behaviour; the behaviour control diagram shows the relationships among machines. A third view would show the relationships among the problem domains induced by their interfaces of shared phenomena, including interfaces to the machines. The form and representation of such an extension is a topic of further work.

The focus on system behaviour provides an intellectual tool for addressing the salient development challenges of cyber-physical systems. The behaviour control tree, of which a trivial example is shown in Fig. 3, allows the complex overall behaviour to be comprehended in a nested structure of potentially concurrent constituent behaviour components. There is a parallel here with the advantages of classical structured programming. The nested behaviour structure establishes a tree of regions of the system's operating envelope[61], each with the accompanying assumptions that justify the chosen formalisations of the problem world properties. Construction of this tree must proceed largely bottom-up. Until a good understanding has been achieved of its components at every level, it is impossible to determine the scope either of proposed invariant requirements or of the validity of proposed formalisations of given problem domain properties.

At the level of a constituent behaviour the approach to complexity is incremental. In a subproblem the behaviour is initially considered in isolation as a complete system in itself. This initial treatment clarifies the simplest case of the behaviour, in which nothing goes wrong and there is no interference from interaction with other behaviours at common problem domains. At later stages the subproblem is revisited to address these and other sources of complexity. For example: deviation from the simplest case to handle a minor exception; modification to ensure compatibility with other behaviours; and interaction with the controlling parent or child behaviours. It may then become necessary to distinguish multiple versions of the behaviour according to the complexities of the context.

The fundamental thesis of this paper is that behaviour is an indispensable concept for developing dependable cyber-physical systems. The approach briefly presented here is still very much a work in progress, aiming to address, directly and effectively, the salient challenges of behavioural design and structuring.

Acknowledgments. Thanks are due to the anonymous reviewer of an earlier draft of this paper for a number of helpful suggestions. The approach described owes much to extended discussions over many years with colleagues and friends, among whom Anthony Hall and Daniel Jackson have been especially patient, encouraging, and insightful.

References

1. Jackson, M.: Problem Frames: Analysing and Structuring Software Development Problems. Addison-Wesley, Boston (2001)
2. O'Halloran, C.: Nose-Gear velocity—a challenge problem for software safety. In: Proceedings of System Safety Society Australian Chapter Meeting (2014)

---

[61] The structure of environment conditions assumed by the subproblems naturally follows the structure of the behaviour control tree and the activation choices of controlling behaviours. The environment conditions of a controlled behaviour imply those of its controlling behaviour. The environment conditions assumed by the machine at the tree root are those of the system's complete operating envelope.

3. von Neumann, J., Morgenstern, O.: The Theory of Games and Economic Behaviour. Princeton University Press, Princeton (1944)
4. Poincaré, H.: Science et Methode; Flammarion 1908; tr Francis Maitland, p. 126, Nelson 1914, Dover 1952, 2003
5. Jackson, M.: Topsy-Turvy requirements. In: Seyff, N., Koziolek, A. (eds.) Modelling and Quality in Requirements Engineering: Essays Dedicated to Martin Glinz on the Occasion of His 60th Birthday. Verlagshaus Monsenstein und Vannerdat, Muenster (2012)
6. Hoare, C.A.R.: Communicating Sequential Processes. Prentice-Hall International, Upper Saddle River (1985)
7. Harel, D., Pnueli, A.: On the development of reactive systems. In: Apt, K.R. (ed.) Logics and Models of Concurrent Systems, pp. 477–498. Springer, New York (1985)
8. Dijkstra, E.W.: On the cruelty of really teaching computer science. Commun. ACM **32**(12), 1398–1414 (1989). (With responses from David Parnas, W L Scherlis, M H van Emden, Jacques Cohen, R W Hamming, Richard M Karp and Terry Winograd, and a reply from Dijkstra)
9. Smith, B.C.: The limits of correctness. In: Prepared for the Symposium on Unintentional Nuclear War; Fifth Congress of the International Physicians for the Prevention of Nuclear War 1985, Budapest, Hungary, 28 June–1 July. ACM SIGCAS Computers and Society, vol. 14,15, Issue 1,2,3,4, pp. 18–26, January 1985
10. Zave, P.: FAQ Sheet on Feature Interaction. AT&T (1999). http://www.research.att.com/ ~pamela/faq.html
11. Calder, M., Magill, E. (eds.): Feature Interactions in Telecommunications and Software Systems VI. IOS Press, Amsterdam (2000)
12. Descartes, R.: Discourse on Method, Part II; Works, vol. VI (1637)
13. Leibnitz, G.W.: Philosophical Writings (Die Philosophischen Schriften), Gerhardt, C.I. (ed.), vol. IV, p. 331 (1857–1890)
14. Jackson, M.A.: Principles of Program Design. Academic Press, Orlando (1975)
15. Polanyi, M.: Personal Knowledge: Towards a Post-Critical Philosophy. Routledge and Kegan Paul, London (1958). (University of Chicago Press, 1974)
16. Turski, W.M.: And no philosopher's stone either. In: Kugler, H.J. (ed.) Proceedings of the IFIP Congress. World Computer Congress, Dublin (1986)
17. Smith, B.C.: The limits of correctness. In: Prepared for the Symposium on Unintentional Nuclear War, Fifth Congress of the International Physicians for the Prevention of Nuclear War, Budapest, Hungary, 28 June–1 July (1985)
18. Jackson, M., Zave, P.: Domain descriptions. In: Proceedings of IEEE International Symposium on Requirements Engineering, January 1993, pp. 56–64. IEEE CS Press (1992)
19. Jackson, M.: Software Requirements & Specifications: A Lexicon of Practice, Principles, and Prejudices. Addison Wesley/ACM, New York (1995)

A Control-Theoretic Approach to Self-adaptive Systems and an Application to Cloud-Based Software

Carlo Ghezzi, Giovanni Paolo Gibilisco, Claudio Menghi$^{(\boxtimes)}$,
and Marco Miglierina

Dipartimento di Elettronica, Informazione e Bioingegneria,
Politecnico di Milano, Milano, Italy
{carlo.ghezzi,giovannipaolo.gibilisco,claudio.menghi,
marco.miglierina}@polimi.it

Abstract. Software systems are usually developed to provide a fixed set of functionalities within given environmental conditions. However, in the last few years, there has been an increasing interest in systems that can autonomously modify their behavior in response to dynamic changes occurring in their execution environment. In one word, they must be *self-adaptive*. Self-adaptation requires the ability to discover and analyze changes, and to react by applying an adequate set of adaptation actions. The choice of the adaptation actions to apply can be performed in a model-driven fashion, that is by evaluating their effectiveness on a model of the system that is kept alive and updated at run-time.

We describe an approach to the design of self-adaptive systems that frames self-adaptation as a control theory problem. Our approach considers the architecture of the application, represented through a Discrete Time Markov Chain (DTMC); the running environment upon which it is deployed, described through a Queuing Model (QM); and a cost model, specified through a Dynamic System. At run-time the system autonomously increases or decreases the amount of resources allocated to different components of the application in response to changes of both workload intensity and distribution, and of performance of the computing resources. The adopted policy both minimizes costs and maintains the desired QoS, in terms of average response time. We evaluate our approach simulating a *cloud computing* application in a cloud infrastructure. This computing environment has been chosen because it allows on-demand access to a configurable pool of resources that can be easily provisioned and released at run-time.

1 Introduction

In the last few years, *adaptive systems* have been gaining increasing interest in the research community. This was mainly motivated by the requirement to design systems that operate in a world that constantly evolves over time [3]. Changes may occur in the environment in which the application is running and their effect

© Springer International Publishing Switzerland 2015
B. Meyer and M. Nordio (Eds.): LASER 2013-2014, LNCS 8987, pp. 63–83, 2015.
DOI: 10.1007/978-3-319-28406-4_3

may lead to violations of the requirements the system is expected to satisfy. To prevent violations, self-adaptive systems can modify their behavior [9]. This is mainly obtained through suitable monitors and reasoning mechanisms, which continuously probe the environment wherein the system is running, and select the most suitable set of adaptation actions to cope with changes, respectively.

A systematic approach to the design of self-adaptive systems can be framed in a *model-driven* way; that is, the strategy employed to manage changes can be based on the use of models. The behavior of the running system is specified through a model that is kept alive and updated at run-time. The model is repeatedly verified to check for possible requirements violations. It is then used by an appropriate controller to compute the most suitable set of adaptation actions to be performed. This arrangement offers several advantages [8,10]. First, describing the system through a formal, mathematical model offers the possibility to better understand the system and its dynamics. Second, models provide a rigorous way to build a controller able to manage changes at run-time.

Self-adaptive systems can be characterized in terms of their flexibility and assurance. *Flexibility* refers to the capability of the system to manage changes. *Assurance* instead refers to the capability of proving the correct behavior of the system at run-time after any change [14]. Flexibility and assurance are usually in conflict and strongly depend on the strategy employed in the controller design. Several approaches require the full definition and the complete tuning of the model of the system and how it reacts to the different changes at design time. In these cases the developer specifies how the system is going to adapt at run-time over a set of predefined changes. These approaches privilege assurance over flexibility, since the behavior of the controller over the set of possible adaptation actions is statically analyzed. In contrast, other approaches autonomously identify and tune the model of the system at run-time. In these cases, the approach is really flexible since the system is able to cope with every type of change, but it may lack assurance about the behavior of the controller. Finally, hybrid approaches combine design-time and run-time techniques to conjugate the flexibility guaranteed by using models at run-time with the assurance gained with the use of design-time models. Usually, in these approaches the developer identifies at design-time a set of parameters that are monitored and used during the run-time adaptation process.

This paper proposes a *hybrid approach* to autonomously regulate the resources allocated to the different components of the system at run-time. The approach explicitly considers the architecture of the application, the running environment upon which the application is deployed and a cost model that describes the monetary charges of the different resources. A Discrete-Time Markov Chain (DTMC) is used to describe the architecture of the application, that is how its different components interact. A Queuing Model (QM) specifies how these components manage the requests once deployed in the running environment and allows us to compute the response time of each of these components. A Dynamic System is used to represent how the costs change over time. Starting from these models, we compute the global specification of the system, which is kept alive and updated at run-time. The specification is used to derive a constraint minimization problem in which the objective function specifies the cost of using the system and the constraint enforces an upper bound to the average response time.

We evaluate our approach using a *Cloud computing* application example, since cloud computing allows on-demand access to a configurable pool of resources that can be easily provisioned and released [21]. The example presented in this work uses the *Infrastructure as a Service (IaaS)* paradigm, which offers the possibility to allocate and de-allocate new virtual machines dynamically at run-time. We assume that the application under design has to comply with a given *Service-Level Agreement* (SLA) that prescribes an upper bound on response time. The goal is to self-adapt by regulating the amount of resources allocated to the different components of the application over time (*scale*) to minimize costs while fulfilling an SLA requirement.

The paper is organized as follows. Section 2 presents an overview of our approach and its main aspects. Section 3 illustrates the case study that is considered throughout this paper. Section 4 provides an overview of the modeling paradigm we used. The proposed controller is presented in Sect. 5. The results we obtained are discussed in Sect. 6. Section 7 describes related works in the context of adaptive systems with a special focus on the Cloud. Finally, Sect. 8 presents the conclusions and outlines future work.

2   Overview of the Approach

This section presents an overview of the proposed *hybrid* approach which is represented in Fig. 1. This approach relies on two different phases: the design-time and the run-time phase.

The *design-time* phase concerns the development of a model of the running system that is used to dynamically modify its behavior at run-time. This model includes (i) a Discrete Time Markov Chain (DTMC) describing the behavior of the application under development, (ii) a Queuing Model (QM) describing how the requests are computed by the different components of the application, and (iii) a Discrete Time Dynamic System (DTDS) describing how the costs associated with the allocation of different resources of the system change over time.

Discrete Time Markov Chains are used to describe how the different components of the application under development interact with each other. A DTMC is a state-based modeling formalism that shows how the configuration of the system changes over time through state transitions. In our approach, each state of the DTMC represents a component. We use the term *component* to indicate any independently running code unit. It might be a *service* in the service-oriented sense. Because the states of a DTMC, which represent components, are represented as graph nodes, when no ambiguity arises, we use the terms *component*, *state*, and *node* interchangeably. Transitions specify how the different requests flow from one component to another. Furthermore, in DTMCs transitions are labeled with probabilities, which specify the likelihood of the transitions to be performed, i.e., the probability of a request to be forwarded from one component to another.

Queuing Models specify how requests are processed in the different nodes. Components can be replicated on a number of virtual machines, which altogether define a *group*[1]. QMs are particularly suitable to effectively analyze the performance of the system. The idea is that at any time a certain number of requests (λ) arrive at a particular node of the system. A request can be immediately processed if a virtual machine is available; otherwise it must be queued. Each virtual machine handles the incoming requests with a given service time. QMs provide a simple, analytic way to compute the waiting time and the response time of different requests in the system.

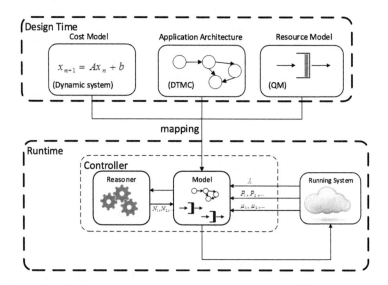

Fig. 1. An overview of the approach

Discrete Time Dynamical Systems (DTDS) are a mathematical formalism that specifies how a system configuration evolves over time. A DTDS represents the current configuration of the system through a vector of variables, which is updated at each time instant. The update function computes its output values in relation with the current configuration and the inputs of the system. A configuration defines the allocation of resources at any time instant, and this can used to reason about the costs involved in using resources over time. Specifically, in our case a configuration describes the allocation of virtual machines to components and the goal we wish to achieve is to satisfy the response time requirements at minimum cost.

The DTMC, QM and the DTDS describe the system under development from different perspectives: the architecture of the application, the response time of

---
[1] An autoscaling group in the Amazon cloud's terminology.

its components, and the costs of the running system. These three models are aggregated during the *mapping* phase into a single, fully comprehensive run-time model of the application. The run-time model of the application allows computation of the *total* response time of the whole application and its cost. In particular, since the different components of the application are deployed on diverse resources, each node of the DTMC is associated to a QM, through which one can compute its response time in relation with the number of allocated resources. Furthermore, each node of the DTMC is associated to a DTDS. The DTDS allows one to compute the costs of the allocated resources and prevents removal of resources from the running system when no benefit are gained (e.g., if resources are allocated on a hourly basis they should be removed only when the hour in which they were activated expires).

The mapping procedure also allows the developer to specify the set of *parameters* (aspects) that can change and to associate these parameters to suitable monitors or estimators. For example, the developer may specify that the probability of performing a certain transition of the DTMC changes at run-time (e.g., the probability of booking mountain hotels increases in snowing days).

During the *run-time* phase the model of the system is used to derive a *constraint optimization problem* which will be solved at run-time to compute the values of $N_1, N_2 \ldots N_n$ that are the number of machines that must be (de-)activated for each component. The optimization problem includes a cost function that specifies how costs change in relation with the number of machines allocated to the different components, and a set of constraints that force the system to guarantee a desired response time. These constraints are generated with regards of the DTMC, the QM and the Discrete Time Dynamic System.

The parameters of run-time models are continuously estimated and the model of the system (and the corresponding constraint optimization problem) is updated consequently. For example, in Fig. 1 the unknown parameters include the incoming workload of the system (λ) the probabilities of forwarding the requests to the different nodes of the application $(p_1, p_2 \ldots p_n)$ and the service time of each of these nodes $(\mu_1, \mu_2 \ldots \mu_n)$. The controller computes the solution of the optimization problem to calculate the set of adaptation actions to be performed in response to changes. In our specific case, the controller acts on the number of machines $(N_1, N_2 \ldots N_n)$ that are allocated for each component. The idea is that the controller increases the number of machines when the total response time of the system violates a desired SLA, while decreases it to reduce costs when the resources allocated to each service are over-provisioned.

3   Case Study

This section introduces the case study used to evaluate our approach, which refers to a web application offering users a way to buy tickets for theatrical events. Users access the application via a browser and interact via HTTP requests. The application is deployed on a cloud environment and exploits the dynamic provisioning of resources to autonomously increase the number of machines that serve the application under the peaks of workload (e.g., when the booking of new theatrical events starts). The different components of the application interact to satisfy users requests. These requests include:

- browsing a set of static pages. For simplicity we consider only the homepage of the web site and the associated request *home*;
- searching for a particular pièce, with the *search* request;
- selecting a seat for the selected performance, with the *pick seat* request;
- purchase the ticket by making an online payment, with the *buy* request.

Figure 2 shows the internal architecture of the application. The application has been divided in two main tiers: a front-end and a back-end. The *front-end* tier contains a web server that is the entry point for all the requests. Some of these requests can be directly handled by accessing a set of static web pages; others require the invocation of the back-end to collect the required information. The *back-end* tier hosts the business logic of the application; it includes the data manager to access a shared database, the seat manager to manage the available seats for each pièce and to avoid conflicts in the reservations, and the payment system that takes care of the charge.

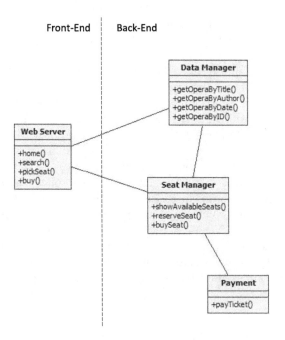

Fig. 2. Architecture of the application

The components of the application illustrated in Fig. 2 interact to provide the desired functionalities. Figure 3 shows the interactions needed to accomplish the *buy* request. The web server sends a *buySeat* request to the seat manager that checks the actual availability of the seat and locks it. The seat manager forwards the request to the payment service responsible for the purchase. Other interactions triggered by the web server, omitted here, may be described in a similar way. Table 1 specifies the set of components necessary to process each request.

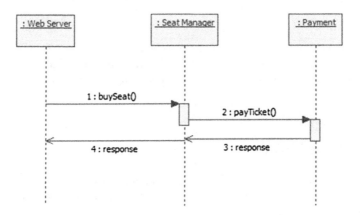

Fig. 3. Buy request processing Sequence Diagram

In our case study, each component of the application is hosted by a dedicated pool of resources (or auto-scaling group). These resources are hosted on a Cloud platform that offers an IaaS solution, such as Amazon EC2. The connectivity, the management of hardware resources and the load balancing among different machines are delegated to the Cloud provider. However, the application administrator is in charge of deciding the number of machines of each auto scaling group and is charged according to a pay-per-hour strategy. Our adaptive solution is able to autonomously allocate and de-allocate machines in the different pool of resources when something change. The case study contemplates the following changes:

– *workload conditions*: the request rate changes over time. For example, there may exists a seasonal relation between the period of the year and the requests of buying certain tickets (e.g., the booking of arena theater tickets increases during summer). Furthermore, the first day a particular ticket is on sale exposes the system to a peak of requests;
– *user preferences*: the likelihood of different user requests is influenced by environmental factors. The first day a particular ticket is sold the probability a user performs a *pick seat* or a *buy* request with respect to a *search* request increases, while usually the user searches for date and periods of particular events (i.e., *search* requests);

Table 1. Set of components necessary to process each request

Request	Necessary components
Home	Web Server
Search	Web Server, Data Manager
Pick seat	Web Server, Seat Manager, Data Manager
Buy	Web Server, Seat Manager, Payment

- *cloud parameters*: the behavior of the cloud environment changes. The processing rate of each resource of the Cloud environment usually increases or decreases when other processes are removed from or deployed on the pool of resources.

4   Modeling Paradigm

This section presents an overview on the modeling formalisms involved in this work and how they are used to design self-adaptive systems considering the case study presented in Sect. 3.

4.1   Discrete Time Markov Chain

Starting from the classical definition of Discrete Time Markov Chain [2] (DTMC), we formalize a DTMC as a tuple $\mathcal{M} = \langle S, P, s_i, s_f\ AP, L \rangle$, where:

- S is a finite set of states;
- $P : S \times S \rightarrow [0, 1]$ is the transition probability function, such that $\forall s \in S$, $\sum_{s' \in S} P(s, s') = 1$;
- $s_i \in S$ is the initial state of the system;
- $s_f \in S$ is the final state of the system[2]. Furthermore, s_f is the only state such that $P(s, s) = 1$. Formally, $\nexists s \in S \mid (P(s, s) = 1) \wedge (s \neq s_f)$;
- AP is the set of atomic propositions;
- $L : S \rightarrow 2^{AP}$ is the labeling function that associates to each state the set of atomic propositions that are true in that state.

The transition probability relation P specifies the probability to move from one state to another in one step, that is, by a single transition. The notation $P(s_j, s_k)$ indicates the entry (j, k) of the matrix P, that corresponds to the probability of moving from the state s_j to the state s_k of $\mathcal{M}$. A state $s \in S$ is *absorbing* if and only if $P(s, s) = 1$. A DTMC is *absorbing* if there exists an absorbing state (that in our case is the absorbing state) and from any state it is possible to eventually reach an absorbing state. A state $s \in S$ is *transient* if and

---

[2] Note that, in general, more final states can be supported. In this work we consider a single final state to represent the successful completion of requests.

only if starting in s there is a non zero probability that we will never return to s. A state is *recurrent* if it is not transient. Note that in an absorbing DTMC the only recurrent states are absorbing states.

An absorbing DTMC can be described using the *canonical form* as specified in Formula 1. The canonical form decomposes the matrix P in four different sub-matrices. Matrix Q $(t \times t)$ contains the transition probabilities between transient states. Matrix R $(t \times r)$ contains the transition probabilities from transient states to absorbing states (i.e., final states). Matrix 0 represents transitions from absorbing states to transient ones, which must be zero for the definition of absorbing state. Matrix I $(r \times r)$ represent transitions between absorbing states, which must be the identity matrix for the definition of absorbing state.

$$P = \begin{pmatrix} Q & R \\ 0 & I \end{pmatrix} \qquad (1)$$

In our case the only absorbing and recurrent state is the final state. This implies that I is a 1×1 matrix and R is a column vector of length t containing the transition probabilities of reaching the final state.

The probability $p_{j,k}^n$ of reaching state s_j from s_k in n steps is the element (i,j) of the matrix P^n. In an absorbing Markov chain, the probability that the process will be absorbed is 1 (i.e., $Q^n \rightarrow 0$ as $n \rightarrow \infty$). For an absorbing Markov chain the matrix Z, computed as specified in Formula 2, is called the *fundamental matrix* for P [18]. The entry $z_{k,j}$ of Z gives the expected number of times that the process is in the transient state s_j if it is started in the transient state s_k. Since in our case requests always enter the system in the initial state s_i, the entry $n_{i,j}$ of Z represents the expected number of time the request visit the state (service) s_j.

$$Z = (I - Q)^{-1} \qquad (2)$$

Therefore, the ith row of Z (i.e., the row corresponding to the initial state) represents the row containing the expected number of times an incoming request transits on each node of the DTMC. We call $\bar{z}$ the transposition of this row vector.

Let us consider the example described in Sect. 3. The architecture of the application illustrated in Fig. 2 is converted into an equivalent DTMC that is illustrated in Fig. 4. Each component of the architecture is mapped on a state of the DTMC. Transitions specify how requests are forwarded through the different components of the architecture. Furthermore, transitions are enriched with probabilities that specify the likelihood of forwarding a request on each of the transitions. Note that an additional state i.e., the final state, is added to specify that the request has been correctly computed and exits the system. Note that the probabilities $p_{1,2}$, $p_{1,3}$ ... are monitored and estimated at run-time as done, for example, by Epifani et al. in [10].

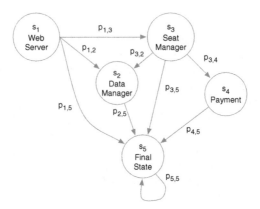

Fig. 4. DTMC of the architecture presented in Sect. 3

4.2   Queuing Models

Queuing models are commonly used to analyze various performance metrics of different kinds of systems (e.g., communication devices, software system, servers) in front of changes in the workload. These systems are usually composed by *processing nodes* that serve requests. Since the processing capacity of these resources is limited, usually, each processing node also contains a *buffer* that stores incoming requests temporarily, until the processing resource becomes available. The queuing model can implement different service policies (e.g., FIFO, LIFO, Processor Sharing) and multiple processing resources sharing the same queue.

Queuing models are usually described using the Kendall notation [19]. This notation represents a queue node as a triple $a/b/c$, where a represents the distribution of the inter-arrival time of requests, b represents the service time distribution, and c the number of resources that are used in each node to process the incoming requests. Usually a and b are replaced by G or M, where G stands for a general distribution and M represents a Markovian process (a Poisson distribution). Other more complex types of distributions can also be specified.

For simplicity in this work we consider each processing resource modeled as pool of $M/M/1$ queues, and we split the incoming workload λ equally among the machines of the pool, this way each queue will have an incoming workload equal to λ/N[3]. The queuing model allows an easy computation of its performance and, more precisely, of the *average service time* (that is the time spent in the queue plus the time needed by the resource to process the request). The average service time ω at the time t is computed using the Formula 3 [1]. The variable $N(t)$ models the number of replicas of the resource, $\mu(t)$ represents the processing rate and $\lambda(t)$ is the arrival rate. Note that the values of N, μ and λ change over time and that Formula 3 is valid only if the denominator is strictly positive.

---

[3] Note that the approach can be easily extended to consider an $M/M/n$ model.

$$\omega(t) = \frac{1}{\mu(t) - \frac{\lambda(t)}{N(t)}} \tag{3}$$

Recalling the DTMC modeling of the service based architecture of Sect. 4.1 each node of the DTMC represents a core service of the application. In our Cloud based deployment of the application each service is hosted on an auto-scaling group, which is modeled by a queue. The *average response time* of each node s_j of the DTMC is given by Formula 4, where $\lambda_j(t)$ is computed by multiplying the incoming workload $\lambda(t)$ with the jth entry of matrix Z given by Formula 2.

$$\omega_j(t) = \frac{1}{\mu_j(t) - \frac{\lambda_j(t)}{N_j(t)}} \tag{4}$$

Given the vector $\overline{\omega}(t)$ that contains the average response time of each node of the DTMC ($\omega_j(t)$), the *total response time* of the application (QM plus DTMC) is computed by multiplying the estimated response time at each node and the number of times an incoming request is expected to transit for that node, and summing all together, as specified in Formula 5^4.

$$\Omega(t) = \overline{\omega}(t)^T \times \overline{z}(t). \tag{5}$$

4.3   Discrete Time Dynamic Systems

Discrete time dynamic systems are a mathematical formalism that is used to describe the system and its *evolution* over time in a rigorous manner. This section only presents the main aspects related to discrete time dynamic systems. The interested reader can refer to [24] for details. The main characteristic of a discrete time dynamic system is the discrete nature of time, that is changes to the values of the system variables occur in distinct separate instants of time. A discrete time dynamic system interacts with the world by means of two different vectors of variables: $\overline{u}$ and $\overline{y}$. The vector $\overline{u} \in \mathcal{R}^p$ contains the set of *input variables*, which affect the actions executed on the dynamic system from external agents. Conversely, the vector $\overline{y} \in \mathcal{R}^n$ contains the set of *output variables*, which usually represent the output of the system or the values of some variables of interest. Finally, the vector $\overline{x} \in \mathcal{R}^n$ contains the set of *state variables*. State variables are used to describe the internal configuration of the dynamic system, i.e., the variables of interest to compute the output of the system. Formally, a discrete time dynamic systems is usually described through a set of equations as specified in Formula 6.

$$\overline{x}(k+1) = f(\overline{x}(k), \overline{u}(k), k) \tag{6a}$$
$$\overline{y}(k) = g(\overline{x}(k), \overline{u}(k), k) \tag{6b}$$

---

[4] The model that is obtained by connecting QMs into a network enriched with the probabilities of moving from one node to another is also known as Jackson Network [16].

Equation 6a, called *state equation*, computes the state of the system at the time instant $k+1$ $(\overline{x}(k+1))$ starting from the state of the system at the time k $(\overline{x}(k))$ and its current input $(\overline{u}(k))$. The value of the next state is computed by an appropriate function $f(\cdot,\cdot,\cdot)$. Equation 6b is the *output equation* and describes the relation between the state of the system $(\overline{x}(k))$, its input $(\overline{u}(k))$ and the output variables $(\overline{y}(k))$ through function $g(\cdot,\cdot,\cdot)$.

In our case, the discrete time dynamic system is used to keep track of how many machines are active and when the different machines have been activated. As previously introduced, each component of the application is deployed on different auto scaling nodes. The set of all the auto scaling nodes of the cloud platform upon which the components of the application are deployed is indicated as $\mathcal{I}$. For each auto scaling node i of the DTMC, the vector $\overline{N}_i$ of length 60, specifies the number of machines that were activated $0, 1, \ldots 59$ minutes earlier. We assume that the pricing model of cloud services is pay-by-the-hour and that the controller is activated every minute. The assumed pricing model reflects a common practice of today's Cloud providers, who charge users for one hour of usage of a single service at the beginning of the hour (e.g., Amazon Web Services pricing model). The assumption on the control period is reasonable, since starting a machine usually takes more than a minute. In this work, we consider very fast startup of machines; if longer time have to be considered the controller period is easily adaptable.

The dynamic behavior of the system is expressed through the *state equations* in Formula 7, which specify the relation between the state of the system at time t and $t+1$. More precisely, at the time instant $t+1$, the number of machines that were been activated j minutes earlier, is stored in the cell j of the vector N_i, that is $N_i(t+1)[j]$. This value is equal to the number of machines that were activated $j-1$ minutes earlier the time instant t plus, possibly, the number of machines that are currently activated or deactivated $N_i^*(t+1)$. The *input* variable $N_i^*(t+1)$ is an integer number (positive or negative) that contains the number of machines that are added (positive) or removed (negative) from the system at the time instant $t+1$. When a machine reaches the 60th minute of operation after its activation, reaching the last cell of the vector $\overline{N}_i$, it re-enters the system in the first cell of vector $\overline{N}_i$. This behavior models the fact that if the machine is not shut down the cost of an entire new hour of utilization is added. The value of $N_i^*(t+1)$ is determined by the controller described in Sect. 5.

$$
\overline{N}_i(t+1) = \begin{bmatrix} 0 & 0 & \cdots & 0 & 1 \\ 1 & 0 & \cdots & 0 & 0 \\ 0 & 1 & \cdots & 0 & 0 \\ \vdots & \vdots & \ddots & \vdots & \vdots \\ 0 & 0 & \cdots & 1 & 0 \end{bmatrix} \times \overline{N}_i(t) + \begin{bmatrix} 1 \\ 0 \\ 0 \\ \vdots \\ 0 \end{bmatrix} \cdot N_i^*(t+1) \tag{7}
$$

The *total number of machines* $(N_i(t+1))$ that are active in each node $i \in \mathcal{I}$ of the DTMC at the time $t+1$ is computed using Formula 8, which sums the number of machines that are activated $0, 1 \ldots 59$ min earlier.

$$N_i(t+1) = \sum_{j \in \{0...59\}} \overline{N}_i(t+1)[j]. \tag{8}$$

5   Runtime Adaptation

The model presented in Sect. 4 is used to trigger the run-time adaptation process. The main idea is that the run-time adaptation mechanism can autonomously modify the overall behavior by allocating and de-allocating resources to the different components of the application, i.e., the number of machines of each auto scaling node, to satisfy the current workload requests. This is done by translating the model described in Sect. 4 into a constrained optimization problem that identifies the number of machines to be allocated or de-allocated from each auto scaling group, guaranteeing the required response time constraint while minimizing costs.

The run-time adaptation procedure presented in this section is also able to manage a set of changes that can occur at run-time. These changes include (i) the probabilities of moving through the different states of the DTMC, (ii) the processing rate $\mu(t)$ of each node and (iii) the current incoming workload. These elements are continuously monitored or estimated at run-time. The estimation of the parameters is out of the scope of this work, the interested reader may refer to [10] for additional information.

Since we assume a pay-by-the-hour pricing model, whenever a machine begins the hour, switching it off before the hour ends will not reduces costs, since the whole hour is already payed. Therefore our controller will not shut down machines before ending the allocated hour. At every periodic control instant (1 min in our experiments) the controller adapts by either switching on or off a certain number of machines. These are modeled by a decision variable $\overline{N}^*$, which is a vector that contains the number of machines added or removed in every auto-scaling group. A positive number specifies that new machines should be added to the ones already running, while a negative number describes the number of machines that should be switched off among those finishing the allocated hour.

$$\mathbf{min}\, \overline{C} \cdot \overline{N}^*(t+1) \tag{9a}$$

$$\Omega(t+1) < T_d \tag{9b}$$

$$\overline{N}^*(t+1) + \overline{N}_f(t) > 0 \tag{9c}$$

$$N_j(t+1) > \frac{\hat{\lambda}_j(t+1)}{\hat{\mu}_j(t+1)} \tag{9d}$$

The constrained optimization problem that our controller periodically solves using iterative methods is specified in Formulae 9a to 9d. The *objective function* in Formula 9a specifies that the solution must minimize the total cost, which is equal to the sum of all the values in vector $\overline{N}^*$, weighted with the cost per machine of the specific auto-scaling group $\overline{C}$. The constraint in Formula 9b imposes that the average service time for a single request $\Omega(t+1)$ should not exceed the given threshold T_d. The constraint in Formula 9c imposes that the number of machines must be positive. $\overline{N_f}$ is the vector of machines ending their payed hour, which is obtained from $\overline{N_i}$. Finally, the constraint expressed by Formula 9d is a necessary condition for Formula 3 to be valid, where $\hat{\lambda}_j(t+1)$ and $\hat{\mu}_j(t+1)$ are the estimated arrival rate and service rate at node j at time $t+1$, respectively, while $N_j(t+1)$ is the total number of machines at node j at time $t+1$, which depends on our control variable according to Formulae 7 and 8.

6   Results

This section presents the results of our run-time adaptation mechanism through-out simulations. The non-ideal nature of an actual cloud deployment is repro-duced by the introduction of artificial noise. Note that the performance of the adaptation mechanism strongly depends on the accuracy of the estimation of the working conditions at the time instant $t+1$. More precisely, the estimation of the workload $(\widehat{\lambda}(t+1))$, the probabilities $(\widehat{Q}(t+1))$ and the service rates $(\widehat{\mu}(t+1))$ are subject to noise. Formally, they are specified as described in For-mula 10 where $\eta_\lambda(t+1)$, $\eta_Q(t+1)$ and $\eta_\mu(t+1)$ are the noise in the workload, probabilities and service rate estimations.

$$\widehat{\lambda}(t+1) = \lambda(t+1) + \eta_\lambda(t+1) \tag{10a}$$

$$\widehat{Q}(t+1) = Q(t+1) + \eta_Q(t+1) \tag{10b}$$

$$\widehat{\mu}(t+1) = \mu(t+1) + \eta_\mu(t+1) \tag{10c}$$

We analyze the behavior of the control mechanism in four different scenarios (i) the workload changes, but the probabilities and the service rate of each auto-scaling group are fixed (ii) the service rate of the different auto-scaling group change, but the workload and the probabilities of the DTMC are fixed (iii) the probabilities change, but the workload and the service rate of each auto-scaling group are fixed (iv) the workload, the probabilities and the service rates change.

Figure 5 shows the behavior of the system when the *workload* changes. If the workload increases (e.g., Fig. 5(a) time instants 500 m–800 m) or decreases (e.g., Fig. 5(a) time instants 200 m–500 m), the controller augments or decreases the number of machines in charge of processing these requests (see Fig. 5(b) time instants 500 m–800 m and 200–500 m, respectively). Note that the controller does not remove a machine if it is not expiring. For example, in Fig. 5(b) no machines are removed in the period included between time instants 360 m–420 m, this is due to the fact that the usage of a machine is priced by the hour even if it is shut down before the end of the hour. This gives at the graph a steps shape. Figure 5(c) shows the response time of the system. Note that in some cases the requirement is violated. This happens because the controller is subject to un-predicted spikes of workload, the $\eta_\lambda(t+1)$, that make the requirement violated. Note that these violations can be prevented by a more precise estimation of $\eta_\lambda(t+1)$.

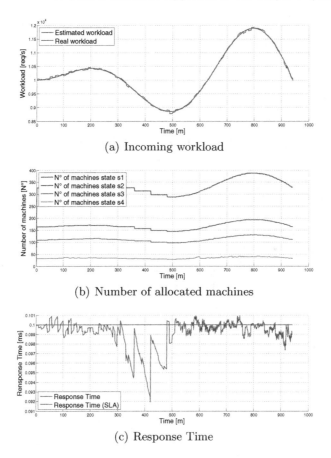

(a) Incoming workload

(b) Number of allocated machines

(c) Response Time

Fig. 5. Behavior of the system when the workload changes

Figure 6 evidences the behavior of the system in response to changes in the *service rate* of the different auto-scaling groups. If the service rate of an auto-scaling group increases (decreases) a set of running machines are removed (added) from the running system. For example, in Fig. 6(a) from time instant 400 m to 700 m the service rate of the auto-scaling group s_2 increases. Therefore, as evidenced in Fig. 6(b) a set of machines are removed from s_2. Note that since we have introduced some noise on the estimation of the service rates of the different nodes (see Fig. 6(a)), in some cases the SLA is violated as depicted in Fig. 6(c). However, this can be handled either by considering the noise in the estimation in the definition of the SLA or by improving the algorithms used to asses the service rates.

Figure 7 evidences the behavior of the run-time adaptation procedure in response to changes in the *probabilities* of the transitions of the DTMC. If the probability of a transition to be performed increases (decreases) the number of machines allocated to the different auto-scaling groups is modified accordingly.

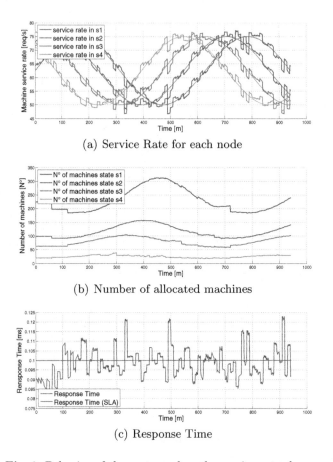

(a) Service Rate for each node

(b) Number of allocated machines

(c) Response Time

Fig. 6. Behavior of the system when the service rate changes

For example, in Fig. 7(a) from time instant 300 m to 500 m the probability of performing the transitions 1–3 ($p_{1,3}$) and 1–2 ($p_{1,2}$) increases and decreases, respectively. Therefore, as evidenced in Fig. 7(b), a set of machines are added (removed) from the auto-scaling group s_2 (s_3). The violations in the SLA evidenced in Fig. 7(c) are, again, caused by errors in the estimation of the probabilities of the DTMC.

Finally, Fig. 8 describes the response time of the system when the probabilities, the service rates and the workload change. Compared to the previously described experiments, in this case, the violations in the SLA increase. The cause is due to the noises that are added on the estimations of the probabilities of the service rates and on the workload.

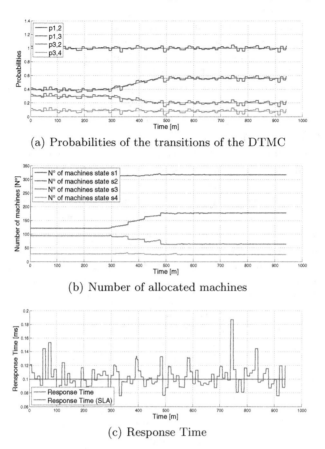

(a) Probabilities of the transitions of the DTMC

(b) Number of allocated machines

(c) Response Time

Fig. 7. Behavior of the system when the probabilities of the DTMC change

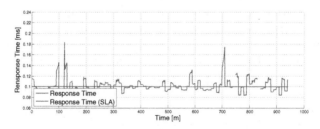

Fig. 8. Behavior of the system when the probabilities, the service rates and the work-load change

7   Related Works

Self adaptive systems have been strongly studied in the last few years due to their ability of autonomously manage changes that occur in their operating environment. The realization of these systems is chained to the solution of a set of sub-problems which include among others, (i) the selection of the adaptation actions to employ after unexpected changes, and (ii) the verification that new configurations of the system are complied with its requirements.

The first problem concerns when and how adaptation is performed. The different approaches proposed in literature exploit theories, such as control theory, models, such as Causal Networks, and procedures, such as optimization algorithms, to select the most suitable set of adaptation actions to apply. For example, Filieri et al. [11] use a control theory based approach to support reliability requirements. Pasquale et al. [4] describe how to realize a requirements-driven adaptation mechanism. More precisely, the requirement model, that is specified using a goal modeling technique, is mapped into a Causal Network that is used at run-time to trigger the adaptation procedure. Ardagna et al. [27] manage adaptation by solving an optimization problem that allows to select the amount of resources to be (de)allocated at run-time in the running system.

The second problem refers to the procedure that is performed, after any change, to verify if the new configuration of the system is aligned with its requirements. One of the possible ways to solve this problem in an efficient way is the generation of constraints [12,15,25]. The developer identifies at design time a set of aspects (e.g., parameters) that can change at run-time. These aspects may include the probabilities of the transitions to be performed, as in [12], or subcomponents of the application [15,25]. Based on these aspects, at design time, a (set of) constraint(s) is pre-computed. At run-time, when something change, instead of verifying everything from scratch, the part that has been modified is only verified against the constraints previously generated, with obvious time advantages.

In the context of the Cloud self adaptiveness refers to the ability of autonomously modify the resources allocated to the different components of the application in response to workload changes. Gambi et al. [14] and Calcavecchia et al. [7] analyze and classify some of these approaches. The former classifies the approaches in relation with their flexibility and assurance which measure the capability of the controller to adapt to unknown or unexpected situations and the capacity of the controller to provide formal guarantees on the behavior of the system, respectively. The latter considers parameter proper of the Cloud, such as their service model (IaaS, PaaS,SaaS), the structure of the controller (e.g., hierarchical, distributed). The works that are discussed in the following provide a high level overview of the current research trends in the area[5].

A first class of approaches concerns the one that provide formal guarantees on the correct behavior of the controller at run-time. A completely specified model representing the real system is required to perform full static analysis before deploying the self-adaptive system. Bi et al. [6] present a dynamic technique to determine the number of virtual machines using a queue model to represent a multi-tier application. The number of machines is chosen as a result of a non-linear constraint optimization problem where only the incoming workload changes. The use of a performance model allows to give formal guarantees

---

[5] For a deeper analysis the interested reader can refer to [7,14].

on the response time of the system. Benanni et al. [5] tackle the provisioning problem by using separate performance models for Online Analytical Processes (OLAP) and Online Transactional Processes (OLTP). The utility function of OLAP processes aims at maximizing the throughput while the one of OLTP minimizes the response time. To assess the performance of a provisioning configuration according to OLAP processes a closed Queue Network (QN) model is used and for OLTP an open QN is preferred.

The second class of approaches consider the model as partially specified, that is several parameters are left unspecified and monitored and updated at run-time. The system is adaptive with respect to variations in the values of these parameters. Calcavecchia et al., [7], proposed a probabilistic and distributed approach where each service is an autonomous agent able to either spawn a new machine or remove itself based on current resource demand. Patikirikorala et al. [23] presented another adaptive mechanism where different models are used at run-time, some of which are static, while others are parametric, and the most suitable one is chosen according to a mechanism they named Multi-Model Switching and Tuning. Miglierina et al. [22] built a dual layer controller to manage both auto scaling of machines and load balancing based on availability constraints, minimizing costs, the model is chosen at design-time but some parameters are updated at run-time.

Finally, the third class concerns approaches that do not rely on a stable representation of the real system. These approaches can manage every type of change, but there is no formal guarantee on their correct behavior. Jiang et al., [17] propose the use different prediction algorithms to estimate the incoming workload and a majority voting algorithm to select between the results of these predictions. Li et al., [20] consider the provisioning problem, using a reinforcement learning approach, and the allocation of the applications of the resources allocated. The Q-Learning algorithm [26] is exploited by servers to distributively learn the best sequence of actions to perform in the different conditions in which the system is operating. Gambi et al., [13] analyzes the same problem using Kriging models, which are surrogate models that are able to efficiently be trained online even with small data sets.

8   Conclusion and Future Work

This paper is a further step toward the realization of systems that are *adaptive*. It presents an approach to develop software that autonomously modifies the amount of resources that serve its components when environmental conditions change. These conditions include (i) the probabilities of requests to be forwarded to the different components of the application (ii) the processing rate of the different resources upon which these components are deployed (iii) the incoming workload that the system has to manage.

The approach requires the developer to define at design time the architecture of the application (its components and their interaction) through a Discrete Time Markov Chain (DTMC); the running environment upon which it is deployed through a Queuing Model (QM); and a cost model through a Dynamic System. These models are aggregated to generate the whole, full-comprehensive, model of the system which is used at run-time to identify the resources to be added or removed from the running system. When something changes, the model is updated and an optimization problem, which is obtained starting from this model, is solved. The solution contains the number of machines to be added or removed, minimizes costs and maintains the desired QoS, in terms of average response time.

We evaluate our approach simulating a *cloud computing* application in a cloud infrastructure. This computing environment has been selected because it allows on-demand access to a configurable pool of resources that can be easily provisioned and released at run-time. The preliminary results obtained in this work encourage further analysis on the applicability of the approach. As future work we aim to evaluate the performance of the approach on a real case study to evidence its advantages. Furthermore, other modeling formalisms, such as more complex queue models (e.g., $M/M/c$) can be considered to specify the system under development.

References

1. Ardagna, D., Panicucci, B., Passacantando, M.: Generalized nash equilibria for the service provisioning problem in cloud systems. IEEE Trans. Serv. Comput. **6**(4), 429–442 (2013)
2. Baier, C., Katoen, J.-P., et al.: Principles of Model Checking, vol. 26202649. MIT Press, Cambridge (2008)
3. Baresi, L., Di Nitto, E., Ghezzi, C.: Toward open-world software: Issue and challenges. Computer **39**(10), 36–43 (2006)
4. Baresi, L., Pasquale, L., Spoletini, P.: Fuzzy goals for requirements-driven adaptation. In: 2010 18th IEEE International Requirements Engineering Conference (RE), pp. 125–134, September 2010
5. Bennani, M., Menasce, D.: Resource allocation for autonomic data centers using analytic performance models. In: ICAC (2005)
6. Bi, J., Zhu, Z., Tian, R., Wang, Q.: Dynamic provisioning modeling for virtualized multi-tier applications in cloud data center. In: Cloud Computing (CLOUD) (2010)
7. Calcavecchia, N.M., Caprarescu, B.A., Nitto, E.D., Dubois, D.J., Petcu, D.: Depas: A decentralized probabilistic algorithm for auto-scaling. CoRR, abs/1202.2509 (2012)
8. Calinescu, R., Ghezzi, C., Kwiatkowska, M., Mirandola, R.: Self-adaptive software needs quantitative verification at runtime. Commun. ACM **55**(9), 69–77 (2012)
9. Di Nitto, E., Ghezzi, C., Metzger, A., Papazoglou, M., Pohl, K.: A journey to highly dynamic, self-adaptive service-based applications. Autom. Softw. Eng. **15**(3–4), 313–341 (2008)
10. Epifani, I., Ghezzi, C., Mirandola, R., Tamburrelli, G.: Model evolution by run-time parameter adaptation. In: IEEE 31st International Conference on Software Engineering, 2009, ICSE 2009, pp. 111–121, May 2009
11. Filieri, A., Ghezzi, C., Leva, A., Maggio, M.: Self-adaptive software meets control theory: a preliminary approach supporting reliability requirements. In: Proceedings of the 2011 26th IEEE/ACM International Conference on Automated Software Engineering, ASE 2011, pp. 283–292. IEEE Computer Society, Washington, DC (2011)

12. Filieri, A., Ghezzi, C., Tamburrelli, G.: Run-time efficient probabilistic model checking. In: Proceedings of the 33rd International Conference on Software Engineering, ICSE 2011, pp. 341–350. ACM, New York (2011)
13. Gambi, A., Toffetti, G., Pautasso, C., Pezze, M.: Kriging controllers for cloud applications. Internet Comput. IEEE **17**(4), 40–47 (2013)
14. Gambi, A., Toffetti, G., Pezzè, M.: Assurance of self-adaptive controllers for the cloud. In: Cámara, J., de Lemos, R., Ghezzi, C., Lopes, A. (eds.) Assurances for Self-Adaptive Systems. LNCS, vol. 7740, pp. 311–339. Springer, Heidelberg (2013)
15. Ghezzi, C., Menghi, C., Sharifloo, A.M., Spoletini, P.: On requirements verification for model refinements. In: 2013 21st IEEE International Requirements Engineering Conference (RE), pp. 62–71. IEEE (2013)
16. Jackson, J.R.: Networks of waiting lines. Oper. Res. **5**(4), 518–521 (1957)
17. Jiang, Y., Perng, C.-S., Li, T., Chang, R.: Self-adaptive cloud capacity planning. In: SCC (2012)
18. Kemeny, J.G., Snell, J.L.: Finite Markov Chains, vol. 210. Springer, New York (1976)
19. Kendall, D.G.: Stochastic processes occurring in the theory of queues and their analysis by the method of the imbedded markov chain. Ann. Math. Stat. **24**, 338–354 (1953)
20. Li, H., Venugopal, S.: Using reinforcement learning for controlling an elastic web application hosting platform. In: ICAC (2011)
21. Mell, P., Grance, T.: The nist definition of cloud computing (draft). NIST Spec. Publ. **800**(145), 1–7 (2011)
22. Miglierina, M., Gibilisco, G., Ardagna, D., Di Nitto, E.: Model based control for multi-cloud applications. In: MiSE (2013)
23. Patikirikorala, T., Colman, A., Han, J., Wang, L.: A multi-model framework to implement self-managing control systems for qos management. In: SEAMS (2011)
24. Robinson, R.C.: An introduction to dynamical systems, vol. 19. AMS Bookstore (2013)
25. Sharifloo, A.M., Spoletini, P.: LOVER: Light-weight fOrmal verification of adaptivE systems at run time. In: Păsăreanu, C.S., Salaün, G. (eds.) FACS 2012. LNCS, vol. 7684, pp. 170–187. Springer, Heidelberg (2013)
26. Watkins, C., Dayan, P.: Technical note: Q-learning. Mach. Learn. **8**(3–4), 279–292 (1992)
27. Zhang, L., Ardagna, D.: Sla based profit optimization in autonomic computing systems. In: Proceedings of the 2nd International Conference on Service Oriented Computing, pp. 173–182. ACM (2004)

Consistency in Distributed Systems

Sebastian Burckhardt[✉]

Microsoft Research, Redmond, USA
sburckha@microsoft.com
http://research.microsoft.com/people/sburckha/

Abstract. Data replication is a common technique for programming distributed systems, and is often important to achieve performance or reliability goals. Unfortunately, the replication of data can compromise its consistency, and thereby break programs that are unaware. In particular, in weakly consistent systems, programmers must assume some responsibility to properly deal with queries that return stale data, and to avoid state corruption under conflicting updates. The fundamental tension between performance (favoring weak consistency) and correctness (favoring strong consistency) is a recurring theme when designing concurrent and distributed systems, and is both practically relevant and of theoretical interest.

In this course, we investigate how to understand and formalize consistency guarantees, and how we can determine if a system implementation is correct with respect to such specifications. We start by examining consensus, a classic problem in distributed systems, and then proceed to study various specifications and implementations of eventually consistent systems.

As more and more developers write programs that execute on a virtualized cloud infrastructure, they find themselves confronted with the subtleties that have long been the hallmark of distributed systems research. Devising message protocols, reading and writing weakly consistent shared data, and handling failures are notoriously challenging, and are gaining relevance for a new generation of developers.

With this in mind, I devised this course to provide a mix of techniques and results that may prove either interesting, or useful, or both. In the first half, I am presenting well-known results and techniques from the area of distributed systems research, including:

- A beautiful, classic result: the impossibility of implementing consensus in the presence of silent crashes on an asynchronous system [7] (Sect. 2.5).
- An algorithm that shows how impossibility is relative, by "achieving the impossible" for all practical purposes: the PAXOS protocol [11] (Sect. 2.6).
- The machinery needed to present these topics: labeled transitions systems and asynchronous protocols (Sect. 2).

In the second half, I focus on the main topic, which are consistency models for shared data. This part includes:

B. Meyer and M. Nordio (Eds.): LASER 2013-2014, LNCS 8987, pp. 84–120, 2015.
DOI: 10.1007/978-3-319-28406-4_4

- A formalization of strong consistency (sequential consistency, linearizability) and a proof of the CAP theorem [1,8] (Sect. 3).
- A general examination and formalization of various models for eventual consistency, which decomposes sequential consistency and introduces the arbitration and visibility relations in its place (Sect. 4.1).
- Several example architectures for implementing various versions of sequential or eventual consistency (Sect. 4.2).

These lecture notes are not meant to serve as a transcript. Rather, their purpose is to complement the slides [2] used in the lectures by providing the technical depth and precision that is difficult to achieve in a lecture. Although the material is technically self-contained, I highly recommend that readers study the slides alongside these lecture notes, because the slides provide additional motivation and contain many more examples and visualizations (such as diagrams or animations) that bring the material to life.

Update: Since giving the original lectures at the LASER summer school, I have expanded and revised much of the material presented in Sects. 3 and 4. The result is now available as a short textbook [3] that provides a thorough introduction to commonly used consistency models and protocols.

1   Preliminaries

We introduce some basic mathematical notations for sets, sequences, and relations. We assume standard set notations for set. Note that we write $A \subseteq B$ to denote $\forall a \in A : a \in B$. In particular, the notation $A \subseteq B$ does neither imply nor rule out either $A = B$ or $A \neq B$. We let $\mathbb{N}$ be the set of all natural numbers (starting with number 1), and $\mathbb{N}_0 = \mathbb{N} \cup \{0\}$. The power set $\mathcal{P}(A)$ is the set of all subsets of A.

Sequences. Given a set A, we let A^* be the set of finite sequences (or "words") of elements of A, including the empty sequence which is denoted ϵ. We let $A^+ \subseteq A^*$ be the set of nonempty sequences of elements of A. Thus, $A^* = A^+ \cup \{\epsilon\}$. For two sequences $u, v \in A^*$, we write $u \cdot v$ to denote the concatenation (which is also in A^*). If $f : A \rightarrow B$ is a function, and $w \in A^*$ is a sequence, then we let $f(w) \in B^*$ be the sequence obtained by applying f to each element of w. Sometimes we write A^ω for the set of ω-infinite sequences of elements of A.

Multisets. A finite multiset m over some base set A is defined to be a function $m : A \rightarrow \mathbb{N}_0$ such that $m(a) = 0$ for almost all a (= all but finitely many). The idea is that we represent the multiset as the function that defines how many times each element of A is in the set. We let $\mathcal{M}(A)$ denote the set of all finite multisets over A. When convenient, we interpret an element a as the singleton multiset containing a. We use the following notations for typical operations on multisets (using a mix of symbols taken from set notations and vector notations), $\emptyset$ for the empty multiset (= the constant 0 function $\lambda a.0$), $m + m'$ for multiset union (meaning $\lambda a.m(a) + m'(a)$), $m \leq m'$ for multiset inclusion (meaning $\forall a \in A : m(a) \leq m'(a)$), $a \in m$ for multiset membership (meaning $m(a) \geq 1$), and $m - m'$ for multiset difference (meaning $\lambda a.max(0, m(a) - m'(a))$).

Relations. A binary relation r over A is a subset $r \subseteq A \times A$. For $a, b \in A$, we use the notation $a \xrightarrow{r} b$ to denote $(a, b) \in r$, and the notation $r(a)$ to denote $\{b \in A \mid a \xrightarrow{r} b\}$. We generalize the latter to sets in the usual way, i.e. for $A' \subseteq A$, $r(A') = \{b \in A \mid \exists a \in A' : a \xrightarrow{r} b\}$. We use the notation r^{-1} to denote the inverse relation, i.e. $(a \xrightarrow{r^{-1}} b) \Leftrightarrow (b \xrightarrow{r} a)$. Therefore, $r^{-1}(b) = \{a \in A \mid a \xrightarrow{r} b\}$ (we use this notation frequently). Given two binary relations r, r' over A, we define the composition $r; r' = \{(a, c) \mid \exists b \in A : a \xrightarrow{r} b \xrightarrow{r'} c\}$. We let id_A be the identity relation over A, i.e. $(a \xrightarrow{\mathrm{id}_A} b) \Leftrightarrow (a = b)$. For $n \in \mathbb{N}_0$, We let A^n be the n-ary composition $A; A \dots; A$, with $A^0 = \mathrm{id}_A$. We let $A^+ = \bigcup_{n \geq 1} A^n$ and $A^* = \bigcup_{n \geq 0} A^n$. For some subset $A' \subseteq A$, and a binary relation r over A, we let $r|_{A'}$ be the binary relation over A' obtained by restricting r, meaning $r|_{A'} = r \cap (A' \times A')$.

Orders. A binary relation r over A is a *partial order* if for all $a, b, c \in A$:

- It is irreflexive: $a \xnrightarrow{r} a$
- It is transitive: $(a \xrightarrow{r} b) \wedge (b \xrightarrow{r} c) \Rightarrow (a \xrightarrow{r} c)$

Note that partial orders are acyclic (if there were a cycle, transitivity would imply $a \rightarrow a$ for some a, contradicting irreflexivity). We often visualize partial orders as directed acyclic graphs. Moreover, in such drawings, we usually omit transitively implied edges, to avoid overloading the picture.

A partial order does not necessarily order all elements. In fact, that is precisely what distinguishes it from a total order: a partial order r over A is a *total order* if for all $a, b \in A$ such that $a \neq b$, either $a \xrightarrow{r} b$ or $b \xrightarrow{r} a$. All total orders are also partial orders.

Many authors define partial orders to be reflexive rather than irreflexive. We chose to define them as irreflexive, to keep them more similar to total orders, and to keep the definition more consistent with our favorite visualization, directed acyclic graphs, whose vertices never have self-loops.

This choice is only superficial and not a deep distinction: consider the familiar notations $<$ and $\leq$. Conceptually, they represent the same ordering relation, but one of them is reflexive, the other one is irreflexive. In fact, if r is a total or partial order, we sometimes write $a <_r b$ to represent $a \xrightarrow{r} b$, and $a \leq_r b$ to represent $(a \xrightarrow{r} b) \vee (a = b)$.

A total order can be used to sort a set. For some finite set $A' \subseteq A$ and a total order r over A, we let $A'.\mathrm{sort}(r) \in A^*$ be the sequence obtained by sorting the elements of A' in ascending $<_r$-order.

2 Models and Machines

To reason about protocols and consistency, we need terminology and notation that helps us to abstract from details. In particular, we need models for machines, and ways to characterize their behavior by stating and then proving or refuting their properties.

2.1 Labeled Transition Systems

Labeled transitions systems provide a useful formalization and terminology that applies to a wide range of machines.

Definition 1. *A* **labeled transition system** *is a tuple* $L = (\mathsf{Cnf}, \mathsf{Ini}, \mathsf{Act}, \rightarrow)$ *where*

- Cnf *is a set of system* configurations, *or system states.*
- $\mathsf{Ini} \subseteq \mathsf{Cnf}$ *is a set of initial states. These represent valid starting configurations of the system.*
- Act *is a set of action labels.*
- $\rightarrow \subset (\mathsf{Cnf} \times \mathsf{Act} \times \mathsf{Cnf})$ *is a ternary transition relation. We write* $x \xrightarrow{a} y$ *to denote* $(x, a, y) \in \rightarrow$.

When using an LTS to model a system, a configuration represents a global snapshot of the state of every component of the system. Actions are abstractions that can model a number of activities, such as sending or receiving of messages, interacting with a user, doing some internal processing, or combinations thereof. Labeled transition systems are often visualized using labeled graphs, with vertices representing the states and labeled edges representing the actions.

We say an action $a \in \mathsf{Act}$ is *enabled* in state $s \in \mathsf{Cnf}$ if there exists a $s' \in \mathsf{Cnf}$ such that $s \xrightarrow{a} s'$. More than one action can be enabled in a state, and in general, an action can lead to more than one successor state. We say an action a is *deterministic* if that is never the case, that is, if for all $s \in \mathsf{Cnf}$, there is at most one $s' \in S$ such that $s \xrightarrow{a} s'$.

Defining an LTS to represent a concurrent system helps us to reason precisely about its executions and their correctness. An *execution fragment* E is a (finite or infinite) alternating sequence of states and actions:

$$s_0 \xrightarrow{a_1} s_1 \xrightarrow{a_2} s_2 \xrightarrow{a_3} \ldots$$

and an *execution* is an execution fragment that starts in an initial state. We formalize these definitions as follows.

Definition 2. *Given some LTS* $L = (\mathsf{Cnf}, \mathsf{Ini}, \mathsf{Act}, \rightarrow)$, *an* **execution fragment** *for* L *is a tuple* $E = (\mathsf{len}, \mathsf{cnf}, \mathsf{act})$ *where*

$$
\begin{aligned}
&\mathsf{len} \in (\mathbb{N}_0 \cup \infty) &&\text{(the length)} \\
&\mathsf{cnf} : \{0 \ldots \mathsf{len}\} \rightarrow \mathsf{Cnf} &&\text{(the configurations)} \\
&\mathsf{act} : \{1 \ldots \mathsf{len}\} \rightarrow \mathsf{Act} &&\text{(the actions)}
\end{aligned}
$$

such that for all $1 \leq i \leq \mathsf{len}$, *we have* $\mathsf{cnf}(i-1) \xrightarrow{\mathsf{act}(i)} \mathsf{cnf}(i)$. *An* **execution** *is an execution fragment* E *satisfying* $E.\mathsf{cnf}(0) \in \mathsf{Ini}$.

We define $\mathsf{pre}(E) = E.\mathsf{cnf}(0)$ and $\mathsf{post}(E) = E.\mathsf{cnf}(E.\mathsf{len})$ (we write $\mathsf{post}(E) = \bot$ if $E.\mathsf{len} = \infty$). Two execution fragments E_1, E_2 can be concatenated to form another execution fragment $E_1 \cdot E_2$ if $E_1.\mathsf{len} \neq \infty$ and $\mathsf{post}(E_1) = \mathsf{pre}(E_2)$.

We say a configuration $c \in$ Cnf is *reachable from* a configuration $c' \in$ Cnf if there exists an execution fragment E such that $c' = \mathsf{pre}(E)$ and $c = \mathsf{post}(E)$. We say a configuration $c \in$ Cnf is *reachable* if it is reachable from an initial configuration.

Reasoning about executions usually involves reasoning about *events*. An event is an occurrence of an action (the same action can occur several times in an execution, each being a separate event). Technically, we define the events of an execution fragment E to be the set of numbers $\mathsf{Evt}(E) = \{1, 2, \ldots, E.\mathsf{len}\}$. Then, for events $e, e' \in \mathsf{Evt}(E)$, $e < e'$ means e occurs before e' in the execution, and $E.\mathsf{act}(e)$ is the action of event e.

Given an execution fragment E of an LTS L, we let $\mathsf{trc}(E) \in (L.\mathsf{Act}^* \cup L.\mathsf{Act}^\omega)$ be the (finite of infinite) sequence of actions in E, called the *trace* of E. If all actions of L are deterministic, then E is completely determined by $E.\mathsf{pre}$ and $E.\mathsf{trc}$. For that reason, traces are sometimes called *schedules*.

In our proofs, we often need to take an existing execution, and modify it slightly by reordering certain actions. Given a configuration c and a deterministic action a, we write $\mathsf{post}(c, a)$ to be the uniquely determined c' satisfying $c \xrightarrow{a} c'$, or $\bot$ if it is not possible (because a is not enabled in c). Similarly, we write $\mathsf{post}(c, w)$, for an action sequence $w \in A^*$, to denote the state reached from c by performing the actions in w, or $\bot$ if not possible. In the remainder of this text, all of our LTS are constructed in such a way that all actions are deterministic.

Working with deterministic actions can have practical advantages. For testing and debugging protocols, we often need to analyze or reproduce failures based on partial information about the execution, such as a trace log. If the log contains the sequence of actions in the order they happened, and if the actions are deterministic, it means that the log contains sufficient information to fully reproduce the execution.

2.2   Asynchronous Message Protocols

An LTS can express many different kinds of concurrent systems, but we care mostly about message passing protocols in this context. Therefore, we specialize the general LTS definition above to define such systems. Throughout this text, we assume that Pid is a set of process identifiers (possibly infinite, to model dynamic creation). Furthermore, we assume that there is a total order defined on the process identifiers Pid. For example, Pid $= \mathbb{N}$.

Definition 3. *A* **protocol definition** *is a tuple*

$$\Phi = (\mathsf{Pst}, \mathsf{Msg}, \mathsf{Act}, \mathsf{ini}, \mathsf{ori}, \mathsf{dst}, \mathsf{pid}, \mathsf{cnd}, \mathsf{rcv}, \mathsf{snd}, \mathsf{upd})$$

where

- Pst *is a set of process states, with a function*

$$\mathsf{ini} : \mathsf{Pid} \to \mathcal{P}(\mathsf{Pst}) \; (\textit{initial states})$$

– Msg *is a set of messages, with properties*

$$\text{ori} : \text{Msg} \to \text{Pid} \ \textit{(the origin)}$$
$$\text{dst} : \text{Msg} \to \text{Pid} \ \textit{(the destination)}$$

– Act *is a set of actions, with properties*

pid : Act → Pid	*(the process)*
cnd : Act → $\mathcal{P}(\text{Pst})$	*(the condition or guard)*
rcv : Act → ⊥ ∪ Msg	*(received message, if any)*
snd : Act × Pst → $\mathcal{M}(\text{Msg})$	*(sent messages)*
upd : Act × Pst → Pst	*(process state update)*

– *the message received by an action targets the same process:*

$$\forall a \in \text{Act} : (\text{rcv}(a) \neq \bot) \Rightarrow (\text{dst}(\text{rcv}(a)) = \text{pid}(a)).$$

– *only finitely many actions apply at a time:*

$$\forall s \in \text{Pst} : \forall m \in (\bot \cup \text{Msg}) : |\{a \in \text{Act} \mid (\text{cnd}(a) \in s) \wedge (\text{rcv}(a) = m)\}| < \infty.$$

We call actions a that receive no message (i.e. $\text{rcv}(a) = \bot$) *spontaneous*. For convenience, given a protocol definition Φ, we write $\Phi.\text{Pst}$, $\Phi.\text{Msg}$, etc. to denote its components.

Definition 4. *Given a protocol definition Φ as above, we construct a corresponding labeled transition system $L_\Phi = (\text{Cnf}_\Phi, \text{Ini}_\Phi, \text{Act}_\Phi, \to_\Phi)$ as follows:*

– Configurations: $\text{Cnf}_\Phi = (\text{Pid} \to \Phi.\text{Pst}) \times \mathcal{M}(\Phi.\text{Msg})$. The meaning is that each configuration is a pair (P, M) with P being a function that maps each process identifier to the current state of that process, and M being a multiset that represents messages that are currently "in flight". For a configuration c, we write $c.P$ and $c.M$ to denote its components.
– Actions: $\text{Act}_\Phi = \Phi.\text{Act}$.
– Initial states: $\text{Ini}_\Phi = \{(P, \emptyset) \mid \forall p \in \text{Pid} : P(p) \in \Phi.\text{ini}(p)\}$
– Transition Relation: define $\to_\Phi$ such that $(P, M) \overset{a}{\to}_\Phi (P', M')$ iff all of the following conditions hold:
  1. the guard is satisfied: $P(\Phi.\text{pid}(a)) \in \Phi.\text{cnd}(a)$
  2. the received message (if any) is removed: either $\Phi.\text{rcv}(a) = \bot$ and $M' = M$, or $\Phi.\text{rcv}(a) \in M$ and $M' = M - \Phi.\text{rcv}(a)$
  3. the sent messages are added to the message pool: $M' = M + \Phi.\text{snd}(a)$
  4. the local state is updated, all other states remain the same:

$$\forall p \in \text{Pid} : \quad P'(p) = \begin{cases} \Phi.\text{upd}(a, P(p)) & \text{if } p = \Phi.\text{pid}(a) \\ P(p) & \text{otherwise} \end{cases}$$

When reasoning about an execution E of L_Φ, we define the following notational shortcut: $E_{p,i} = E.\text{cnf}(i).P(p)$.

process state
| **preference** : $\{0, 1\}$;   // initially one of $\{0, 1\}$
| **decision** : $\{\bot, 0, 1\}$;   // initially $\bot$
messages
| Proposal(p : Pid, b : $\{0, 1\}$)   //sent from p to l
| Announcement(q : Pid, b : $\{0, 1\}$) //sent from l to q
action propose(p : Pid) **at** p
| **sends** Proposal(p, **preference**)
action announce(p : Pid, b : $\{0, 1\}$) **at** l
| **receives** Proposal(p, b)
| **condition** decision $= \bot$
| **sends** $\sum_{q \in \text{Pid}}$ Announcement(q, b)
| **updates** decision $\leftarrow b$
action learn(q : Pid, b : $\{0, 1\}$) **at** q
| **receives** Announcement(p, b)
| **updates** decision $\leftarrow b$

Fig. 1. Example strawman protocol for a leader-based consensus, with a fixed leader $l \in$ Pid.

Example. Consider a simple protocol where the processes try to reach consensus on a single bit. We assume that the initial state of each process contains the bit value it is going to propose. We can implement a simple leader-based protocol to reach consensus by fixing some leader process $l \in$ Pid. The idea is based on a "race to the leader", which works in three stages: (1) each process sends a message containing the bit value it is proposing to the leader, (2) the leader, upon receiving any message, announces this value to all other processes, and (3) upon receiving the announced message, each recipient decides on that value.

We show how to write pseudocode for this protocol in Fig. 1. Our notation is somewhere between pseudocode and formulae (see Fig. 1). It defines all the components of Φ listed in Definition 3 in several sections with the following meanings:

- In the **process state** section, we define the set Pst_Φ and the initial state function ini_Φ. The process state is expressed as a product of several named typed variables, and we show the initial value of each variable in the comment at the end of each line.
- In the **messages** section, we define the set Msg and the functions ori and dst. Each message has a name and several named typed parameters. We show how the functions ori and dst (which determine the origin and destination of each message) are defined in the comment at the end of each line.
- The remaining sections define the actions, with one section per action. The entries have the following meaning:
  - The first line of each **action** section defines the action label, which is a name together with named typed parameters. All action labels together constitute the set Act. The comment at the end of the line defines the pid function, which determines the process to which this action belongs.

- The **receives** section defines the rcv function. If there is a receives line present, it defines the message that is received by this action, and if there is no receives line, it specifies that this action is spontaneous.
- The **sends** section defines the snd function. It specifies the message, or the multiset of messages, to be sent by this action. We use the multiset notations as described in Sect. 1, in particular, the sum symbol is used to describe a collection of messages. We omit this section if no messages are sent.
- The **condition** section defines the cnd function, representing a condition that is necessary for this action to be performed. It describes a predicate over the local process state (i.e. over the variables defined in the process state section). We omit this section if the action is unconditional.
- The **updates** section defines the upd function, by specifying how to update the local process state. We omit this section if the process state is not changed.

One could conceivably formalize these definitions and produce a practically usable programming language for protocols; in fact, this has already been done for the programming language used by the Murϕ tool [6], an explicit-state model checker that is suitable for model checking protocols defined in this style, and which inspired our pseudocode formalization.

Consider the consensus protocol shown in Fig. 1. Is this a good protocol? Not really. It's not all that bad: we shall see that it is actually a correct consensus in the absence of failures, and it works even if there are crash failures as long as only non-leader processes fail. However, it is susceptible to leader failures. Also, it has some oddities: participants can keep sending inordinate numbers of propose messages. The decision value is written twice on the leader. Perhaps worst: the protocol is more complicated than necessary. The leader could just send its own proposal immediately to everyone.

2.3   Consensus Protocols

What makes a protocol a consensus protocol? Somehow, we start out with a bit on each participant describing its preference. When the protocol is done, everyone should agree on some bit value that was one of the proposed values. And, there should be progress eventually, i.e. the protocol should terminate with a decision.

We now formalize what we mean by a consensus protocol, by adding functions to formalize the notions of initial preference and of decisions.

Definition 5. *A consensus protocol is a tuple*

$$(\mathsf{Pst}, \mathsf{Msg}, \mathsf{Act}, \mathsf{ini}, \mathsf{ori}, \mathsf{dst}, \mathsf{pid}, \mathsf{cnd}, \mathsf{rcv}, \mathsf{snd}, \mathsf{upd}, \mathsf{pref}, \mathsf{dec})$$

such that

– $(\mathsf{Pst}, \ldots, \mathsf{upd})$ *is a protocol.*

- pref *is a function* Pid $\times$ $\{0,1\}$ $\rightarrow$ Pst *with the following meaning:* pref(p,b) *is the initial process state to be used for a process whose initial preference is b. We require that for all p,* ini(p) = $\{$pref$(p,0)$, pref$(p,1)\}$.
- dec *is a function* Pst $\rightarrow$ $\{\perp, 0, 1\}$; *For a process state s,* dec(s) = $\perp$ *means no decision has been reached, otherwise* dec(s) *is the decision that has been reached.*

For example, for the strawman protocol, we define pref(p,b).preference = b and pref(p,b).decision = $\perp$, and we define dec(s) = s.decision.

Next, we formalize the correctness conditions we briefly outlined at the beginning of this section, and then examine if they hold for our strawman. For an execution E, we define the following properties:

1. **Stability.** If a value is decided at a process p, it remains decided forever:

$$\forall p \in \text{Pid} : \forall i < E.\text{len} : (\text{dec}(E_{p,i}) \neq \text{dec}(E_{p,i+1})) \Rightarrow (\text{dec}(E_{p,i}) = \perp)$$

2. **Agreement.** No two processes should decide differently:

$$\{0,1\} \not\subseteq \{\text{dec}(E_{p,i}) \mid i \leq E.\text{len and } p \in \text{Pid}\}$$

3. **Validity.** If a value is decided, this value must match the preference of at least one of the processes:

$$\{\text{dec}(E_{p,i}) \mid i \leq E.\text{len and } p \in \text{Pid}\} \subseteq \{\perp\} \cup \{b \mid \exists p : \text{pref}(p,b) = E_{p,0}\}$$

4. **Termination.** Eventually, a decision is reached on all correct[1] processes:

$$\forall p \in (\text{Pid} \setminus F) : \{0,1\} \cap \{\text{dec}(E_{p,i}) \mid i \leq E.\text{len}\} \neq \emptyset$$

Does our strawman protocol satisfy all of these properties, for all of its executions? Certainly, this is true for the first three.

1. **Strawman satisfies agreement and stability.** There can be at most one announce event, because only the leader can perform the announce action, and the leader sets the decided variable to true after doing the announce, which prevents further announce actions. Therefore, all decide actions must receive a Announcement message sent by the same announce event, thus all the actions that write a decision value write the same value. Decision values are stable: there is no action that writes $\perp$ to the decision variable.
2. **Strawman satisfies validity.** Any announce event (for some bit b) receives a Proposal message that must have originated in some propose event (with the same bit b), which has as a precondition that the variable proposal = b. Thus, b matches the preference of that process.

Termination is however not satisfied for all executions. For example, in an execution of length 0, no decision is reached. Perhaps it would be more reasonable to restrict our attention to complete executions:

---

[1] We talk more about failures later. For now, just assume that the set F of faulty processes is empty.

Definition 6. *An execution fragment E is* complete *if it is either infinite or terminated, i.e. if either E.len $= \infty$, or if no actions are enabled in E.post.*

Does the strawman satisfy termination on all complete executions? The answer is again no. For example, consider an initial configuration where the preference of process p is 0. Then we can have an infinite execution

$$\mathsf{propose}(p, 0) \; \mathsf{propose}(p, 0) \; \mathsf{propose}(p, 0) \; \mathsf{propose}(p, 0) \; \ldots$$

Clearly, no progress is made and an unbounded number of messages is sent. No decision is reached.

Still, it appears that this criticism is not fair! It is hard to imagine how *any* protocol can achieve termination unless the transport layer and the process scheduler cooperate. Clearly, if the system simply does not deliver messages, or never executes actions even though they are enabled, nothing good can happen. We need *fairness*: some assumptions about the "minimal level of service" we may expect.

Informally, what we want to require is that messages are eventually delivered unless they become undeliverable, and that spontaneous actions are eventually performed unless they become disabled. We say an action $a \in \mathsf{Act}$ *receives* message $m \in \mathsf{Msg}$ if $\mathsf{rcv}(a) = m$. We say $m \in \mathsf{Msg}$ is *receivable* in a configuration s if there exists an action a that is enabled and that receives m.

Definition 7. *A message m is* **neglected** *by an execution E if it is receivable in infinitely many configurations, but received by only finitely many actions. A spontaneous action a is* **neglected** *by an execution E, if it is enabled in infinitely many configurations, but performed only finitely many times.*

Definition 8. *An execution E of some protocol Φ is* **fair** *if it does not neglect any messages or spontaneous actions.*

Definition 9. *A consensus protocol is a* **correct consensus protocol** *if all fair complete executions satisfy stability, agreement, validity, and termination.*

Strawman is Correct. We already discussed agreement and validity. Termination is also satisfied for fair executions, for the following reasons. Because the propose action is always enabled for all p, it must happen at least once (in fact, it will happen infinitely many times for all p). After it happens just once, announce is now enabled, and remains enabled forever if announce does not happen. Thus announce must happen (otherwise fairness is violated). But now, for each q, decide is enabled, and thus must happen eventually.

Fair Schedulers. The definition of fairness is purposefully quite general; it does not describe how exactly a scheduler is guaranteeing fairness. However, it is useful to consider how to construct a scheduler that guarantees fairness. One way to do so is to schedule an action that has maximal seniority, in the sense that it is executing a spontaneous action or receiving a message that has been waiting (i.e. been enabled/receivable but not executed/received) the longest:

Definition 10. *Let Φ be a protocol, let E be a finite execution of L_Φ, and let $a \in \mathsf{Act}_\Phi$ be an action that is enabled in $\mathsf{post}(E)$. Then, we define the **seniority** of a to be the maximal number k such that either (1) some message m in $\mathsf{rcv}(a)$ is receivable in $E.\mathsf{cnf}(E.\mathsf{len} - k)$ but has not been received by any action $E.\mathsf{act}(j)$ where $E.(E.\mathsf{len} - k) < j \leq E.\mathsf{len}$, or (2) a is a spontaneous action that is enabled in $E.\mathsf{cnf}(E.\mathsf{len} - k)$ but is not equal to any $E.\mathsf{act}(j)$ where $(E.\mathsf{len} - k) < j \leq E.\mathsf{len}$.*

Lemma 1. *If a scheduler always picks the most senior enabled action, the resulting schedule is fair.*

Proof. Assume to the contrary that there exists an execution that is not fair, that is, neglects a message or spontaneous action.

First, consider that a message m is neglected. This means that the message is receivable infinitely often, but received only finitely many times. Consider the first configuration where it is receivable after the last time it is received, say $E.\mathsf{cnf}(k)$. Since m is receivable in infinitely many configurations $\{E.\mathsf{cnf}(k') \mid k' > k\}$ but never received, there must be infinitely many configurations $\{E.\mathsf{cnf}(k') \mid k' > k\}$ where some enabled action is more senior than the one that receives m (otherwise the scheduler would pick that one). However, an action can only be more senior than the one that receives m if it is either receiving some message that has been waiting (i.e. has been receivable without being received) at least as long as m, or a spontaneous action that has been waiting (i.e. has been enabled without being performed) at least as long as m. But there can only be finitely many such messages or spontaneous actions, since there are only finitely many configurations $\{E.\mathsf{cnf}(j) \mid j \leq k\}$, and each such configuration has only finitely many receivable messages and enabled spontaneous actions, by the last condition in Definition 3; thus we have a contradiction.

Now, consider that a spontaneous action is neglected. We get a contradiction by the same reasoning. □

Independence. The notion of *independence* of actions and schedules is also often useful. We can define independence for general labeled transition systems as follows:

Definition 11. *Let $L = (S, I, \mathsf{Act}, \rightarrow)$ be a LTS. Two actions $a, a' \in L$ are called independent if for all configurations $c \in \mathsf{Cnf}$ in which both a and a' are enabled, the following conditions are true:*

- *They do not disable each other: a is enabled in $\mathsf{post}(c, a')$ and a' is enabled in $\mathsf{post}(c, a)$.*
- *Their effect commutes: $\mathsf{post}(c, a \cdot a') = \mathsf{post}(c, a' \cdot a)$.*

For protocols, actions performed by different nodes are independent. This is because executing an action for process p can only remove messages destined for p from the message pool, it can thus not disable any actions on any other process. Actions by different processes always commute, because their effect on the local state targets local states by different processes, and their effects on the message pool commute.

We call two schedules $s, s' \in \mathsf{Act}^*$ independent if for all $a \in s$ and $a' \in s'$, a and a' are independent. Note that if two schedules s, s' are independent and possible in some configuration c, then $\mathsf{post}(c, s \cdot s') = \mathsf{post}(c, s' \cdot s)$. Visually, this can be seen by doing a typical tiling argument.

2.4   Failures

As we probably all know from experience, failures are common in distributed systems. Failures can originate in the transport layer (a logical abstraction of the network, including switches, links, proxies, etc.) or the nodes (computers running the protocol software). Sometimes, the distinction is not that clear (for example, messages that are waiting in buffers are conceptually in the transport layer, but are subject to loss if the node fails).

We now show how, given a protocol Φ and its LTS as defined in Sect. 2.2, Definition 3, we can model failures by adding failure actions to the LTS defined in Definition 4.

Modeling Transport Failures. Failures for message delivery often include (1) reordering, (2) loss, (3) duplication, and (4) injection of messages. In our protocol model, reorderings are already allowed, thus we do not consider them to be a failure. To model message loss, we can add the following action to the LTS:

$$\mathsf{Act}_\Phi^{\mathsf{lose}} = \mathsf{Act}_\Phi \cup \{\mathsf{lose}(m) \mid m \in \mathsf{Msg}\}$$
$$(P, M) \xrightarrow{\mathsf{lose}(m)} (P', M') \Leftrightarrow ((P = P') \wedge (m \in M) \wedge (M' = M - m))$$

Similarly, we can add an action for message duplication:

$$\mathsf{Act}_\Phi^{\mathsf{duplicate}} = \mathsf{Act}_\Phi \cup \{\mathsf{duplicate}(m) \mid m \in \mathsf{Msg}\}$$
$$(P, M) \xrightarrow{\mathsf{duplicate}(m)} (P', M') \Leftrightarrow ((P = P') \wedge (m \in M) \wedge (M' = M + m))$$

We can also model injection of arbitrary messages:

$$\mathsf{Act}_\Phi^{\mathsf{invent}} = \mathsf{Act}_\Phi \cup \{\mathsf{invent}(m) \mid m \in \mathsf{Msg}\}$$
$$(P, M) \xrightarrow{\mathsf{invent}(m)} (P', M') \Leftrightarrow ((P = P') \wedge (M' = M + m))$$

However, we will not talk more about the latter, which is considered a *byzantine* failure, and which opens up a whole new category of challenges and results.

Masking Transport Failures. Protocols can mask message reordering, loss, and duplication by affixing sequence numbers to messages, and using send and receive buffers. Receivers can detect missing messages in the sequence and re-request them. In fact, socket protocols (such as TCP) use this type of mechanism (e.g. sliding window) to achieve reliable in-order delivery of a byte stream. In practice, however, just using TCP is not always good enough, because TCP connections can themselves fail. Often, resilience against transport failures needs to be built into the protocol in some form.

A common trick to tolerate message duplication in services is to design the service calls to be *idempotent*, meaning that executing a message twice has the same effect as executing it just once. For example, setting the value of some parameter twice is harmless. Properly written REST protocols use the verb PUT to mark such requests as idempotent, allowing browsers and proxies to duplicate them.

Modeling Node Failures. Typical node failures considered by protocol designers are *crash failures* (a process permanently stops at some point), and *crash-recovery* failures (a process stops at some point, then recovers later). Sometimes, byzantine failures are also considered, where faulty nodes exhibit arbitrary behavior, but we are skipping that topic. Typical terminology is to call a process correct if it does never experience a crash failure, and if it encounters only finitely many crash-recovery failures. We let $F \subset \mathsf{Pid}$ be the subset of faulty processes, i.e. processes that *may* be incorrect (it is acceptable for processes in F to be actually correct in any given execution).

In a crash failure, the process state is permanently lost, and the process never takes another action. In a crash-recovery failure, the process can recover some or all of its state from some form of durable storage (if it cannot, there is little reason for a process to continue under the same identity). The part of the state that is lost in crashes is called "soft state". Often, message buffers are soft state, thus it is possible that messages are lost or duplicated if the crash occurred during a transition that receives or sends messages.

In asynchronous systems, it is often important to distinguish between *silent* crashes and *noisy* crashes. Silent crashes mean that other processes have no way to distinguish between a slow response and a crashed process, which can be a real problem as we shall see below. Noisy crashes mean that other processes can use *failure detectors* to get information about whether a crash occurred. In some situations (e.g. inside a data center), it is often quite feasible to build failure detectors, in particular approximate failure detectors, and they can be very helpful for designing protocols. However, in other situations failure detection is impossible. For example, if a server loses contact to a JavaScript app running in somebody's browser, it does not know if this was a temporary connection failure and the app will reconnect at some future time, or if the user has closed the browser and will never return.

In the following, we consider only silent crash failures. To model them, we use a modified definition of fairness: we allow executions to be 'unfair' if this unfairness is consistent with processes crashing, in the sense that crashed processes perform no more actions and receive no more messages after they crash.

Definition 12. *An execution E of L_Φ for some Φ is a* **complete F-fair execution** *if there exists a partial function* $\mathsf{fails} : F \to \perp \cup \{0 \ldots E.\mathsf{len}\}$ *such that*

- *Crashed processes take no steps after they crash: If* $\mathsf{fails}(p) \neq \bot$ *for some p, then* $\mathsf{pid}(E.\mathsf{act}(j)) \neq p$ *for all* $j > \mathsf{fails}(p)$.
- *E is complete: either* $E.\mathsf{len} = \infty$, *or for all actions a that are enabled in* $\mathsf{post}(E)$, $\mathsf{fails}(\mathsf{pid}(a)) \neq \bot$.
- *E is fair for correct processes: it does not neglect any spontaneous actions a except if* $\mathsf{fails}(\mathsf{pid}(a)) \neq \bot$, *and it does not neglect any messages m except if* $\mathsf{fails}(\mathsf{dst}(m)) \neq \bot$.

2.5 Asynchronous Consensus Under Silent Crash Failures is Impossible

We now show the famous impossibility result for asynchronous consensus protocols under just 1 silent crash failure, following the same proof structure as in Fischer, Lynch and Paterson [7]. Their proof assumes a limited form of protocol where for each process, there is exactly one receive action per message, exactly one spontaneous action, and the actions do not have conditions. We first prove the theorem under the same limitation, and then show how to generalize it to the more general protocols defined above.

Definition 13. *A* **simple consensus protocol** *is a consensus protocol*

$$(\mathsf{Pst}, \mathsf{Msg}, \mathsf{Act}, \mathsf{ini}, \mathsf{ori}, \mathsf{dst}, \mathsf{pid}, \mathsf{cnd}, \mathsf{rcv}, \mathsf{snd}, \mathsf{upd}, \mathsf{pref}, \mathsf{dec})$$

such that the only actions are:

$$\mathsf{Act} = \{\mathsf{receive}(p, m) \mid p \in \mathsf{Pid}, m \in \mathsf{Msg}\} \cup \{\mathsf{run}(p) \mid p \in \mathsf{Pid}\},$$

and such that:

$$\mathsf{rcv}(\mathsf{receive}(p, m)) = m \quad \mathsf{rcv}(\mathsf{run}(p)) = \bot \quad \mathsf{pid}(\mathsf{receive}(p, m)) = \mathsf{pid}(\mathsf{run}(p)) = p$$

and where the actions have no guard:

$$\mathsf{cnd}(\mathsf{receive}(p, m)) = \mathsf{cnd}(\mathsf{run}(p)) = \mathsf{Pst}.$$

Theorem 1. *Let* Φ *be a simple consensus protocol and let* Pid *contain at least two processes. Then,* Φ *is not correct in the presence of silent crash failures: in particular, its labeled transition system* $L_\Phi = (\mathsf{Cnf}_\Phi, \mathsf{Ini}_\Phi, \mathsf{Act}_\Phi, \rightarrow_\Phi)$ *has a complete F-fair execution that violates either validity, agreement, stability, or termination, and where* $|F| = 1$.

Proof. Assume to the contrary that all F-fair executions with $|F| \leq 1$ satisfy validity, agreement, stability, and termination. We then prove (using a sequence of lemmas) that a contradiction results.

The key to the proof is the idea of examining the *valence* of system configuration, meaning how many different decisions are possible when starting in that configuration. For a system configuration $c \in \mathsf{Cnf}_\Phi$, we define $V(c) \subseteq \mathsf{Cnf}_\Phi$ to be the set of decisions reachable from c:

$$V(c) = \{\mathsf{dec}(c'.P(p)) \mid c' \text{ reachable from } c \text{ and } p \in \mathsf{Pid}\} \setminus \{\bot\}$$

Since we assume that the protocol is correct, in particular, terminating, we know that $|V(c)| \geq 1$ for all reachable configurations c. We call a configuration *bivalent* if $|V(c)| = 2$, *univalent* if $|V(c)| = 1$, *0-valent* if $V(c) = \{0\}$, and *1-valent* if $V(c) = \{1\}$.

Lemma 2. Φ *has a bivalent initial configuration.*

Proof. Assume not; then all configurations are univalent. For $b \in \{0, 1\}$, let c_b be the initial configuration where all processes have preference b. Because the protocol satisfies termination and validity, it must be true for both choices of $b \in \{0, 1\}$ that $b \in V(c_b)$, and thus that c_b is b-valent. Let us call two initial configurations c, c' *adjacent* if they differ only in the initial value of a single process, i.e. iff $c.P(p) = c'.P(p)$ for all but one $p \in \mathsf{Pid}$. Since c_0 must be connected to c_1 by a chain of adjacent configurations, there must exist adjacent initial configurations c, c' such that c is 0-valent and c' is 1-valent. Let p be the process on which c, c' differ. Now, run a $\{p\}$-fair scheduler that schedules actions fairly, except that p takes no steps at all. Since p takes no steps, the initial state of p cannot influence the outcome, thus we can run the same schedule with the same outcome on both c and c', contradicting the assumption that c is 0-valent and c' is 1-valent.

Lemma 3. *Let c be a bivalent configuration, and let a be an action that is enabled in c. Then there exists an action sequence $w \in \mathsf{Act}^*$ such that $\mathsf{Exec}(c, w \cdot a).\mathsf{post}$ is a bivalent configuration.*

Proof. For the given c and a, let $C(c, a) \subseteq \mathsf{Cnf}$ be the set of configurations that are reachable from c without performing the action a. Note that a must be enabled in all configurations in $C(c, a)$, since it is either a receive operation (which stays enabled until it is performed, no matter what other actions are performed meanwhile), or a run operation (which is always enabled). Let $D(c, a)$ be the set of configurations reachable from a configuration in $C(c, a)$ by performing a. If $D(c, a)$ contains a bivalent configuration, we are done. Otherwise, we assume $D(c, a)$ contains only univalent configurations and proceed to provide a contradiction.

First, let's find two configurations c_0, c_1 in $C(c, a)$ such that $c_0 \xrightarrow{a'} c_1$ for some $a' \neq a$, and such that the respective a-successors $d_0 = \mathsf{post}(c_0, a)$ and $d_1 = \mathsf{post}(c_1, a)$ (which are both in $D(c, a)$ and are thus both univalent) have different valence.

- Consider $\mathsf{post}(c, a)$. Since it is in $D(c, a)$, it must be univalent, say b-valent.
- Since c is bivalent, it must be possible to reach a $(1 - b)$-valent configuration c' from c. Let c'' be the last configuration on this path that is still in $C(c, a)$. Then, $x = \mathsf{post}(c'', a)$ must be $(1 - b)$-valent as well: either $c'' = c'$, in which case x is a successor of the $(1 - b)$-valent configuration c' and thus also $(1 - b)$-valent, or $c'' \neq c'$, in which case x is a univalent conf (because it is in $D(c, a)$) from which a $(1 - b)$-valent configuration (c') can be reached, thus x is also $(1 - b)$-valent.

– Since we have a path from c to c'' entirely within $C(c, a)$, and where $\mathsf{post}(c, a)$ has different valence than $\mathsf{post}(c'', a)$, there must exist c_0, c_1 as claimed.

Now, distinguish cases.

1. If $\mathsf{pid}(a') \neq \mathsf{pid}(a)$, then a and a' are independent actions, thus $d_0 = \mathsf{post}(c_0, a) = \mathsf{post}(c_1, a) = d_1$ which is impossible because d_i are both 1-valent with different valence.
2. If $\mathsf{pid}(a') = \mathsf{pid}(a) = p$ for some $p \in \mathsf{Pid}$, then run some $\{p\}$-fair schedule, starting in c_0, in which p takes no steps, until some decision is reached in a configuration $x = \mathsf{post}(c_0, s)$ for some schedule $s \in \mathsf{Act}^*$ containing no actions by p. Now:
   – The schedule s and the action a are independent, thus $y_0 := \mathsf{post}(c_0, s{\cdot}a) = \mathsf{post}(c_0, a \cdot s)$. Therefore, y_0 is reachable from both $x = \mathsf{post}(c_0, s)$ and $d_0 = \mathsf{post}(c_0, a)$. Because x and d_0 are both univalent, this implies that they have the same valence.
   – Also, the schedule s and the schedule $a' \cdot a$ are independent, thus $y_1 := \mathsf{post}(c_0, s \cdot a' \cdot a) = \mathsf{post}(c_0, a' \cdot a \cdot s)$. Therefore, y_1 is reachable from both $x = \mathsf{post}(c_0, s)$ and $d_1 = \mathsf{post}(c_0, a'{\cdot}a)$, which are both univalent, implying that x and d_1 have the same valence.
   – The previous two points together imply that d_0 and d_1 have the same valence which is a contradiction.   □

Using the two lemmas, we will now construct an infinite, fair execution consisting entirely of bivalent configurations, which contradicts the correctness of the protocol.

– We start with some bivalent initial configuration, whose existence is guaranteed by Lemma 2.
– We pick the most senior enabled action a (as defined in Definition 10).
– We execute the action sequence $w \in \mathsf{Act}^*$ (whose existence is guaranteed by Lemma 3), then the action a, and end up in another bivalent configuration.
– Continue with step 2.5.

This construction yields an infinite execution; it is fair because we pick the most senior enabled action in step 2.5 and then execute it after a few more other steps w, which means that there is no neglect (as explained in the proof of Lemma 1). □

Finally, we can lift the restriction and allow general protocols as defined in Definition 5.

Corollary 1. *Let Φ be a consensus protocol and let Pid contain at least two processes. Then, Φ is not correct in the presence of silent crash failures: If $|F| > 1$, then L_Φ contains a complete F-fair execution that violates either validity, agreement, stability, or termination.*

Proof (Sketch only). The idea is to construct a simple consensus protocol $\overline{P}$ that simulates P, and whose F-fair executions correspond to F-fair executions of P. Thus, P can not be correct, otherwise we could use it to build a correct simple consensus protocol which we know does not exist.

The messages are the same ($\overline{\mathsf{Msg}} = \mathsf{Msg}$). The local state $\overline{\mathsf{Pst}}$ stores (1) the process state Pst, (2) an "inbox", i.e. a multiset representing messages that are available, and (3) a step counter recording how many times this process has taken a step, and (4) a data structure recording the timestamps (i.e. step counts) for messages in Msg and spontaneous actions in Act, used to calculate the seniority of actions as defined in Definition 10. On $\overline{\mathsf{receive}}(p, m)$, the received message is simply added to the inbox. On $\overline{\mathsf{run}}(p)$, we look for the most senior action, and execute it.

The key requirement is that for every fair execution $\overline{E}$ of $\overline{P}$ we find a corresponding fair execution E of P. Consider a message m: if it does not get neglected in $\overline{E}$, it must be received, meaning that it reaches the inbox; and because $\overline{\mathsf{run}(\mathsf{dst}(m))}$ does not get neglected in $\overline{E}$, it executes infinitely many times. Because the scheduler that is simulated by run is fair, as shown by Lemma 1, the simulated execution is fair as well. $\square$

Ways Around Impossibility. Impossibility results are often called negative results, but in fact, they usually help us to discover new ways in which to change our approach or our definitions, in order to succeed. There are many ways to work around the impossibility result we just proved:

- The result applies only to asynchronous systems. We can solve consensus in synchronous systems, e.g. if we have some bounds on message delays.
- The result assumes that crashes are silent. We can solve consensus if we have failure detectors (for an extensive list of various consensus algorithms, see [5]).
- The result assumes an adversarial scheduler: this means that our proof constructs an extremely contrived schedule to prove nontermination.

The last item is perhaps the most interesting. In the next section, we show an asynchronous protocol for consensus that can be tuned to terminate quite efficiently in practice.

2.6   The PAXOS Protocol

We now have a closer look at the PAXOS protocol for asynchronous consensus by Leslie Lamport [11]. It is a standard mechanism to provide fault tolerance in distributed systems, and variations of the classic protocol are used in many practical systems, e.g. in the Chubby lock service [4] or in Zookeeper [9].

The basic idea is to perform a leader-based consensus: a leader p performs a voting round (whose goal is to reach consensus on a bit) by sending a proposal for a consensus value to all participants, and if p gets a majority to agree with the proposal, p informs all participant about the winning value. Voting rounds can fail for various reasons, but a leader can always start a new round, which can still succeed (i.e. the protocol never gets stuck with no chance of success).

The trick is to (1) design the protocol to satisfy agreement, validity, and stability even if there are many competing leaders, and (2) make it unlikely

types
| Round $= (\mathbb{N}_0 \times \mathsf{Pid})$ using lexicographic order
| Vote $= (\mathsf{Round} \times \{0,1\})$ using lexicographic order

process state
| state : $\{N, Q, P\}$ initially N (leader)
| inbox : $\mathcal{P}(\mathsf{Msg})$ initially $\emptyset$ (leader)
| lasttried : $\mathbb{N}_0$ initially 0 (leader)
| quorum : $\mathcal{P}(\mathsf{Pid}_a)$ initially $\emptyset$ (leader)
| lastpromise : Round   initially $(0, \mathsf{pid})$ (acceptor)
| lastvote :   Vote   initially $((0, \mathsf{pid}), b_{\mathsf{pid}})$ for $b_{\mathsf{pid}} \in \{0,1\}$ (acceptor)
| decision : $\{\bot, 0, 1\}$ initially $\bot$ (learner)

messages
| Inquiry$(n : \mathbb{N}, p : \mathsf{Pid}_l, q : \mathsf{Pid}_a)$ //sent from leader p to acceptor q
| LastVote$(n : \mathbb{N}, p : \mathsf{Pid}_l, q : \mathsf{Pid}_a, v : \mathsf{Vote})$ //sent from acceptor q to leader p
| Proposal$(n : \mathbb{N}, p : \mathsf{Pid}_l, q : \mathsf{Pid}_a, b : \{0,1\})$ //sent from leader p to acceptor q
| Vote$(n : \mathbb{N}, p : \mathsf{Pid}_l, q : \mathsf{Pid}_a, b : \{0,1\})$ //sent from acceptor q to leader p
| Winner$(p : \mathsf{Pid}_l, q : \mathsf{Pid}_r, b : \{0,1\})$ //sent from leader p to learner q

Fig. 2. Types, states and messages for the basic PAXOS consensus protocol.

(using ad-hoc heuristics) that there are many competing leaders at a time, thus termination is likely in practice.

There are three roles of participants (leaders, acceptors, learners) which we represent by three different process subsets $\mathsf{Pid}_l, \mathsf{Pid}_a, \mathsf{Pid}_r$ of Pid. Leaders conduct the organizational part of a voting round (solicit, collect, and analyze votes); acceptors perform the actual voting; and learners are informed about the successful outcome, if any. It is perfectly acceptable (and common in practice) for a process to play multiple roles. If everybody plays every role we have $\mathsf{Pid}_l = \mathsf{Pid}_a = \mathsf{Pid}_r = \mathsf{Pid}$. The number of acceptors must be finite ($|\mathsf{Pid}_a| < \infty$) so that they can form majorities.

Some key ideas include:

- Voting rounds are identified by a unique *round* identifier. This identifier is a tuple (n, p) consisting of a sequence number n and the process identifier p of the leader for this round. There is just one leader for each round, but different rounds can be initiated by different leaders, possibly concurrently.
- Each round has two and a half phases. In the first phase, the leader sends an inquiry message to all acceptors. The acceptors respond with a special message containing the last vote they cast (in a previous round), or a pseudo-vote containing their initial preference (if they have not cast any votes in a real round yet).
- When the leader has received a last-vote message from a quorum (i.e. at least half) of acceptors, it starts the second phase. In this phase, it proposes a consensus value and asks the quorum to vote for it.
- If the leader receives votes from all members of the quorum, it informs all learners about the successful outcome.

action answer$(n : \mathbb{N}, p : \mathrm{Pid_l}, q : \mathrm{Pid_a}, v : \mathrm{Vote})$ **at** q (acceptor)
| **receives** Inquiry(n, p, q)
| **condition** $(\texttt{lastpromise} < (n, p)) \wedge (\texttt{lastvote} = v)$
| **sends** LastVote(n, p, q, v)
| **updates** $\texttt{lastpromise} \leftarrow (n, p)$

action accept$(n : \mathbb{N}, p : \mathrm{Pid_l}, q : \mathrm{Pid_a}, b : \{0, 1\})$ **at** q (acceptor)
| **receives** Proposal(n, p, b)
| **condition** $\texttt{lastpromise} = (n, p)$
| **sends** Vote(n, p, q, b)
| **updates** $\texttt{lastvote} \leftarrow ((n, p), b)$

action learn$(q : \mathrm{Pid_r}, b : \{0, 1\})$ **at** q (learner)
| **receives** Winner(p, q, b)
| **updates** $\texttt{decision} \leftarrow b$

Fig. 3. The acceptor actions and the one learner actions for the basic PAXOS consensus protocol.

action inquire$(n : \mathbb{N}, p : \mathrm{Pid_l})$ **at** p (leader)
| **condition** $(\texttt{state} = N) \wedge (\texttt{n} = \texttt{lasttried} + 1)$
| **sends** $\sum_{q \in \mathrm{Pid_a}}$ Inquiry(n, p, q)
| **updates** $\texttt{state} \leftarrow Q; \texttt{lasttried} \leftarrow n$

action propose$(n : \mathbb{N}, p : \mathrm{Pid_l}, b : \{0, 1\}, Q : \mathcal{P}(\mathrm{Pid_a}), lv : Q \rightarrow \mathrm{Vote})$ **at** p (leader)
| **condition** $\texttt{inbox} \geq \sum_{q \in Q}$ LastVote$(n, p, q, lv(q))$
| **condition** $(\texttt{state} = Q) \wedge (\texttt{lasttried} = n) \wedge (|Q| > |\mathrm{Pid_a}|/2)$
| **condition** $\max\{lv(q) \mid q \in Q\} = (\_, b)$
| **sends** $\sum_{q \in Q}$ Proposal(n, p, q, b)
| **updates** $\texttt{state} \leftarrow P; \texttt{quorum} \leftarrow Q; \texttt{inbox} \leftarrow \emptyset$

action announce$(n : \mathbb{N}, p : \mathrm{Pid_l}, b : \{0, 1\}, Q : \mathcal{P}(\mathrm{Pid_a}))$ **at** p (leader)
| **condition** $\texttt{inbox} \geq \sum_{q \in Q}$ Vote(n, p, q, b)
| **condition** $(\texttt{state} = P) \wedge (\texttt{lasttried} = n) \wedge (\texttt{quorum} = Q)$
| **sends** $\sum_{q \in \mathrm{Pid_r}}$ Winner(p, q, b)
| **updates** $\texttt{state} \leftarrow N; \texttt{inbox} \leftarrow \emptyset$

action receive$(m : \mathrm{Msg})$ **at** dst(m) (leader)
| **receives** m
| **updates** $\texttt{inbox} \leftarrow \texttt{inbox} + m$

action abandon$(n : \mathbb{N}, p : \mathrm{Pid_l})$ **at** p (leader)
| **condition** $(\texttt{lasttried} = n) \wedge (\texttt{state} \in \{P, V\})$
| **updates** $\texttt{state} \leftarrow N; \texttt{inbox} \leftarrow \emptyset$

Fig. 4. The leader actions for the basic PAXOS consensus protocol.

We show the definitions of local states (for each role) and of message formats in Fig. 2. The actions are shown in Figs. 3 and 4.

The following properties of the protocol are key to ensure consensus even under concurrent voting rounds:

- Rounds are totally ordered (lexicographically based on the order, then the process id). Participants are no longer allowed to participate in a lower round once they are participating in a higher round.
- When transitioning from the first phase (gather last vote messages) to the second phase (send out proposal messages), the leader chooses the consensus value belonging to the highest vote among all the last-vote messages. This ensures that if a prior round was actually successful (i.e. it garnered a majority of votes), the new round uses the same bit value.

The following lemma formalized these intuititons, and constitutes the core of the correctness proof.

Lemma 4 (Competing Leaders). *If E is an execution and*

$$\mathsf{announce}(n, p, b, Q) \in \mathsf{trc}(E) \quad and \quad \mathsf{propose}(n', p', b', Q', lv) \in \mathsf{trc}(E),$$

and $(n, p) < (n', p')$, *then* $b = b'$.

Proof. By contradiction. Assume the lemma is not true, then there exist E, p, n, b, Q, p', n', b', Q', lv falsifying the condition, and without loss of generality we can assume (n', p') are chosen minimal among all such. To perform $\mathsf{propose}(n', p', b', Q', lv)$, the leader p' received several LastVote messages; Let $((n'', p''), b') = \max_{q \in Q} lv(q)$ be the maximal vote received. Distinguish cases:

- $(n'', p'') < (n, p)$ this is impossible: because Q and Q' must intersect, there exists $q \in Q \cap Q'$. Since q must have voted for the round (n, p) before answering in the round (n', p') (otherwise it would not have voted), the LastVote message sent from q to p' must contain a vote whose round is no lower than (n, p) (note that the `lastvote` variable is always monotonically increasing).
- $(n'', p'') = (n, p)$ in that case, $b' = b$ because all votes for the same round have the same bit value. Contradiction.
- $(n'', p'') > (n, p)$. Because p is at least 1, so is p'', thus $((n'', p''), b')$ is a vote for a non-zero round, so there must exist some $\mathsf{propose}(n'', p'', b', \_, \_)$ in the execution. Because we chose (n', p') minimal among all such violating the lemma, this implies that $b = b'$. Contradiction.

The following lemma shows that no matter how many crashes occur, how many messages are lost, or how many leaders are competing, safety is always guaranteed.

Theorem 2. *All executions of PAXOS satisfy agreement, validity, and stability.*

Proof. Validity is easy because all votes can be tracked back to some initial vote, which is the preference of some processor. Stability and agreement follow because if we had two $\mathsf{announce}(n, p, b, Q)$ and $\mathsf{announce}(n', p', b', Q')$ with $b \neq b'$, and suppose that $(n, p) < (n', p')$ without loss of generality, then there must also be a $\mathsf{propose}(n', p', b', Q', lv')$, which contradicts Lemma 4.

Of course, termination is not possible for arbitrary fair schedules in the presence of failures because of Theorem 1. However, the following property holds: success always remains possible as long as there remains some non-crashed leader, some non-crashed learner, and at least $\lceil |\mathsf{Pid_a}/2| \rceil$ non-crashed acceptors. The reason is that:

- A leader cannot get stuck in any state: if it is waiting for something (such as the receipt of some message), and that something is not happening (for example, due to a crash), the leader can perform the spontaneous action abandon to return to a neutral state, from which it can start a new, higher round.
- If a leader p starts a new round (n, p) that is larger than any previous rounds, and if no other leaders are starting even higher rounds, and if at least $\lceil |\mathsf{Pid_a}/2| \rceil$ acceptors remain, and if there are no more crashes, then the round succeeds.

The PAXOS algorithm shown, and the correctness proof, are both based on the original paper by Lamport [11]. Since then, there have been many more papers on the subject, and many alternative (e.g. disk-based) and optimized (e.g. for solving continuous consecutive consensus problems) versions of PAXOS exist.

3 Strong Consistency and CAP

In this section we examine how to understand the consistency of shared data. We explore the cost of strong consistency (in terms of reliability or performance). We develop abstractions that help system implementors to articulate the consistency guarantees they are providing to programmers.

3.1 Objects and Operations

We assume that the shared data is organized as a collection of named *objects* Obj. As in the last section, we assume a set of *processes* Pid. The sets of objects and processes may be infinite, to model their dynamic creation. Processes interact with the shared data by performing *operations* on objects. Each object $x \in \mathsf{Obj}$ has a *type* $\tau = \mathsf{type}(x) \in \mathsf{Type}$, whose *type signature* $(\mathsf{Op}_\tau, \mathsf{Val}_\tau)$ determines the set of supported operations Op_τ and the set of their return values Val_τ. We assume that a special value $\perp \in \mathsf{Val}_\tau$ belongs to all sets Val_τ and is used for operations that return no value.

Example 1. An **integer register** intreg can be defined as follows: $\mathsf{Val}_{\mathsf{intreg}} = \mathbb{Z} \cup \{\perp\}$, and $\mathsf{Op}_{\mathsf{intreg}} = \{\mathsf{rd}\} \cup \{\mathsf{wr}(a) \mid a \in \mathbb{Z}\}$

Example 2. A **counter object** ctr can be defined as follows: $\mathsf{Val}_{\mathsf{ctr}} = \mathbb{Z} \cup \{\perp\}$, and $\mathsf{Op}_{\mathsf{ctr}} = \{\mathsf{rd}, \mathsf{inc}\}$.

Sequential Semantics. The type of an object, as defined above, does not actually describe the semantics of the operation, only their syntax. We formally specify the sequential semantics of a data type τ by a function

$$\mathcal{S}_\tau : \mathsf{Op}_\tau \times \mathsf{Op}_\tau^* \to \mathsf{Val}_\tau,$$

which, given an operation and sequence of prior operations, specifies the expected return value. For a register, read operations return the value of the last preceding write, or zero if there is no prior write. For a counter, read operations return the number of preceding increments. Thus, for any sequence of operations ξ:

$$
\begin{aligned}
\mathcal{S}_{\mathtt{intreg}}(\mathbf{rd}, \xi) &= a, \quad \text{if } \mathbf{wr}(0)\,\xi = \xi_1\,\mathbf{wr}(a)\,\xi_2 \text{ and} \\
&\qquad \xi_2 \text{does not contain } \mathbf{wr} \text{ operations;} \\
\mathcal{S}_{\mathtt{ctr}}(\mathbf{rd}, \xi) &= (\text{the number of } \mathtt{inc} \text{ operations in } \xi);
\end{aligned}
$$

Our definition of the sequential semantics uses sequences of prior operations (representing all earlier updates), rather than the current state of an object, to define the behavior of reads. This choice is useful: for many implementations, there are multiple versions of the state, and these versions are often best understood as the result of using various update sequences (such as logs), subsequences, or segments.

Moreover, for objects such as the integer register, only the last update matters, since it overwrites completely all information in the object. For the counter, however, all updates matter. Similarly, if considering objects that have multiple fields and support partial updates, e.g. updates that modify individual fields, it is not enough to look at the last update to determine the current state of the object.

In general, operations may both read and modify the state. Operations that return no value are called *update-only* operations. Similarly, we call an operation o of a type τ *read-only* if it has no side effect, i.e. if for all $o' \in \mathsf{Op}_\tau$ and $u, v \in \mathsf{Op}_\tau^*$, we have $\mathcal{S}_\tau(o', u \cdot o \cdot v) = \mathcal{S}_\tau(o', u \cdot v)$.

What is an Object? There is often some ambiguity to the question of what we should consider to be an object. For example, consider a cloud table storage API that provides tables that store records (consisting of several fields that have values) indexed by keys. Then:

- We can consider each record to be an object, named by the combination of the table name and the key, and supporting operations for reading and writing fields or removing the object.
- We can consider the whole table to be an object, named by the table name. Operations specify the key (and the field, if accessing individual fields).
- We can consider each field to be an object, named by the combination of the table name, the key, and the field name. This approach seems most consistent with the types shown above (integer registers, counters).
- We can consider the entire storage to be a single object, and have operations to target a specific (table, key, field) combination.

We propose the following definition, or perhaps we should say guideline:

- An object is the largest unit of data that can be written atomically without using transactions.
- A transactional domain is the largest unit of data that can be written atomically by using transactions.

Traditional databases follow a philosophy without objects (nothing can be written outside of a transaction) and large transactional domains (the entire database), which requires strong transaction support. Cloud storage and web programming rely more commonly on moderately to large sized objects, and transactional domains that do not contain all data (transaction support is typically nonexistent, or at best limited). The reason is that the latter approach is easier to guarantee as a scalable service. Unfortunately, it is also harder to program.

3.2 Strong Consistency

Intuitively, programmers expect operations on shared data to be *linearizable*. Informally, this means that when they call into some API to read or write a shared value, they expect a behavior that is consistent with (i.e. observationally undistinguishable from):

- a single copy of the shared data being maintained somewhere.
- the read or write operations being applied to that copy somewhere in between the call and the return.

Unfortunately, guaranteeing these conditions can be a performance and reliability problem, if communication between processes is expensive and/or unavailable. Many systems thus relax the consistency. A good test to see whether a system is indeed linearizable (in fact, sequentially consistent) is shown in Fig. 5. On an linearizable or sequentially consistent system, when running programs A and B (one time each), there is at most one winner. Why? Informally, it is because under sequential consistency, *all* operations are organized into some global sequence. In this case, it means that the two writes must happen in *some* order — we don't know which one, but the system will decide on one or the other, which implies that either A or B (or both) do not win:

- If the system decides that A's write to x happens before B's write to y, then it must also happen before B's read from x, thus the value read must be 1, so B does not win.
- If the system decides that B's write to y happens before A's write to x, then it must also happen before A's read from y, thus the value read must be 1, so A does not win.

This reasoning seems still a bit informal - talking about 'happens before' without a solid foundation can get quite confusing. In order to give a more rigorous reasoning, we first need a precise definition of what sequential consistency and linearizability mean.

Program (A)	Program (B)
| $x.\mathtt{wr}(1);$ $//a_1$ | if $(y.\mathtt{rd} = 0)$ $//a_2$ | | print "A wins";	| $y.\mathtt{wr}(1);$ $//b_1$ | if $(x.\mathtt{rd} = 0)$ $//b_2$ | | print "B wins";

Fig. 5. The Dekker Litmus test, using two integer registers x, y (which are initially 0). If we run these two concurrently on a sequentially consistent or linearizable system, there is at most one winner.

Abstract Executions. To specify consistency models, we use *abstract executions*. The basic idea is very simple:

1. A consistency model is formalized as a set of abstract executions, which are mathematical structures (visualized using graphs) consisting of operation events (vertices) and relations (edges), subject to conditions. Abstract executions capture "the essence" of an execution (that is, what operations occurred, and how those operations are related), without including low-level details (such as exactly what messages were sent when and where).
2. We describe what it means for a concrete execution of a system to *correspond* to an abstract execution.
3. We say that a system is correct if *all* of its concrete executions correspond to some abstract execution of the consistency model.

The advantage of this approach is that we can separately (1) determine whether programs are correct for a given consistency model, without needing to know details about the system architecture, and (2) determine whether a system correctly implements some consistency model, without knowing anything about the program that is running on it. Consistency models can be thought of as a contract between the programmer and the system implementor.

For sequential consistency, we define abstract executions in two steps. First, we define operation graphs.

Definition 14. *An operation graph is a tuple* $(\mathsf{Evt}, \mathsf{pid}, \mathsf{obj}, \mathsf{op}, \mathsf{rval}, \mathsf{po})$ *where*

- Evt *is a set of events.*
- $\mathsf{pid} : \mathsf{Evt} \to \mathsf{Pid}$ *describes the process on which the event happened.*
- $\mathsf{po} \subseteq \mathsf{Evt} \times \mathsf{Evt}$ *is a partial order (called process order) that describes the order in which events happened on each process. We require that po is a union of total orders for each process, that is, there exist for each $p \in \mathsf{Pid}$ a total order $\mathsf{po}_p \subseteq (\mathsf{pid}^{-1}(p) \times \mathsf{pid}^{-1}(p))$ such that po is their union: $\mathsf{po} = \bigcup_{p \in \mathsf{Pid}} \mathsf{po}_p$.*
- $\mathsf{obj}, \mathsf{op}, \mathsf{rval}$ *are event attributes (i.e. functions Evt) describing the details of the operation: each event $e \in \mathsf{Evt}$ represents an operation $\mathsf{op}(e) \in \mathsf{Op}_{\mathsf{type}(\mathsf{obj}(e))}$ on an object $\mathsf{obj}(e) \in \mathsf{Obj}$, which returns the value $\mathsf{rval}(e) \in \mathsf{Val}_{\mathsf{type}(\mathsf{obj}(e))}$.*

Operation graphs capture the relevant interactions between the system and the client program. However, they do not explain the underlying reasons. Looking just at the operation graph, it can be difficult to determine the order in which the system processed operations. Abstract executions contain this additional information: in the case of sequential consistency, a total order over all operations:

Definition 15. *Define the set $\mathcal{A}_{SC}$ of sequentially consistent abstract executions to consist of all tuples*
$(\mathsf{Evt}, \mathsf{pid}, \mathsf{obj}, \mathsf{op}, \mathsf{rval}, \mathsf{po}, \mathsf{to})$, *where*

- $(\mathsf{Evt}, \ldots, \mathsf{po})$ *is an operation graph.*
- $\mathsf{to} \subseteq \mathsf{Evt} \times \mathsf{Evt}$ *is a total order.*
- to *is consistent with process order:* $\mathsf{po} \subseteq \mathsf{to}$.
- *The return value of each operation matches the sequential specification $\mathcal{S}_\tau$ (as defined in Sect. 3.1), applied to the sequence of to-prior operations:*

$$\forall e \in \mathsf{Evt} : \mathsf{rval}(e) = \mathcal{S}_{\mathsf{type}(\mathsf{obj}(e))}(\mathsf{op}(e), (\mathsf{to}^{-1}(e) \cap \mathsf{obj}^{-1}(\mathsf{obj}(e))).\mathsf{sort}(\mathsf{to}))$$

In pictures, we usually draw abstract executions by (1) creating a vertex for each event, and aligning events into columns corresponding to process identifiers, and (2) adding arrows to represent to ordering edges.

We can now define sequential consistency; note that we purposefully omit a precise definition of what a concrete execution is, but simply assume that it contains operation events that can be meaningfully related to the abstract execution.

Definition 16. *A concrete execution of some system is sequentially consistent if there exists an abstract sequentially consistent execution, with corresponding operation events, process order, and attributes.*

Dekker Explanation. We can now explain why under sequential consistency, there can never be two winners in the Dekker litmus test (Fig. 5). Suppose there were two winners. This would mean that in the corresponding abstract execution, there are four events $\{a_1, a_2, b_1, b_2\}$ (meaning that $\mathsf{pid}(a_1) = \mathsf{pid}(a_2) = a$, $\mathsf{pid}(b_1) = \mathsf{pid}(b_2) = b$, $\mathsf{obj}(a_1) = \mathsf{obj}(b_2) = x$, $\mathsf{obj}(b_1) = \mathsf{obj}(a_2) = y$, $\mathsf{op}(a_1) = \mathsf{op}(b_1) = \mathsf{wr}(1)$, $\mathsf{op}(a_2) = \mathsf{op}(b_2) = \mathsf{rd}$, $\mathsf{rval}(a_2) = \mathsf{rval}(b_2) = 0$, and $\mathsf{po} = \{(a_1, a_2), (b_1, b_2)\}$).

Now we can argue that there is no way to construct to without creating a cycle and thus a contradiction:

- Because $\mathsf{rval}(a_2) = 0$, it cannot be the case that $b_1 \xrightarrow{\mathsf{to}} a_2$ (because that would imply a return value of 1). Therefore, because to is a total order, $a_2 \xrightarrow{\mathsf{to}} b_1$.
- Because $\mathsf{rval}(b_2) = 0$, it cannot be the case that $a_1 \xrightarrow{\mathsf{to}} b_2$ (because that would imply a return value of 1). Therefore, because to is a total order, $b_2 \xrightarrow{\mathsf{to}} a_1$.
- Because $\mathsf{po} \subseteq \mathsf{to}$, $a_1 \xrightarrow{\mathsf{to}} a_2$ and $b_1 \xrightarrow{\mathsf{to}} b_2$.

Linearizability. Sometimes, systems use a slightly stronger consistency model than sequential consistency, called *linearizability*. The difference is that for linearizability, we additionally require that the order to must not contradict the order of operation calls and operation returns in the concrete execution.

Definition 17. *A concrete execution of some system is* linearizable *if there exists a corresponding abstract sequentially consistent execution, such that for any two operations $e, e' \in$ Evt in the abstract execution satisfying $e \xrightarrow{\text{to}} e'$, it is not the case that* return$(e') <$ call(e) *in the concrete execution.*

Note that any linearizable concrete execution is also sequentially consistent. The converse is not true in general; we will show an example in the next section.

There is an alternative popular interpretation of linearizability that roughly goes as follows: The abstract execution must be consistent with a placement of *commit events* of operations, which are placed somewhere in between call and return. The two definitions are equivalent: (1) if the order matches commit events, then it cannot violate the condition above, and (2) if the condition above is not violated, we can find a commit event placement.

3.3   CAP Theorem

The CAP theorem explores tradeoffs between **C**onsistency, **A**vailability, and **P**artition tolerance, and concludes that, while it is possible to provide any two of these properties, it is impossible to provide all three. It was conjectured by Brewer [1] and proved by Gilbert and Lynch [8]. Our proof here follows the same simple reasoning as the one by Gilbert and Lynch, but we use sequential consistency instead of linearizability.

We use the following meaning of the three terms. *Consistency* means sequential consistency as defined above. *Availability* means that all operations on objects eventually complete. *Partition Tolerance* means that the system keeps operating even if the network becomes *permanently partitioned,* i.e. if there exists a subset of isolated processes Iso $\subseteq$ Pid such that the processes in Iso and the processes in Pid \ Iso cannot communicate in any way.

Theorem 3 (CAP). *No system with at least two processes can provide sequential consistency, availability, and partition tolerance.*

Proof. Assume such a system exists. Consider two processes $a, b \in$ Pid and a permanent network partition Iso $= \{a\}$ that isolates process a. We run three independent experiments, called A, B, and AB. In experiment A, process a runs the program (A) shown in Fig. 5, while process b does nothing. In experiment B, process b runs the program (B) shown in Fig. 5, while process a does nothing. In experiment AB, both processes run the respective program. Then:

- In experiment A, availability and partition tolerance imply that the code executes to completion. Consistency means that process a prints "A wins" (because there is only one process accessing the data, the semantics is equivalent to standard sequential semantics).
- There is no way for process a to distinguish between experiments A and AB, thus it must print "A wins" in experiment AB as well.
- For the symmetric reason, process b must print "B wins" in experiment AB.

– Thus, in experiment AB, both "A wins" and "B wins" are printed, which is not sequentially consistent. Contradiction.

Although the theorem above is narrowly stated, the proof reveals a somewhat wider impact:

– The proof reveals the performance impact of strong consistency: it shows that the partitions *have to talk to each other* before completing the execution of the program. Thus, if communication is expensive (for example, if two data centers have to talk to each other across a far distance), clients are forced to wait.
– Simply knowing about the partition is not helpful. Even if the processes have perfect information about the existence of a network partition, the above reasoning holds. This is different from the situation with consensus in asynchronous systems with crash failures, where the impossibility of distinguishing between failure and slow response is key, and a perfect failure detector can make consensus possible.

C+A is Possible. Consistency and Availability can be easily guaranteed. A whole range of solutions are possible:

– (Single Copy). The simplest idea is to just pick one process to store the data, then forward all read and write operations to that process. In the absence of partitions, we can always reach this process from everywhere.
– (Primary Replication). In this case, we allow all processes to store a copy of the data, and to also read data locally. However, (1) all writes must be first performed on a designated replica, the *primary* replica, before applying them to a secondary replica, and (2) all writes must be applied to the secondary replicas in the same order that they were applied to the primary replica. Primary replication can greatly enhance the latency and the throughput of read operations, but write operations remain slow.

C+P is Possible. We can guarantee consistency and partition tolerance by simply stalling the execution of write requests if the primary copy cannot be reached.

A+P is Possible. It is trivial to guarantee availability and partition tolerance without consistency, for example, by giving each process its own isolated copy of the data. However, this is hardly meaningful.

C'+A+P' is Possible. The most useful approximation to CAP is to use a weaker form of consistency (eventual consistency) in conjunction with a weaker from of partition tolerance (resilience against temporary network partitions). Informally, it means that the shared data remains available for reading and writing even in the presence of network partitions. When the network partition heals, processes reconcile conflicting updates that happened during the network partition, and converge to a common state. Understanding specifications and implementations of eventual consistency is the main topic for the remainder of this course.

4 Eventual Consistency Models and Mechanisms

Weakening the consistency guarantees can improve performance and availability, but it can also create problems for unaware programmers. Understanding exactly what can go wrong, and how to write programs that are resilient, remains an important challenge. One of the key difficulties is that there are many subtle variations of consistency models, and myriads of architectures and optimizations that all have slightly different effects. We study this problem by approaching it from two sides:

- In Sect. 4.1, we show how to generalize sequentially consistent abstract executions to eventually consistent abstract executions, and show how to express various guarantees (causality, consistent prefix, read my writes, monotonic reads) and combinations of guarantees.
- In Sect. 4.2, we take a closer look at a few selected architectures that implement some form of consistency, and show how to specify their behavior using abstract executions.

4.1 Eventual Consistency Models

The following simple definition of quiescent consistency is often used to describe eventually consistent systems:

> if clients stop issuing update requests, then the replicas will eventually reach a consistent state.

However, quiescent consistency is very weak. For example, it (1) does not specify what happens if clients never stop issuing updates, which is common in reactive systems such as services, and (2) does not in any way restrict the intermediate values. Few programs will work correctly under quiescent consistency, and most architectures provide much stronger guarantees. Thus, we need a better way to define eventual consistency models.

To devise a better model for eventual consistency, we start by deconstructing our definition of sequential consistency (Definition 15). In that definition, we use a total order to to figure out what value an operation e on some object $x = \mathsf{obj}(e)$ should return:

$$\forall e \in \mathsf{Evt} : \mathsf{rval}(e) = \mathcal{S}_{\mathsf{type}(x)}(\mathsf{op}(e), (\mathsf{to}^{-1}(e) \cap \mathsf{obj}^{-1}(x)).\mathsf{sort}(\mathsf{to})) \qquad (1)$$

The key observation is that the total order to is playing two independent roles:

1. It is used to determine what prior operations are *visible* to e. In (1), this is the part $\mathsf{to}^{-1}(e)$, which returns the set of all operations e' such that $e' \xrightarrow{\mathsf{to}} e$.

2. It is used to *arbitrate* between conflicting operations. In (1), this is the part $\mathsf{sort}(\mathsf{to})$: it ensures that everyone is using the same order to sort conflicting operations (e.g. multiple writes to the same location).

Definition 18. *Given a type τ, we say two operations $o_1, o_2 \in \mathsf{Op}_\tau$ are write-conflicting if there exists an operation $o \in \mathsf{Op}_\tau$ and operation sequences $u, w \in \mathsf{Op}_\tau^*$ such that $\mathcal{S}_\tau(o, u \cdot o_1 \cdot o_2 \cdot w) \neq \mathcal{S}_\tau(o, u \cdot o_2 \cdot o_1 \cdot w)$. Given an operation graph $(\mathsf{Evt}, \ldots, \mathsf{obj}, \mathsf{op}, \ldots)$, we say that two events $e_1, e_2 \in \mathsf{Evt}$ are write-conflicting (written as $\mathsf{wconflict}(e_1, e_2)$) if (1) $\mathsf{obj}(e_1) = \mathsf{obj}(e_2)$, and (2) $\mathsf{op}(e_1)$ and $\mathsf{op}(e_2)$ are write-conflicting.*

We now define eventually consistent abstract executions, similar to (Definition 15), but using two separate relations; a *visibility relation* is used to determine what operations are visible, and an *arbitration order* is used to determine how to order conflicting operations.

Definition 19. *Define the set $\mathcal{A}_{\mathrm{EC}}$ of eventually consistent abstract executions to consist of all tuples $(\mathsf{Evt}, \mathsf{pid}, \mathsf{obj}, \mathsf{op}, \mathsf{rval}, \mathsf{po}, \mathsf{vis}, \mathsf{ar})$, where*

1. *$(\mathsf{Evt}, \ldots, \mathsf{po})$ is an operation graph.*
2. *The visibility relation $\mathsf{vis} \subseteq \mathsf{Evt} \times \mathsf{Evt}$ is an acyclic, irreflexive relation.*
3. *Operations become eventually visible: for all $e \in \mathsf{Evt}$, $e \xrightarrow{\mathsf{vis}} e'$ for almost all $e' \in \mathsf{Evt}$ (i.e. all but finitely many).*
4. *The arbitration order $\mathsf{ar} \subseteq \mathsf{Evt} \times \mathsf{Evt}$ is a partial order.*
5. *The arbitration order orders all conflicting operations that are visible to another operation: for all $e_1, e_2, e \in \mathsf{Evt}$:*

$$((e_1 \xrightarrow{\mathsf{vis}} e) \wedge (e_2 \xrightarrow{\mathsf{vis}} e) \wedge \mathsf{wconflict}(e_1, e_2)) \Rightarrow ((e_1 \xrightarrow{\mathsf{ar}} e_2) \vee (e_2 \xrightarrow{\mathsf{ar}} e_1))$$

6. *There are no causal cycles: $\mathsf{po} \cup \mathsf{vis}$ is acyclic.*
7. *The return value of each operation matches the sequential specification $\mathcal{S}_\tau$ applied to visible operations in arbitration order:*

$$\forall e \in \mathsf{Evt} : \mathsf{rval}(e) = \mathcal{S}_{\mathsf{type}(\mathsf{obj}(e))}(\mathsf{op}(e), (\mathsf{vis}^{-1}(e) \cap \mathsf{obj}^{-1}(\mathsf{obj}(e))).\mathsf{sort}(\mathsf{ar}))$$

Note how the return value is determined in condition 7: first, it determines the set of visible events on the same object $\mathsf{vis}^{-1}(e) \cap \mathsf{obj}^{-1}(\mathsf{obj}(e))$, then it sorts this set into a sequence using ar, and then applies the sequential semantics. Although the sorting is not quite deterministic (since ar is not necessarily a total order), the value of the whole expression *is* deterministic because condition 5 ensures that ar determines at least the order of write-conflicting operations.

For an abstract eventually consistent execution A, we define the *happens-before order* hb_A, sometimes also called the *causal order*, to be the partial order $\mathsf{hb}_A = (A.\mathsf{po} \cup A.\mathsf{vis})^+$ (note that we rely on the acyclicity guaranteed by condition 6). The happens-before order tracks potential causal dependency chains:

if two operations are issued by the same process ($a \xrightarrow{\text{po}} b$), or if the first operation is visible to the second ($a \xrightarrow{\text{vis}} b$), the second may causally depend on the first.

How do these concepts map into practical implementations? Consider a typical implementation where each process maintains a replica of the shared state. Updates performed on a replica are broadcast to other replicas in some way. Visibility and arbitration are often determined in one of the following ways:

- Arbitration is typically determined either by (1) some timestamp, or (2) the order in which updates are processed on some primary replica.
- Visibility is typically determined by two factors, (1) the timing of when a process learns about an update (a process learns about a local update immediately, and about a remote update when it receives a message), and (2) the time at which a process chooses to make that update visible to subsequent queries (which could be as soon as it learns about it, or delayed, for example until an update is confirmed by the primary replica).

Eventual consistency is much stronger than quiescent consistency, but still quite weak. Most of the time, systems guarantee additional properties. In particular, the following guarantees are common. We start with a table giving the formal definition, and explain them below. These guarantees are not mutually exclusive; quite to the contrary, most systems provide a combination.

Guarantee	Condition
Sequential consistency	$\text{vis} = \text{ar}$
Read my writes	$\text{po} \subseteq \text{vis}$
Consistent prefix	ar is total, and $\forall e : \exists e' : \text{vis}^{-1}(e) = \text{ar}^{-1}(e')$
Monotonic reads	$(\text{vis}; \text{po}) \subseteq \text{vis}$
Causal visibility	$\text{hb} \subseteq \text{vis}$
Causal arbitration	$\text{hb} \subseteq \text{ar}$

Sequential Consistency. We already defined this in the last section. Formally, sequential consistency means that arbitration and visibility are one and the same.

Read My Writes. If the same process performs two operations, it may expect that the first operation is visible to the second. For example, if we increment and then read a counter on the same process, read-my-writes guarantees that the read does not return zero.

Consistent Prefix. Sometimes it is acceptable to read a stale value, as long as that value appears as a past value of some timeline of values that everyone agrees on. Consistent prefix means just that: (1) a timeline is maintained (ar is a total order), and (2) the visible updates for any event e match some prefix of ar.

Monotonic Reads. One may except that once an update has become visible to an operation on some process, it should remain visible to all future operations on the same process.

Causal Visibility. If an operation has a causal chain to another operation, we may expect the second operation to see the first. Causal Visibility implies monotonic-reads and read-my-writes.

Causal Arbitration. If an operation has a causal chain to another operation, we may expect that the second one is ordered after the first in arbitration order.

We now illustrate these guarantees on a couple of examples.

Score Example. First, let us look at a sports example (following Doug Terry's baseball example [13]). Consider a match in which a home team and a visitors team score points, and the respective scores are stored in integer registers $\{h, v\} \subseteq$ Obj. Furthermore, assume that we are using a system where ar is a total order based on timestamps that reflect the real time at which operations are performed. Now, consider an abstract execution in which there are seven write events and two read events, ordered by ar as follows (note that we are not assuming that they are all issued by the same process):

$$h.wr(1)$$
$$v.wr(1)$$
$$h.wr(2)$$
$$h.wr(3)$$
$$v.wr(2)$$
$$h.wr(4)$$
$$h.wr(5)$$
$$\text{print } (v.rd() + \text{"-"} + h.rd())$$

How do the various guarantees impact what possible scores could be printed at the end? Here is a table listing all the possibilities:

Sequential Consistency	2-5
Eventual Consistency	0-0, 0-1, 0-2, 0-3, 0-4, 0-5,
	1-0, 1-1, 1-2, 1-3, 1-4, 1-5,
	2-0, 2-1, 2-2, 2-3, 2-4, 2-5
Consistent Prefix	0-0, 0-1, 1-1, 1-2, 1-3, 2-3, 2-4, 2-5

What if a process prints the score twice? By default, each read can print any of the options above. However, if the system guarantees monotonic reads or causal visibility, the second read can only report scores that are higher than they were in the first read.

Causality Example. Not all systems guarantee causal arbitration or causal visibility. This can lead to odd behaviors. For example, consider a chat application where participants {Alice, Bob, Carol} ⊆ Pid append to a list (the "wall"), or read the list. Alice asks a question, and Bob sees it and answers it. Finally, Carol looks at the chat and sees Bob's answer. But what about Alice's question?

Alice	Bob	Carol
e_1: wall.append("Anyone?")	e_2: print wall.rd	e_4: print wall.rd
	e_3: wall.append("Bob here.")	

Since Bob saw Alice's question, we know $e_1 \xrightarrow{\text{vis}} e_2$, and since Carol saw Bob's answer, we know $e_3 \xrightarrow{\text{vis}} e_4$. However:

- If the system does not guarantee causal visibility, then it is possible that $e_1 \xrightarrow{\text{vis}} e_4$. Thus, Carol does not see Alice's question, even though she saw Bob's answer. However, if the system *does* guarantee causal visibility, then $e_1 \xrightarrow{\text{vis}} e_2 \xrightarrow{\text{po}} e_3 \xrightarrow{\text{vis}} e_4$ implies $e_1 \xrightarrow{\text{hb}} e_4$ which implies $e_1 \xrightarrow{\text{vis}} e_4$.
- If the system does not guarantee causal arbitration, then it is possible that Carol sees both appends ($\{e_1, e_3\} \subseteq \text{vis}^{-1}(e_4)$), but that they appear in the wrong order ($e_3 \xrightarrow{\text{ar}} e_1$). However, if the system *does* guarantee causal arbitration, then $e_1 \xrightarrow{\text{vis}} e_2 \xrightarrow{\text{po}} e_3 \xrightarrow{\text{vis}} e_4$ implies $e_1 \xrightarrow{\text{hb}} e_4$ which implies $e_1 \xrightarrow{\text{ar}} e_4$.

Causal visibility is easily violated in systems that do not use primary replication, but broadcast updates directly. However, even in such systems, causal visibility guarantees are possible and sensible, as shown in the COPS paper and algorithm, titled "Don't settle for eventual" [12].

Causal arbitration can easily be violated if arbitration is based on physical timestamps (i.e. timestamps provided by physical clocks on the various devices), and if those clocks exhibit skew. Often, systems use logical clocks (such as Lamport clocks) which are by construction consistent with the happens-before relation, thus avoiding this problem.

4.2   Eventual Consistency Mechanisms

We now discuss four protocols $\Phi_a, \Phi_b, \Phi_c, \Phi_t$ that provide various levels of consistency, as shown in the table below:

Eventually Consistent Protocol Φ_t. First, we look at the protocol with the weakest guarantees, which is quite simple (Fig. 6). Each process keeps a set known of known updates. When performing an update, this update is added to the local set, and also broadcast to all other processes; when they receive the update, they add it to their set. All updates are timestamped, using Lamport's scheme based on logical clocks [10]. When computing the return value of an operation,

	Primary replication			Direct broadcast
	Φ_a	Φ_b	Φ_c	Φ_t
Sequential consistency	✓	—	—	—
Read my writes	✓	—	✓	✓
Consistent prefix	✓	✓	—	—
Monotonic reads	✓	✓	✓	✓
Causal visibility	✓	✓	✓	—
Causal arbitration	✓	✓	✓	✓
Available under partitions	—	✓	✓	✓

types
| Update = $\mathbb{N}_0 \times$ Pid $\times$ Obj $\times$ Op ordered lexicographically
process state
| known : $\mathcal{P}(\text{Update})$ // initially $\emptyset$
| clock : $\mathbb{N}_0$ // initially 0
messages
| Inform$(u : \text{Update}, q : \text{Pid})$ //sent from u.second to q
  action perform$(p : \text{Pid}, n : \mathbb{N}_0, x : \text{Obj}, o : \text{Op}, r : \text{Val})$ **at** p
  condition $(n = \text{clock}) \wedge (r = \mathcal{S}_{\text{type}(x)}(o, \text{ops}_x(\text{known}).\text{sort}))$
| **sends** $\bigcup_{q \in \text{Pid}} \text{Inform}((n, p, x, o), q)$
  updates known $\leftarrow$ known $\cup \{(n, p, x, o)\}$; clock $\leftarrow$ clock $+ 1$;
  action learn$(u : Update, q : \text{Pid})$ **at** q
| **receives** Inform(u, q)
  updates known $\leftarrow$ known $\cup \{u\}$; clock $\leftarrow \max\{\text{clock}, (u.\text{first} + 1)\}$;

Fig. 6. Eventually consistent protocol Φ_t based on direct broadcast and Lamport timestamps.

the updates are sorted according to timestamps, and filtered according to the object they target (we define the function ops_x to filter updates from a sequence that target object x), then fed into the function $\mathcal{S}$ which tells us what value to return.

It is easy to show that this protocol is eventually consistent; to construct a corresponding abstract execution, we simply use one event per perform action. For the arbitration order, we use the lexicographic order over timestamps. For the visibility order, we say that e is visible to e' if the update tuple for e is in the known set when e' is performed.

Without further optimizations, this protocol is not practical since it consumes too much space. However, it is easy to see that for most data types, we can reduce the known set. For example, when working with registers, it is enough to keep only the latest update for each object, without altering the semantics. This is known as Thomas' rule [14].

types
| $\mathsf{Update} = \mathsf{Pid}_{\mathsf{sec}} \times \mathsf{Obj} \times \mathsf{Op} \times \mathbb{N}_0$

process state
| busy : $(\bot \cup \mathsf{Update})$ initially $\bot$ (secondary)
| localcount : $\mathbb{N}_0$ initially 0 (secondary)
| confirmed : Update^* initially ϵ (secondary)

messages
| $\mathsf{Update}(u : \mathsf{Update})$ //sent from secondary u.first to primary p
| $\mathsf{Inform}(u : \mathsf{Update}, q' : \mathsf{Pid}_{\mathsf{sec}})$ //sent from primary p to secondary q'

action $\mathsf{read}(q : \mathsf{Pid}_{\mathsf{sec}}, x : \mathsf{Obj}, o : \mathsf{Op}, r : \mathsf{Val})$ **at** q (secondary)
| **condition** $(\mathtt{busy} = \bot) \wedge (o$ is a read-only operation)
| **condition** $r = \mathcal{S}_{\mathrm{type}(x)}(o, \mathsf{ops}_x(\mathtt{confirmed}))$

action $\mathsf{update}(q : \mathsf{Pid}_{\mathsf{sec}}, x : \mathsf{Obj}, o : \mathsf{Op}, l : \mathbb{N}_0)$ **at** q (secondary)
| **condition** $(\mathtt{busy} = \bot) \wedge (o$ is a update-only operation) $\wedge (l = \mathtt{localcount})$
| **sends** $\mathsf{Update}(q, x, o, l)$
| **updates** $\mathtt{busy} \leftarrow (q, x, o, l); \mathtt{localcount} \leftarrow \mathtt{localcount} + 1;$

action $\mathsf{perform}(u : \mathsf{Update})$ **at** p (primary)
| **receives** $\mathsf{Update}(u)$
| **sends** $\bigcup_{q' \in \mathsf{Pid}} \mathsf{Inform}(u, q')$

action $\mathsf{learn}(u : \mathsf{Update}, q' : \mathsf{Pid}_{\mathsf{sec}})$ **at** q' (secondary)
| **receives in-order** $\mathsf{Inform}(u)$
| **updates** $\mathtt{confirmed} \leftarrow \mathtt{confirmed} \cdot u$
| **updates** if $\mathtt{busy} = u$ then $\mathtt{busy} \leftarrow \bot$

Fig. 7. Sequentially consistent protocol Φ_a based on primary replication, supporting local reads on secondaries, for some primary process $p \in \mathsf{Pid}$ and secondary processes $\mathsf{Pid}_{\mathsf{sec}} \subseteq \mathsf{Pid}$.

Sequentially Consistent Protocol Φ_a. Figure 7 shows a protocol based on primary replication. Operations are performed at the secondary replicas, with identifiers $\mathsf{Pid}_{\mathsf{sec}} \subseteq \mathsf{Pid}$. Each secondary replica stores a sequence confirmed of updates it received from the primary replica, using in-order delivery. Read-only operations are performed locally on secondary replicas, by consulting the updates stored in confirmed. Other operations issued on secondary replicas are broken down into beginoperation and endoperation. beginoperation sends the update to the primary. Nothing else can happen on the secondary, until this same update is confirmed by the primary.

Executions are sequentially consistent. To obtain an abstract execution, define the events to be the actions read and perform, and define $\rightarrow$ to be the total order that we obtain by (1) taking the total order in which the perform events appear in the execution, and (2) inserting read into this chain anywhere after the last update confirmed before the local read, and before the next update confirmed after the local read.

types
| Update $=$ Pid$_{\text{sec}} \times$ Obj $\times$ Op $\times$ $\mathbb{N}_0$

process state
| localcount : $\mathbb{N}_0$ initially 0 (secondary)
| confirmed : Update* initially ϵ (secondary)

messages
| Update(u : Update)   //sent from secondary u.first to primary p
| Inform(u : Update, q' : Pid$_{\text{sec}}$) //sent from primary p to secondary q'

action read(q : Pid$_{\text{sec}}, x$: Obj, o : Op, r : Val) **at** q (secondary)
| **condition** (o is a read-only operation)
| **condition** $r = \mathcal{S}_{\text{type}(x)}(o, \text{ops}_x(\text{confirmed}))$

action update(q : Pid$_{\text{sec}}, x$: Obj, o : Op, l : $\mathbb{N}_0$) **at** q (secondary)
| **condition** (o is a update-only operation) $\wedge$ ($l = $ localcount)
| **sends** Update(q, x, o, l)
| **updates** localcount $\leftarrow$ localcount $+ 1$

action perform(u : Update) **at** p (primary)
| **receives in-order** Update(u)
| **sends** $\bigcup_{q' \in \text{Pid}}$ Inform(u, q')

action learn(u : Update, q' : Pid$_{\text{sec}}$) **at** q' (secondary)
| **receives in-order** Inform(u)
| **updates** confirmed $\leftarrow$ confirmed $\cdot u$

Fig. 8. Consistent prefix protocol Φ_b based on primary replication, for some primary process $p \in$ Pid and secondary processes Pid$_{\text{sec}} \subseteq$ Pid.

Note that Φ_a is not linearizable, even though it is sequentially consistent. The reason is that it is possible that a read operation o_1 is logically ordered before a write operation o_2 by the order $\rightarrow$ (i.e. the read does not see the write), but that the completion of the write operation endoperation($q, \_, o_2 \_$) appears before the beginning (=ending) of the read operation read($q, \_, o_1, \_$) in the execution, thus contradicting the definition of linearizability.

Consistent Prefix Protocol Φ_b. Figure 8 shows another protocol based on primary replication. This time around, the protocol supports availability even in the presence of network partitions: both reads and writes are satisfied locally (assuming that all operations are either read-only or update-only operations). The protocol is similar to Φ_a, but update operations do not block, but allow the client to continue immediately. Update notifications are sent to the primary using in-order delivery, and broadcast back. They are received in-order and appended to the confirmed sequence.

The protocol is eventually consistent: we construct the arbitration order the same way as for Φ_a. For the visibility order, we define vis$^{-1}(o)$ to be ar$^{-1}(u)$

types
| $\text{Update} = \text{Pid}_{\text{sec}} \times \text{Obj} \times \text{Op} \times \mathbb{N}_0$

process state
| `localcount` : $\mathbb{N}_0$ initially 0 (secondary)
| `pending` : Update^* initially ϵ (secondary)
| `confirmed` : Update^* initially ϵ (secondary)

messages
| $\text{Update}(u : \text{Update})$ //sent from secondary $u.\text{first}$ to primary p
| $\text{Inform}(u : \text{Update}, q' : \text{Pid}_{\text{sec}})$ //sent from primary p to secondary q'

  action $\text{read}(q : \text{Pid}_{\text{sec}}, x : \text{Obj}, o : \text{Op}, r : \text{Val})$ **at** q (secondary)
| | **condition** (o is a read-only operation)
 | **condition** $r = \mathcal{S}_{\text{type}(x)}(o, \text{ops}_x(\texttt{confirmed}) \cdot \text{ops}_x(\texttt{pending}))$

  action $\text{update}(q : \text{Pid}_{\text{sec}}, x : \text{Obj}, o : \text{Op}, l : \mathbb{N}_0)$ **at** q (secondary)
 | **condition** (o is an update-only operation) $\wedge$ ($l = \texttt{localcount}$)
 | **sends** $\text{Update}(q, x, o, l)$
 | **updates** $\texttt{localcount} \leftarrow \texttt{localcount} + 1; \texttt{pending} \leftarrow \texttt{pending} \cdot (q, x, u, l)$

  action $\text{perform}(u : \text{Update})$ **at** p (primary)
| | **receives in-order** $\text{Update}(u)$
 | **sends** $\bigcup_{q' \in \text{Pid}} \text{Inform}(u, q')$

  action $\text{learn}(u : \text{Update}, q' : \text{Pid}_{\text{sec}})$ **at** q' (secondary)
| | **receives in-order** $\text{Inform}(u)$
 | **updates** $\texttt{confirmed} \leftarrow \texttt{confirmed} \cdot u;$ if $q = q'$ then $\texttt{pending} \leftarrow \texttt{pending}.\text{remove}(u)$

Fig. 9. Read-my-writes protocol Φ_c based on primary replication, for some primary process $p \in \text{Pid}$ and secondary processes $\text{Pid}_{\text{sec}} \subseteq \text{Pid}$.

where u is the last operation in `confirmed` at the time o is performed. Thus, the protocol satisfies consistent prefix.

Read-My-Writes Protocol Φ_c. Figure 9 shows yet another protocol based on primary replication. This time, we want to support read-my-writes, so we locally store a sequence `pending` of operations that have been sent to the primary, but not confirmed yet. When performing reads or writes locally, we use not only the updates in `confirmed`, but also append the updates in `pending`.

References

1. Brewer, E.A.: Towards robust distributed systems (abstract). In: PODC 2000 (2000)
2. Burckhardt, S.: Consistency in distributed systems. LASER Summer School Slide Decks (2013). http://sdrv.ms/1dWFsBQ
3. Burckhardt, S.: Principles of eventual consistency. Found. Trends Program. Lang. 1(1–2), 1–150 (2014)
4. Burrowsm, M.: The Chubby lock service for loosely-coupled distributed systems. In: Operating Systems Design and Implementation, pp. 335–350 (2006)

5. Cachin, C., Guerraoui, R., Rodrigues, L.: Introduction to Reliable and Secure Distributed Programming, 2nd edn. Springer, Heidelberg (2011)
6. Dill, D.L.: The murphi verification system. In: Computer Aided Verification, pp. 390–393 (1996)
7. Fischer, M.J., Lynch, N.A., Paterson, M.S.: Impossibility of distributed consensus with one faulty process. J. ACM **32**, 374–382 (1982)
8. Gilbert, S., Lynch, N.: Brewer's conjecture and the feasibility of consistent, available, partition-tolerant web services. SIGACT News **33**(2), 51–59 (2002)
9. Hunt, P., Konar, M., Junqueira, F.P., Reed, B.: Zookeeper: wait-free coordination for internet-scale systems. In: Proceedings of the 2010 USENIX Conference on USENIX Annual Technical Conference, USENIXATC 2010, p. 11. USENIX Association, Berkeley (2010)
10. Lamport, L.: Time, clocks, and the ordering of events in a distributed system. Commun. ACM **21**(7), 558–565 (1978)
11. Lamport, L.: The part-time parliament. ACM Trans. Comput. Syst. **16**, 133–169 (1998)
12. Lloyd, W., Freedman, M.J., Kaminsky, M., Andersen, D.G.: Don't settle foreventual: scalable causal consistency for wide-area storage with COPS. In: SOSP 2011 (2011)
13. Terry, D.: Replicated Data Consistency Explained Through Baseball (2011)
14. Thomas, R.H., Beranek, B.: A majority consensus approach to concurrency control for multiple copy databases. ACM Trans. Database Syst. **4**, 180–209 (1979)

Software Mining Studies: Goals, Approaches, Artifacts, and Replicability

Sven Amann[1]($\boxtimes$), Stefanie Beyer[2], Katja Kevic[3], and Harald Gall[3]

[1] TU Darmstadt, Darmstadt, Germany
amann@cs.tu-darmstadt.de
[2] Alpen-Adria University Klagenfurt, Klagenfurt, Austria
[3] University of Zurich, Zurich, Switzerland

Abstract. The mining of software archives has enabled new ways for increasing the productivity in software development: Analyzing software quality, mining project evolution, investigating change patterns and evolution trends, mining models for development processes, developing methods of integrating mined data from various historical sources, or analyzing natural language artifacts in software repositories, are examples of research topics. Software repositories include various data, ranging from source control systems, issue tracking systems, artifact repositories such as requirements, design and architectural documentation, to archived communication between project members. Practitioners and researchers have recognized the potential of mining these sources to support the maintenance of software, to improve their design or architecture, and to empirically validate development techniques or processes. We revisited software mining studies that were published in recent years in the top venues of software engineering, such as ICSE, ESEC/FSE, and MSR. In analyzing these software mining studies, we highlight different viewpoints: pursued goals, state-of-the-art approaches, mined artifacts, and study replicability. To analyze the mining artifacts, we (lexically) analyzed research papers of more than a decade. In terms of replicability we looked at existing work in the field in mining approaches, tools, and platforms. We address issues of replicability and reproducibility to shed light onto challenges for large-scale mining studies that would enable a stronger conclusion stability.

1 Motivation

Software archives, such as source control systems, defect tracking systems, or archived communication among project members, are used to help managing the progress of software projects. Since about a decade, the software engineering community exploits the potential benefit of mining this information to support the evolution of software systems, improve software design and reuse, and empirically validate novel ideas and techniques. Research has now proceeded to uncover the ways in which mining these archives can help to understand software development, to support predictions about software properties, and to plan software projects. Researchers regularly exchange their results and present novel tools at

© Springer International Publishing Switzerland 2015
B. Meyer and M. Nordio (Eds.): LASER 2013-2014, LNCS 8987, pp. 121–158, 2015.
DOI: 10.1007/978-3-319-28406-4_5

conferences and symposia, such as MSR[1], MSA 2010,[2] ASDS 2013,[3] or MSR Vision 2020.[4]

Mining software archives (MSA) is one kind of software analytics that deals with investigating repositories that are used during software development to store all kinds of information about the software. Examples are version control systems, issue trackers, task management, project management, software forges (such as BitBucket or GitHub), Q&A sites (such as StackOverflow), or communication archives (such as emails, instant messages, or social-media data).

MSA has evolved from applying data mining to all kinds of data about a software system to a discipline of data-driven analysis that today is known as software analytics [69]. Software analytics is more than just data mining software versions. It is about obtaining insights into the actual development and evolution of software systems. These insights shall enable the observer to take actions in terms of changing practices, tooling, or infrastructures to improve productivity of software developers.

One example for such insights into evolutionary aspects of software is defect prediction, i.e. discovering code components (modules, classes, methods, etc.) that are likely defect-prone. Actions following from that can be redesign, refactoring, or even reengineering. Another example are so-called recommender systems that provide help for code completion, suggest good code examples, or support understanding code. Other examples are software effort prediction [112] or test-code impact analysis [127].

The major conference for researchers to publish their latest mining results is the Working Conference on Mining Software Repositories (MSR).[5] Analyzing the proceedings of past MSR conferences confirmed previous analyses [16] and revealed that the mined artifacts have become manifold.

In the first editions of the MSR conference, about ten years ago, only data from CVS repositories was investigated, whereas today researchers mine data from a broad range of resources, such as Git repositories, Q&A sites, blogs, emails, tutorials, and Twitter. The prominence of version repositories has declined over the years, but augments towards "social" artifacts, focusing more on the individual developer.

Kagdi et al. [49] surveyed the field and provide a good overview of the areas of MSR that cover dimensions of information sources, representation (type and granularity, as well as context), purpose of studies, methodology, and evaluation. Besides a comprehensive discussion of approaches and their classification, it is remarkable that in 2007 (looking back for about a decade) only few threats to (internal and external) validity were discussed in MSR studies. We argue that, with the manifold techniques and mined artifacts, the dimensions of reproducibility and replicability have not been addressed adequately. This opens new avenues for systematic mining studies.

---

[1] http://msrconf.org.
[2] http://www.ifi.uzh.ch/seal/events/msa2010.html.
[3] http://www.ifi.uzh.ch/seal/events/ASDS-2013.html.
[4] http://msrcanada.org/msrvision2020/.
[5] http://MSRconf.org.

In this chapter, we address the question of systematic mining studies by looking at two aspects in particular: reproducibility and replicability. A special focus will be given to the latter with investigating approaches, techniques, and platforms published at the major conferences in the field in the recent past—in particular ICSE, ESEC/FSE, and MSR—that claim to deal with this challenge to some extent. We look into what makes a good mining study, then describe techniques for mining, and further study replicability and systematic mining studies. We also take a look onto how these challenges are taken up in recent fields, such as green mining, sentiment analysis, and studies covering human aspects.

2 Mining Studies

This section introduces two approaches where to place the field of mining software repositories into data analytics and data science. This is followed by an overview what characterizes a mining study. The main focus is on the setup for the study, the process, and the interpretation of the results. Then, we discuss the threats of mining software repositories, in particular for bug prediction on biased datasets, sample size, stable rankings, and time variance. Approaches, languages and tools that support researchers in mining software repositories, for instance, to share data, to improve reproducibility and to avoid redundant preprocessing of data are presented. Finally, we discuss the reproducibility of mining studies.

2.1 Meta-Studies on Mining Software Repositories

Mining software repositories evolved a lot in the last decade and the question about the relation of MSR to data science and software analytics needs to be addressed.

Mining Software Repositories and Data Science. Mockus [74] discussed in his keynote at the MSR conference in 2014 the relationship between mining software repositories, operational data, and data science. Mining software repositories focuses on extracting knowledge from software data. Both use operational data, so he concludes that mining software repositories actually is data science.

Mining software repositories and data science have similar goals, namely to identify laws by extracting knowledge from data. The data used for data science is often experimental data, such as temperatures of sensors. Accordingly, for mining software repositories mainly software data is analyzed.

Operational data are digital traces which are not primarily created for analysis, such as logs of mobile phones that are not created to be measured, but may be used for data science. However, the use of operational data brings along multiple challenges, such as missing data or even wrong data. Therefore, the challenge is to identify data laws to segment information, impute missing information and correct the data. Traditional data may be taken into account to fill the gaps of operational data. Tools that create operational data are, for instance, version control systems, such as SVN or git, as well as issue-trackers, such as BugZilla or JIRA. Mockus argues that it is worth to research on operational data because there is so much data that also map the human activities to the digital domain. Furthermore, data is *treacherous* [74] and may have multiple contexts, missing data, and faked data.

The aims for mining software repositories and data science are similar: approaches or tools to engineer operational data with a software system to ensure integrity of results, to get more effectively results, and simplify the building of software systems to analyze operational data in order to increase the quality of the data. Therefore, operational data are common in both, data science and mining software repositories. The conclusion is that mining software repositories is indeed data science.

Software Analytics. Menzies and Zimmermann [69] describe the changing goals of software analytics over time, as well as the different methods of data analytics, and the principles to perform a good study. They point out that the main goal is to give 'relevant advice' to the audience. Who should benefit from the outcome of the analysis? Analytics for testers and developers may require different tools and techniques than analytics for managers or even researchers. The claims of data analytics are to share information, or more concrete, to share models, insights, data, and methods. The main goal about 40 years ago was to find 'the model of software engineering.' By the time, this goal has changed, since one model cannot fit all software projects. So the focus shifted to find methods of a particular system that may be transferred to other systems. The most important factors for data analysis are the choice of the right usage patterns for the data, as well as the user itself who should profit from this analysis. The right choice of tools, for instance to visualize data or draw conclusions automatically from data might influence the data analysis positively. However, tools, algorithms, as well as a suitable hardware for analysis are not the key components.

The Seven Principles for Software Analytics. By Menzies and Zimmermann give advice on how to perform data analytics. To apply data analysis effectively, the users' goals and needs must be well known and understood. If possible, early and continuous feedback of the users should be considered. The system built for data analysis should be able to repeat the analysis several times. The possibility of growing datasets should be taken into account. If the approaches did not work out it is often helpful to be open-minded for other directions. Evaluation of the data plays a very important role. One of the main evaluation principles is to repeat the analysis various times with different percentage of the data and see if the results change. Furthermore, preprocessing of data is often required and should not be neglected. The last principle guides to use a wide range of technologies. Tools that are constantly updated with the implementation of new methods make this easier.

The analysis of data has widespread goals and different focus. Therefore, Menzies and Zimmermann differentiate between several kinds of analytics. First, they distinguish *internal* and *external analytics.* For internal analytics the access to data is easier than for external analytics that requires more effort, since the data typically has to be anonymized to keep privacy. Second, they distinguish the *quantitative* and the *qualitative* method. The former is applied automatically by using several data mining tools and statistics; the latter is mainly applied by investigating the data manually. Lastly, they point out the necessity to distinguish *exploratory* and *deployment analytics*. In exploratory analytics, the goals often are not clear and the research might not result in prominent findings. However, if results are found and the goals are clear, it is possible to use deployment analytics to build tools and systems to use the findings.

2.2   What is a Mining Study?

Let us explain a mining study first by looking at a recent experiment in the field of defect prediction [28]: We train models to predict defect-prone source files of the next release of a software system. For that we use product, process, and organizational measures and then apply machine-learning techniques to training the models. The result is a model (basically a set of coefficients for a function or set of functions) that fits the data best. This model can then be used for predicting the defect-prone modules of the next release. Typical models are regressions or decision trees; however a huge variety of machine learners can be used for such an experiment.

While the setup and the process of such a mining study might be clear, it is less clear what the essential ingredients of a *good* study are. We might view that it is all about the data; it is of course data-driven, but at the same time it is as much about the research hypothesis and the underlying assumptions of the experiment: Typically, the starting point is a research question that tries to relate (or correlate) some property X (e.g. code churn) with another property Y (e.g. defects), to check whether there exists a statistically significant correlation. Other setups might investigate how some property Z (e.g. code ownership) has developed over time, by looking at the version history of a software system. Phenomenons, such as code ownership or networks of developers, often are related to quality aspects of the software system, such as defect proneness, code irregularity, or complexity.

A mining study typically starts with a research hypothesis, then prepares the data to be investigated, analyzes the data, and continues to interpreting the results. The granularity of studies can vary quite a bit, ranging from factors influencing some particular property (such as buggy commits) to comprehensive quality measures (such as proper design or architecture).

With any such mining study, it is important to check whether the process of analysis, mining, and interpretation can be reproduced or replicated. *Reproducibility* means that the study description provides all the data, tooling, and configuration settings to validate the experiment. *Replicability* means that the study can be performed with different data sets and projects to gain a broader conclusion. Basic criteria for studies are:

Stability: The algorithms and tools run stable without crashing.

Reliability: The same results can be achieved with same data over and over again.

Efficiency: The results can be produced in reasonable amount of time given the volume of the data.

Auxiliary tasks to be supported: Added value of the data can be provided, for example in the form of models or higher-level abstractions.

Essential for all mining studies is the data preparation and data cleansing, which includes analyzing spurious values in the data and eliminating outliers that would impact or even distort the results. Data filtering is the primary key for a successful study; it deals with selecting subsets of data based on defined selection criteria (dependent on the research question to be investigated). Data binning is one such technique that tries to reduce the effects of minor observation errors by using intervals. Original values that fall in a given interval, a bin, are used as representative for a central value. For example, this is done in defect prediction, where files (or classes etc.) are put into bins to represent defect prone or non-defect prone files.

More details on proper design of mining studies can be found, for example, in the Cross Industry Standard Process for Data Mining (CRISP-DM) documentation [105].

2.3   Threats to the Validity in Mining Software Repositories

Next, we discuss some threats of mining studies. In particular, we discuss four approaches to address threats in bug prediction concerning stable rankings of estimation methods, sample size and bias in datasets, and time variance. Any of these can result in distorted or even questionable predictions.

Stable Rankings for Different Effort-Estimation Models. Menzies *et al.* [68] investigated 158 software effort estimation methods concerning their stability across different evaluation cirteria on various datasets and randomly selected features of COCOMO. The goal was to find a ranking among the estimation methods, since previously conducted studies suffered from 'conclusion instability' [107]. They use the COSEEKMO effort-estimation workbench that combines preprocessors to prune rows or columns, learners, such as local calibration, model trees, and standard linear regression, as well as different nearest-neighbor algorithms. Menzies *et al.* evaluated the performance of the methods by applying the model to a training set and then to a test set, as well as by collecting performance statistics using AR (Absolute Residual), MRE (Magnitude of Relative Error), or MER (Magnitude of Error Relative to the estimate), and counting the number of times a method loses with the Mann-Withney U test. They found that Local Calibration (LC), COCOMIN + LC, COCOMIN + LOCOMO + LC, and LOCOMO + LC perform better than all the other combination of methods and conclude that the combination of nearest neighbors with other methods is quite powerful.

Sample Size vs. Bias in Defect Prediction. Rahman *et al.* [95] performed a study how bias and size influence the results of mining studies on defect prediction. They sampled a dataset of high quality to several small 'biased and polluted sub-datasets,' to see if there is an effect on the bias of the defect prediction. They considered five kinds of bias for defect prediction: experience of the defect-fixer, severity of the defect, proximity to the next release deadline, the time to fix a bug, and the cardinality in size of the commits for each defect. Meta-models are used to evaluate if there are differences between the types of bias and their effect on the results. They found, that the type of bias does not have a significant influence on the prediction results. Furthermore, they investigated how bias, pollution, and size effect the prediction results. Size is at least as important as bias and pollution. Considering the performance metrics AUC and F50 it is even significantly more important.

Bias in Bug-Fix Datasets. Bird *et al.* [8] investigated how biased datasets influence the performance of bug prediction techniques. A biased dataset is a dataset where links between the code repository and the bugs tracker are missing. In their study they considered the severity of the bugs, as well as the experience of the developer who fixed the bug. They found that severe bugs are most likely fixed by experienced users, since there exist often links between the bug-fix and the issue-tracker. Bird *et al.* tested their hypotheses on BUGCACHE, a bug prediction tool for biased datasets. By sampling the dataset, they found that if BUGCACHE is trained on a certain level of severity, it performs well for this severity, but badly for other severities. The usage of a model, considering biased data and trained for trained for all kind of bugs, is reflected in the performance of the bug-prediction model.

Time Variance and Variability in Defect Prediction. Ekanayake *et al.* [18] investigated the problem of variability in the accuracy of a bug prediction-model over time. They looked into four large open source projects and empirically identified various project features that influence the defect-prediction quality. In particular, they observed that a change in the number of authors of a file and the number of defects fixed by these authors influence the prediction quality. As a major conclusion their experiments showed that there exist periods of stability and variability of prediction quality. As a result, one should use approaches such as the one proposed to assess the model's accuracy in advance. These findings have a major consequence in that prediction quality is highly dependent on the time interval one selects for training the data to then make predictions. The accuracy of the predictions, therefore, can range from poor to high just depending on the selected time slices. Still, it remains open how to pick time intervals that represent stable (versus variable) phases in the software development.

2.4 Approaches, Languages, and Platforms for Mining

There are many possibilities how to support the mining of software repositories. Here, we introduce approaches, languages, and platforms that support, for instance, data sharing, the examination of mining software repositories from different aspects, and the use of domain-specific languages (DSLs). Extracting and preprocessing data from software archives is time intensive and, therefore, need to be assisted by tools. For that, several platforms and tools have been developed that we briefly introduce in this section.

SeCold, TA-RE, iSPARQL, and *EvoONT* address this problem by providing the possibility of data sharing and making the replication of studies easier. *SeCold,* implemented by Keivanloo *et al.* [52,53], is "an open and collaborative platform for sharing software datasets." It provides research data online, to avoid that researchers preprocess the same data several times. The data is collected from issue trackers, such as BugZilla, Issuezilla, or JIRA, as well as from version control systems, such as SVN, CVS, or Git. This data then is merged to an abstract representation that mirrors the main concepts of these approaches. SeCold can also be used to find code duplicates as well as source-code-license violations. Studies and experiments in data mining are often not replicable due to the lack of shared knowledge about how the data is extracted. The results also depend highly on the selected parameters and heuristics. The goal of *TA-RE* is to address this issue. The corpus of *TA-RE* consists of the extracted data of software repositories and of an exchange language to share additional data that influences the results of the studies, but is not contained in the data itself, such as heuristics or parameter settings. The data may be further used to benchmark experiments. Kiefer *et al.* [56] extended SPARQL to *iSPARQL* and added the possibility to query for similar software entities, such as classes or methods. Furthermore, they developed EvoONT, based on the Web Ontology Language (OWL) that includes software, releases and bug-related data. It is possible to extend EvoOnt and integrate existing tools. With the combination of iSPARQL and EvoONT it is possible to mine software repositories that are represented in OWL. This combination supports the visualization and counting of code changes between versions, the localization of bad code smells or orphan methods, and the recommending of refactorings, as well as the computation of design metrics, such as size and complexity.

Mining software repositories includes a variety of aspects, concerning the evolution, the granularity of data, and meta-data of the projects, such as development process or team information. Yamashita *et al.* developed *E-CUBE,* an analysis tool for mining software repositories [125]. E-CUBE addresses platform evolution, target evolution, and scale evolution. They use FODA (Feature Oriented Domain Analysis) to create a DSL for E-CUBE. To target platform evolution, abstract types for bug repositories or code repositories are defined, instead of using a concrete repository. To address target evolution E-CUBE structures the data in a way so that it may be observed on several levels of granularity, such as file-level or method-level. The DSL provides the functionality to link projects to deal with the massive amount of data and the time for analysis. Spacco *et al.* [111] used software-repository mining to find better ways to teach and learn programming. They proposed the tool Marmoset. Marmoset collects snapshots of code, that are committed on saving operations. These fine grained code changes are collected in a database with a data schema that allows one to apply lots of queries to get information about fine-grained code evolution [111]. *CVSgrab* [120] provides the possibility to visualize the evolution of large software projects. It uses evolution similarity metrics to group files with similar evolution patterns. CVSgrab may be used to get information about the evolution of the team and development process, as well as for the localization of development issues.

In [45] Huang *et al.* describe their approach to use Alloy (a language and tool for relational models) to build a family of DSLs, similar to SQL, to address the various applications of mining software repositories. For this, they applied FODA (feature oriented domain analysis) to get the feature model of MSR. The feature model is then transformed to a logical formula using Alloy, which is used to derive automatically the language elements of the DSL.

In [122] Würsch *et al.* developed a pyramid of ontologies for software evolution analysis named *SE-ON*,[6] in particular to support mining studies. These ontologies model the domains of software versions, issues, developers, and the like. As such, they constitute a common vocabulary for tools to work on and exchange mining results. For software evolution analysis, Ghezzi and Gall devised a framework and platform for software analysis as a service, named *SOFAS* [26,27]. This approach enables systematic and reproducible software evolution analyses that exploit semantic descriptions of software, bugs, and versions using ontologies, semantic web services, and a RESTful architecture. This constitutes a major milestone for reproducibility in software mining studies [25]. The backbone for software analysis services is based on the pyramid of software evolution ontologies named SE-ON [122] and, for example, is used for developer support in Hawkshaw [123,124].

3   Revisiting a Decade of Software Mining Studies

Reasons to mine software repositories are manifold. Work related to mining software repositories spans from feature location, to better understanding development processes, to improve power consumption of software. We present a comprehensive overview of existing works in the field. In particular, we present a systematic literature review of research topics and methods applied from the past two years, followed by a lexical analysis of the research papers from eleven years of the Mining Software Repositories conference.

3.1   Why Researchers Mine Software Repositories

Over the past years, many research fields adopted MSR approaches as a new means to achieve their respective goals or to improve existing approaches. We reviewed the MSR research published at MSR 2014, ICSE 2014, ICSE 2013, and FSE 2013, to better understand what problems can be tackled through mining

---

[6] http://www.se-on.org/.

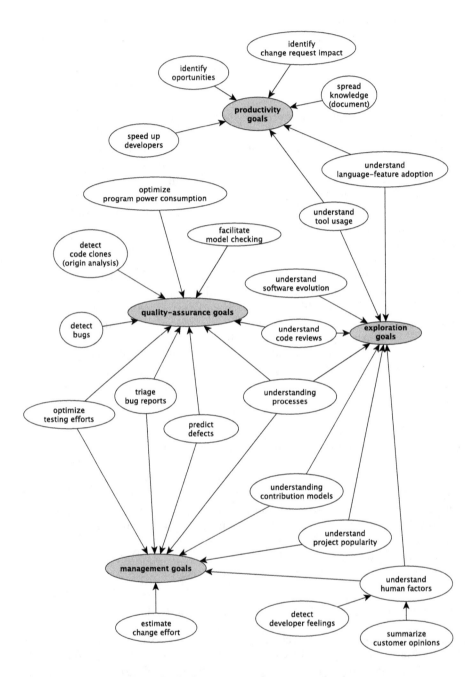

Fig. 1. Goals for mining software repositories

software repositories and to gain an insight on the datasets used in the field. Figure 1 summarizes the goals that the reviewed work pursues. We identified three high-level goals: productivity goals, quality-assurance goals, and management goals. All three goal categories subsume concrete software engineering tasks that researchers try to support by developing targeted approaches and tools. In addition, the reviewed research includes exploratory studies to understand different aspects of software projects better, and meta-studies that aim at improving MSR methodologies.

Productivity Goals. Much past research aims at tools helping developers write better code faster, thus, pursuing the ultimate goal to make developers more productive. A category of such tools commonly referred to as *Recommender Systems for Software Engineering* [99] received much attention over the last decade. These recommender approaches typically mine code repositories [10, 40, 44, 83], version-control systems [75], or even more fine-grained sequences of code changes to identify usage patterns [55, 80]. Other productivity-enhancing approaches identify code locations that are likely to be affected by change requests from interaction- and version-control histories [129].

Another line of research focuses on the documentation of software systems. This research ranges from exploring the common forms of documentation [116], to enriching existing documentation with information about common pitfalls from bug trackers [51], examples from StackOverflow [115], or usage patterns from large code bases [81], to the automated creation of feature models for better software understanding [15, 104].

In the light of the ever increasing amounts of data, e.g., due to the number and size of publicly available projects or additional data sources, such as Q&A-sites, it becomes even more difficult to find a specific piece of information. Lemos *et al.* [62] automatically expand code-search queries to increase the probability of finding the desired code snippets in the presence of potential vocabulary mismatch, i.e., when query and code use alternative terminology. Ponzanelli *et al.* [90] automatically look up relevant StackOverflow threads based on the developer's current coding context. Both approaches aim at faster knowledge accessibility and less need for context switching.

Exploratory work in the field includes the investigation of how developers use GitHub's pull requests to better understand change-management processes [33, 97]. Other work focuses on the adoption of language features over time [17, 98]. In the long run, such work will discover which kind of support developers need in learning and migrating to new language features. To improve widely used question-and-answer sites like StackOverflow, researchers investigated techniques to identify frequently asked questions [4] and reasons why questions remain unanswered [101].

Quality-Assurance Goals. Much research is dedicated to support developers in ensuring functional correctness of code, enhancing maintainability of code, and optimizing code. There are many different goals and approaches, which we discuss subsequently.

Bug detection is one of the most prominent areas in MSR. The goals are to detect previously unknown bugs [12, 22, 81], localize reported bugs in source code [34, 82], and identify potential fixes for bugs [38]. Johnson *et al.* investigated on shortcomings of current bug-detection tools that keep developers from using them in practice [48]. They found that developers are dissatisfied by the additional effort required to use such tools and by the number of false positives they produce. They collected possible improvements to address the usability aspect.

Many evaluations of bug-detection approaches use FindBugs[7] as a test oracle. Therefore, researchers applied FindBugs to large sets of projects, to create benchmark datasets [72, 102]. Other evaluations of bug detection approaches use issue trackers as oracles to test whether actually reported bugs would have been found by the respective approach. However, Chen *et al.* [14] identified a systematic bias in this evaluation technique, due to bugs reported only much later than introduced. Rahman *et al.* [94] compare static bug finders and statistical prediction methods to identify and discuss synergy potentials between these two fields.

Code clone detection and origin analysis are considered as further quality-assurance goals. Both identify code locations that are similar in terms of their structure or semantics. Mondal *et al.* [75] identify source code locations that are likely to require changes, based on their similarity to recently changed locations. Kevic *et al.* [55] identify locations that a bug report or change request most likely impacts, based on the impact of previous reports. Steidl *et al.* [113] present a framework for incremental origin analysis that scales even for very large code bases to make such approaches feasible in practice. Different oracles have been proposed to evaluate code clone detection approaches [59, 76].

Tulsian *et al.* apply MSR methods to facilitate model checking in practical application [117]. Though model checking has improved significantly, it remains challenging to select the right checker for a given program and property. They prove that statistical evidence for correlations between checkers and program-property pairs can be mined. To the best of our knowledge, this is the first work to combine model checking and MSR.

Another rising new area of MSR research aims at the optimization of program power consumption on code level. Hindle [42] named this area Green Mining. Pinto *et al.* [88] explored which power-consumption-related questions matter to software developers. Other pioneering work investigates on frameworks for further research [43] and on evaluation benchmarks [130].

McIntosh *et al.* [67] inspected modern (lightweight) code-reviews in OSS projects. They find that reviews positively influence software quality, if review coverage is high and reviewers are involved in the development process. Beller *et al.* [6] find that the changes triggered from review processes are surprisingly similar between OSS and industrial projects. They analyze what kind of changes are triggered from reviews and what triggers them.

Management Goals. Some research from the MSR community tackles management related goals. As management is a cross-cutting concern, some of these

---

[7] http://findbugs.sourceforge.net/.

goals are also related to aspects such as the triaging of bug reports or quality assurance in general.

Bug triaging encompasses tasks such as finding report duplicates [2,57,60, 61], automatic identification of non-reproducible bug reports [19], or predicting blocking bugs [119] and bugs that are eventually fixed [128]. Closely related research automatically infers bug-management processes from issue trackers [35], this exploratory work could help to detect differences between the intended and the actual process and identify potential for improvement.

Moreover, MSR techniques are used to estimate the effort (in terms of resources) required to realize an incoming change request based on historical change requests [100,132]. Other work investigates on how such effort models can be transferred between companies [71].

A different, quality-assurance-related management goal is the allocation of hardware resources for testing. Especially large industry projects face the problem that execution of all their regression tests takes too long for timely feedback. Therefore, Anderson et al. [3] and Shi et al. [108] propose approaches to rank tests according to their likelihood of identifying the next bugs.

Another closely related area is defect prediction. Its goal is to predict code modules (e.g. files, classes, or methods) that are likely to contain a bug, in order to optimize quality assurance efforts. While some defect-prediction research still explores new algorithms [47], most current effort is concerned with building cross-project defect-prediction models [24,79,131]. Lewis et al. [63] investigated the impact of defect-prediction tools on practitioners. They found that the predictors are rarely used, since, like the bug-prediction tools discussed above, they are to imprecise and investigating on their findings is much effort. Furthermore, the tools miss to present rationales for their findings to the users. In research on defect prediction, bug trackers are often used as oracles to evaluate the prediction quality. Herzig et al. analyze how misclassified bugs in such trackers impact evaluation results [41].

Recently, considering human factors becomes more and more important in software engineering research. The goal is to gain insight on the feelings of developers or other stakeholders involved in software development [37,77]. Such approaches are often referred to as Sentiment Analysis. Recent work has analyzed sentiments involved in discussions [89] and commit messages [36] on GitHub projects. Chen et al. [13] mine customers' opinions about software changes from reviews in mobile-app marketplaces.

Exploratory research aims at understanding how software and processes evolve over time, given changes in requirements, technologies, staff, and such. Past research has, for example, investigated feature churn on the basis of large source-code repositories [5,87] and changes of dependencies between modules in large software systems [9]. Other work focuses specifically on correlations between database-schema and code changes [93]. Brunet et al. [11] investigated whether developers discuss design on GitHub, in commits messages, issues comments, or pull requests.

More exploratory work looked on reasons for project success and downfall [1,64]. Yamashita *et al.* [126] researched what makes developers contribute to OSS projects, while Matragkas *et al.* [66] explored indicators for a healthy OS community. Other research looked at how developers contribute to OSS projects on GitHub [86,106] and how they collaborate [118].

Meta Studies. A significant part of MSR research is to support the community itself and to bring it forward in terms of replicability and reproducibility [92]. Researchers have created large datasets of GitHub project (meta) data [32,121] and version histories [23] together with platforms to access them, as a basis for future research. Others investigated on scalable infrastructure and algorithms to perform analyses and searches on todays huge datasets [21,58].

To mitigate risks to the validity of evaluations, Kalliamvakou *et al.* [50] discuss common pitfalls and respective counter-measures of studies based on GitHub data. Linares-Vasquez *et al.* [65] looked at datasets from Google Play and discuss bias introduced by reusable app-modules. Merten *et al.* [70] discuss strategies to efficiently separate code from unstructured text in large datasets.

3.2   Characteristics of the Data Sources Used

MSR research has long passed the point of mining only software repositories. Alongside traditional sources, such as code repositories and version-control systems, many other knowledge bases, such as issue trackers, Q&A sites, and developers itself, are the target of mining approaches. Researchers collect data from a multitude of companies and projects, from the very small to the very large. They creat datasets of various sizes and with regard to different criteria. Many of these datasets are tailored to answer specific research questions, others to reproduce previous results, and others again to enable reproducibility and comparability of future work.

In the majority, researchers evaluate their approaches using one or multiple software projects as exemplary subjects. Depending on the respective approach, they retrieve different types of data from these projects, e.g., sources of test and production code, execution traces, change histories, bug reports, developer or user discussions, and even energy-consumption traces. The data sources from which this data can be retrieved and the effort required to do so varies greatly.

This section first gives an overview of which data sources have been exploited and how and why they were selected. Second, it presents some filtering strategies applied to extract data from these sources and the properties of the resulting datasets. Last, it discusses the limitations of these datasets and the experiments performed on them as well as the issue of reusability of those datasets.

Data Sources. Datasets have a huge impact on the validity of MSR experiments. Oftentimes, datasets qualify for the generalizability of the findings. Thus, to reduce the threats on external validity, researchers constitute big datasets that include diverse data [78]. The datasets' diversity can stem, for example, from small and large change sets or from a lot of different developers.

To create big datasets, researchers often mine the source-code repositories of large OSS projects, because this data is publicly accessible and contains many data points. Popular examples of such projects are Eclipse [19,24,60,61,119,128], Firefox [19,128,130], and the Linux kernel [34,70,87]. However, all data points in such datasets originate from the same project and might not be representative for other projects.

To increase the diversity within datasets, researchers mine different projects from meta-repositories, such as Apache Projects [12,14,77], the Eclipse Marketplace [121], the Gentoo Repository [9], or Google Play [51,57]. Many of these contain more diverse projects, ranging over multiple sizes and maturity levels. Since all projects in meta-repositories are accessible in the same way, the effort to extend datasets is manageable. However, diversity may still be limited, since projects in such repositories often either belong to the same domain or are developed by the same organization. This issue was discussed by Nagappan et al. [78] who presented an approach to select diverse sets of projects for evaluations, in order to increase external validity. Proksch et al. [92] further discussed how to use this idea for a standardized platform of evaluation datasets.

Recently, the emergence of mega-repositories, such as SourceForge [62,98, 131], GitHub [32,121], or Google Code [131], helped researchers more easily access large quantities of projects. Mega-repositories contain a huge variety of projects, targeting all kinds of platforms. However, researchers showed that the variety of projects in such repositories can bias datasets. Kalliamvakou et al. [50] show, for example, that the majority of the projects on GitHub are personal and inactive; that GitHub is also used for free storage and as a Web hosting service; and that almost 40 % of all pull requests do not appear as merged, even though they were.

In addition, researchers have investigated on closed-source, commercial products [19,22,63,82,96,132]. Some research could show similarities, other differences between commercial and OS software. A general problem with evaluations on commercial products is the availability of the datasets, which is mostly limited by legal restrictions. Therefore, such evaluations are typically not reproducible.

Besides repositories, benchmark datasets, like the Nasa PROMISE repository,[8] are valuable data sources. These are specialized datasets that contain precomputed metadata used in the evaluations of respective tools. In contrast to the non-standardized way of retrieving data from repositories, benchmark datasets enable the comparability of results.

To further investigate on software projects, MSR was complemented with the mining of issue trackers, such as JIRA [19,77] or BugZilla [19,24,34], Q&A sites, such as StackOverflow [4,88,90], as well as email discussions [37,114], discussion threads [11,89], documentation sites [1,116], code reviews [6,67], change requests [129], and customer reviews [13]. To fully exploit these as data sources, the linking between issues and source code changes became a research target in its own right [113,129].

---

[8] http://openscience.us/repo/.

A further data source constitutes observational studies, which capture, for instance, interaction traces of developers within the source code [55] or interactions with specific tools [63]. The effort to obtain such datasets is especially high, since it requires the contribution of large numbers of developers and the legal and privacy matters are particularly present.

Data Sampling. Much of the reviewed work does not specify why one data source was selected over the other. Mostly, the selection seems guided by the specific requirements of the respective approach. The generalizability of the results is pursued by increasing the datasets' size. Large project sets (up to 140 k projects) are often sampled from mega-repositories, e.g., in [11,13,77,86,98], while smaller sets (1–50 projects) are also collected manually, e.g., in [19,24,38,57,61,119]. The number of projects is limited by the manual effort and time required to include further projects.

The primary filtering criteria is the availability of required (amounts of) data about the projects and the format this data is available in. For example, Erfani Joorabchi *et al.* [19] filter for projects that use either BugZilla or JIRA as their issue trackers, because the prototype implementation of their approach supports these two platforms; Kechagia *et al.* [51] select clients of the BugSense SDK, as crash reports are available for these projects; Brunet *et al.* [11] select projects with more than 50 discussion threads on GitHub, as they want to detect design discussions; Aggarwal *et al.* [1] select popular projects from GitHub that have documentation, as they want to investigate on relations between popularity and documentation.

Some work considers the diversity of their sample, with respect to dimensions such as the programming languages [3,131], the project domain [13,24,46,63], project size [13,46,63], project maturity (age, size, quality measures) [41,46], and open-source vs. industrial software [116].

After the selection of a project set follows the extraction of data from those projects, e.g., by analyzing source code [59], change history [80,87], discussions [77,88], or bug reports [2,57]. In this process, again, different sampling strategies are applied. For example, researchers often limit datasets to datapoints with certain properties, like closed bug reports [2,14,41,57,61,128], answered questions [4] or discussions with certain keywords [88], code entities with online documentation [51], or issue reports with links to code changes [67,129]. Work that uses historical data, like change history or discussions, often limits the considered time period [3,13,77,128,129].

A special case in data sampling is the interaction with developers. For surveys, the most common strategy is to just take all received answers [59,90,113, 118]. Researchers also include validation questions, to filter participants, especially when calling out to the general public. The driving factor seems the need for a sufficiently large number of participants.

Reusability. When looking at the availability of datasets, we found that only 27 publications (about 29 %) make the respective datasets available for reuse. We counted only those papers that provided an explicit link or instructions on how to obtain the dataset. Another 2 publications (about 2 %) name legal issues in the context of industry cooperations as the reason for not publishing the dataset.

Only 10 publications (less than 11 %) actually reuse a dataset from previous studies. Unfortunately, it is difficult to understand why this is the case, as we did not encounter any work that discusses problems or shortcomings of available datasets as the reason for coming up with a new one. Future work should identify reasons for this low reuse rate, e.g. insufficiencies of the datasets, and respective mitigation strategies.

The remaining 58 % of the work does not mention availability at all. This shows that reusability is not generally considered by the community.

3.3   A History of Artifacts in Mining Research

The artifact selection has a great impact on the replicability and reliability of an experiment's result. To better understand which factors influence the selection of artifacts within previous experiments, we investigated the proceedings of the past MSR conferences. Specifically, we conducted a lexical analysis on all accepted papers of the past eleven MSR conferences to answer the following questions:

Q1: At which point in time were particular artifacts more popular? How do technical developments influence MSR research?

Q2: Which artifacts will be used most likely in future?

Procedure. In our effort investigating these questions, we created for each past MSR conference a list including the most popular terms of each paper. To elicit each year's list of most popular terms, we first collected the proceedings of the past eleven years. To establish our dataset, we only considered full- and short-papers, disregarding other paper types, such as papers related to mining challenges. Parsing the remaining 297 papers into strings,[9] enabled to analyze the content of each paper. First, we eliminated the text, which follows the last occurrence of the term "references". Then, we split these strings into tokens, according to the whitespaces in the text. To improve the accuracy of our analysis, we performed well-known text-preprocessing steps, which included stop word removal and stemming. Specifically, we removed stop words included in an English stop word list of the Journal of Machine Learning Research.[10] For stemming the tokens, we used the Porter stemming algorithm [91], which strips suffixes from terms. To find the most popular terms within each paper, we counted the occurrences of each remaining token, producing a set of the top-ten terms per paper. Finally, we combined for each year the top-ten lists of each paper to a map, which includes pairs of terms associated to the count of appearance in a top-ten list.

---

[9] We used the java PDF library Apache PDFBox, https://pdfbox.apache.org/.

[10] http://jmlr.csail.mit.edu/papers/volume5/lewis04a/a11-smart-stop-list/english. stop.

Q1: At which point in time were particular artifacts more popular? How do technical developments influence MSR research? Overall, we identified 15 distinct sources of artifacts which are used for mining. These resources include *cvs, git, mercurial, github, svn, jazz, bug, commit, patch, message, stackoverflow, email, twitter, blog,* and *tutorial.* There are resources which are closely related to the source code, such as source code repositories. In contrast, other resources are more generic, not targeting particularly towards software engineering. To examine the appearance and popularity of the different kinds of artifacts, we plotted the artifacts' popularity metric along a timeline, see Fig. 2. The diagram depicts in the upper part technologies for versioning source code, while the remaining artifacts and sources for artifacts are represented in the lower part of the diagram.

When looking at the popularity of different version control systems over the years, the data indicates that in first experiments of the MSR conference *cvs* was used predominantly. Then, in 2009, several version control systems, were mentioned a lot in papers: *jazz, svn,* and *git.* However, from 2009 onwards version control systems were not as prominent as before. Our dataset indicates that terms like *github* and *mercurial* gained popularity.

Various terms related to communication channels started to appear more frequently from 2009 onwards. While terms like *email* and *message* started to be mentioned already in 2006, another category of artifact sources, namely social media, started to appear predominantly in 2011. From 2011 a conglomerate of various artifacts from different sources were included in MSR experiments.

Our data indicates that more and more diverse artifacts are considered in a mining study. The consideration of more and diverse artifacts highlights different aspects within the programming tasks of developers. It potentially converges more and more to the actual environment in which a developer works. However, the introduction of new artifact sources reduces the reproducibility and replicability as each experimenter then selects a particular combination of artifacts to be mined out of the set of available artifacts.

Q2: Which artifacts will be used most likely in future? To make a qualified guess which artifacts will become even more prominent in future, we analyzed which subtopics of MSR are currently emerging and would potentially involve new artifacts. Hence, we filtered our dataset for terms which appeared for the first time at most three years ago. The terms revealed by our filtering scheme can be categorized into three major topics:

- **Green Mining**, indicated through terms, such as *energy, consumption, green, power, watt,* and *energy-greedy*
- **Mobile Software Engineering**, indicated through terms, such as *mobile, chrome,* and *browser*
- **Human Aspects in Software Engineering/ Social Mining**, indicated through terms, such as *emotion, behavior, twitter,* and *stackoverflow*

Interestingly, the term *nonisolated* appears as well in this filtered list, further indicating that the examination of several integrated artifacts bears further potential.

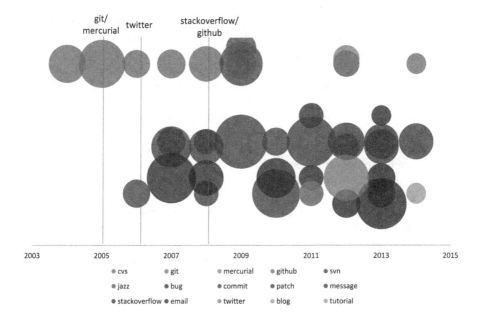

Fig. 2. Popularity of artifacts and artifact-sources in MSR since 2004.

These three research areas uncover artifacts which could potentially become more prominent. As example, related to green mining, artifacts about CPU, I/O, and memory traces are particularly interesting. Advanced technologies, which necessarily require energy-aware applications, such as the Google Glass, might unravel even further artifacts. Considering mobile software engineering, uncovers that, for example, data gathered through Web IDEs could become relevant for further experiments. To better understand human behavior within the software development process, a variety of data sources can be mined. Data sources to better understand developers capture either data about the developer itself, as example through psycho-physiological measurements in particular situation while coding, or capture data about social interactions of developers. Devices, such as eye trackers, electrodermal activity, electrocardiodiagrams, or electroencephalograms, allow detailed insights about individual behaviors during a programming task. Communication threads in *emails* or *messages* were part of early experiments in the MSR community. However, in recent years the range of these artifacts has increased. Recent experiments mine Twitter feeds, so it is conceivable that social networks, such as Facebook, will eventually become a mining artifact for software engineering as well.

3.4   Discussion

We performed a survey of the MSR research published at MSR 2014, ICSE 2014, ICSE 2013, and FSE 2013 and performed a lexical analysis on the proceedings of the last decade (2004–2014)of the MSR proceedings. Comparing the used approaches and artifacts supports our hypothesis that MSR research questions change over time. We hypothesize that there is a constant development of ongoing research, driven by two main factors: First, MSR research solves software engineering problems and respective tools emerge and spread. Second, new and evolving tools present new features, which pose new possibilities and challenges to MSR research.

We observed that today's artifacts hold more and more data about individuals in software engineering processes. Researchers have shown that modern mining techniques are able to extract valuable information from such data. This enables more personalized investigation approaches and tools in the future. However, it also gives rise to new problems, such as the major privacy concerns that come with the mining of data from social media.

The survey shows that MSR research already came a long way towards representativity of evaluation datasets and generalizability of respective results. However, more work is required to further increase the diversity and to improve reusability of evaluation datasets which can increase the comparability of results.

4   Replication of Mining Studies

The replication of studies in mining software repositories is essential to compare different mining techniques and their results across many projects. The study of Ghezzi and Gall [25,27] reported that the replication of these studies is still at a rather early stage. However, the replication of mining studies is just as fundamental as the studies themselves.

Very few studies can be reproduced because of the lack of availability of the tools or the data used [30] for the study: The tools used in the studies are accessible only for approximately 20 % of all the studies and for another 20 % they are only partially accessible. Even when publicly available, they are difficult to set up and use. As a matter of fact, they are mostly prototypes (or a collection of scripts) and work only under rather specific operating systems and settings.

Data can be divided into raw and processed data. Raw data can be directly retrieved from publicly available sources such as version control systems, issue trackers, plain source code, mailing lists, etc. Preprocessed data, which is what is actually used to perform the mining, is the result of the retrieval and processing of raw data. While raw data is usually widely available (at least in the case of OSS projects), processed data is not.

Different approaches have been proposed to address this problem. But these efforts are mainly aimed at creating large, internet accessible, data repositories, such as PROMISE [103]. Some of these internet repositories offer a query-able static collection of data for specific projects fetched from single [73] or multiple sources [84,85]; other online repositories allow the user to interactively run specific analyses on her own projects of interest [29,31].

Large static software data repositories such as PROMISE[11], Krugle[12], or Open Hub (formerly known as Ohloh)[13], provide third party applications with a common body of knowledge to build analyses upon. They could also be useful to provide benchmark data to test and compare similar tools/analysis that use such data. However, they do not target the *replication* of analyses and are based on static data of a multitude of software projects. The interactive features of these online repositories limit the user to only the pre-defined analyses the platform offers by design. Replicability is thus still limited to very few and specific cases. While these online repositories are certainly a step into the right direction, a more systematic approach to replicability is required [25].

4.1   Platform Support for Mining Studies

Platforms to support mining studies have been developed, although their number is still very low, given that the effort to spend on providing a mature platform is pretty high and that scientifically such an achievement is hardly rewarding.

SOFAS (Software Analysis as a Service) is a platform developed at the University of Zurich that enables a systematic and replicable analysis of software projects by providing extensible and composable analysis workflows [26]. These analysis workflows can be applied repeatedly and in the same manner on a multitude of software projects, facilitating the replication and scaling of mining studies.

Using SOFAS, Ghezzi *et al.* investigated the mining studies of the MSR conference from 2004 to 2011 [27] and found that from 88 studies published in the MSR proceedings in that time frame, they could fully replicate 25 empirical studies using their platform. Additional 27 studies could be replicated to a large extent. The remainder of 36 studies could not be replicated due to lack of tool support or automation of the models or that were proposed in the studies. A platform such as SOFAS that focuses on analyses services up to the level of statistical analysis can support (and automate) close to 60 % of the published studies. This shows that there is a high potential for such platforms to support the automation and replication of mining studies.

Dyer *et al.* developed Boa [16], which is a mining tool for large code repositories, which translates queries formulated in a domain specific language into parallelized code that runs on a Hadoop cluster. It is one of the few tools that address a systematic extraction of data from code repositories. For that, it offers a domain-specific language and infrastructure that supports the testing of hypotheses and the re-running of mining experiments. It can be used to mine repository metadata as well as source code across thousands of software projects. Formulating queries in the Boa DSL enable to look for the existence of particular code fragments (e.g., assert statements or specific class names), but not to perform more elaborate investigations, such as complexity computations, code clone or code smell detection or other more complex structural analyses.

---

[11] www.promisedata.org.

[12] www.krugle.org.

[13] www.openhub.net.

However, it is certainly a major contribution to the field of replicating software mining studies as it provides a web-based interface to its infrastructure and a DSL as query language.

Kenyon developed by Bevan *et al.* [7] is a platform designed to facilitate the fact extraction from code archives and configuration management systems. Its features enable a multi-project analysis of repositories by providing a common set of importers from various kinds of archives. As such it can be seen as one of the early platforms to deal with the peculiarities of different archiving systems in version control, issue tracking, or configuration management. It is mainly a toolbox to build one's analyses on top, but by itself does not provide specific mining features. It can be seen as a middleware between the specifics of software archives and the applications that actually perform the mining parts.

4.2   Replication of Software-Mining Studies

The importance of replication has long been recognized in other fields, such as statistics, field research, or psychology. We highlight the following quote about replication taken from [39]:

> "Replication is the key to the support of any worthwhile theory. Replication involves the process of repeating a study using the same methods, different subjects, and different experimenters. It can also involve applying the theory to new situations in an attempt to determine the generalizability to different age groups, locations, races, or cultures. [..]
> Replication, therefore, is important for a number of reasons, including (1) assurance that results are valid and reliable; (2) determination of generalizability or the role of extraneous variables; (3) application of results to real world situations; and (4) inspiration of new research combining previous findings from related studies" [39]

According to [109], replication can be divided in two main categories: exact and conceptual replication. *Exact replication* is when the procedures of the experiment are followed as closely as possible. *Conceptual replication* is when the experimental procedure is not followed strictly, but the same research questions or hypotheses are evaluated, e.g. different tools or algorithms are used or some of the variables are changed.

In [25], a mining study was considered replicable whenever it could be replicated, either conceptually or exactly, using mining and analysis services available in the mining platform *SOFAS*. Table 1 describes how many of the analyzed studies published in the MSR conference 2004–2011 could be replicated and to which extent.

As a result, 52 out of the analyzed 88 mining studies (i.e. 59 %) could be fully or at least partially replicated with mining services offered by *SOFAS*. The replication of these studies typically requires basic services such as import from various version control or issue tracking systems; it further requires composite

Table 1. Replicability of MSR studies from 2004–2011; source: [25]

Study category	Number of studies (%)	Replicable	Partially replicable	Not replicable
Version history mining	8 (9 %)	4	0	4
History mining	17 (20 %)	0	8	9
Change analysis	13 (15 %)	5	6	2
Social networks and people	19 (22 %)	6	5	8
Defect analysis	19 (22 %)	8	6	5
Bug prediction	8 (9 %)	2	2	4
	88 (100 %)	25 (30 %)	27 (32 %)	32 (38 %)

services such as change coupling analysis or linking issues to fixes in the code, all of which can be supported by a platform such as *SOFAS*. The details of how each study category can be replicated are given in the paper [25].

In terms of case studies that have been investigated in the MSR conferences, a study by Gonzalez-Barahona *et al.* [30] reported the following most often analyzed projects until 2010: PostgreSQL (18), ArgoUML (16), Eclipse (15), Apache Web Server (10), Gnome and Linux (7). The study shows that there are rather few studies that have been frequently analyzed, but it also shows that some of them could be used as reference projects for further replication studies.

4.3   Performance of Prediction Studies

With any mining study, its performance is essential. For that, we briefly look into some of their performance aspects, in particular for prediction studies.

Time Variance. It depends on the time interval chosen for training whether a (defect) prediction study has better or worse performance. Studies such as [18] investigate time variance dependencies by taking different time intervals (such as 1 or 2 months etc.) and computing the prediction model.

Calibration of Learners. It also depends on the calibration of the (machine) learners used and the coefficients computed for coming up with a highly accurate prediction. This means that data preparation (data cleansing, binning, filtering, etc.) in combination with the proper configuration of learners is essential for reproducible and replicable studies. Keung *et al.* analyze aspects of learner calibration for selecting the best effort predictor in software effort estimation [54].

Data Preparation. Data distribution analysis, outlier elimination, and binning (failure-prone, non failure prone) are essential. As for binning there are quasi standards in the MSR community that are widespread and accepted, for example, failure-proneness classification is based on the median of failure distributions; this however is a model that could be more fine-tuned to the data and less binary. Learning about the data (including its visualization) are key practices in data mining (see CRISP-DM [105]) and need to be part of any mining study.

Benchmarking. Results of a mining study are typically not benchmarked, but at most compared to some "baseline technique". This however has a bias in terms of what is considered such a baseline technique and whether this is representative for the kind of data, the research question, and the case studies to compare with. As there is lots of data sources available (such as PROMISE, or the MSR Mining Challenge datasets), unfortunately, there is no benchmark data (results of mining studies) out there. This asks for an intensive investigation, as being performed, for example in our most recent SNF project named "Whiteboard."

4.4   Replicating Mining Studies with SOFAS

For replicating a mining study one has to take the dataset of the experiment, prepare the data according to the published data preparation mechanisms (e.g., distribution analysis, filtering outliers, binning, etc.) and then start with the same dataset the modeling; one would typically use functions for importing data, preprocessing it, and delivering models to start with for data mining and machine learning. The latter would be outside a mining platform, but be embedded features of machine learning software. As such, the machine learning parts are outside a platform, such as SOFAS, but the platform would provide interfaces to the machine learner.

Fully replicable with SOFAS means that the published study can fully be computed inside the platform including the presentation of the results. 25 out of 84 studies (i.e. 30 %) in our set were fully replicable.

Partially replicable means that platforms such as SOFAS would provide all functionality until it gets to the machine learning or statistics parts. In the replication study, 27 out of 84 (i.e. 32 %) fell in that category.

This left 32 out of 84 (i.e. 38 %) in the residual of non-replicable studies. Summing up the fully and partly replicable studies this amounts to 52 out of 88 (i.e. 59 %) of all the published studies by then. This clearly shows the potential for such platforms as they can be considered major contributors to the replicating software mining studies.

Given a mining platform such as *SOFAS*, the replication of an already published study is just one aspect. A further substantial benefit is that the original study can be extended rather easily in at least two ways:

– Extending a study by adding more software systems to the dataset
– Extending a study by refining or adding research questions to the analysis

Given the goals of replication (assuring that results are valid and reliable; determining the generalizability of extraneous variables; applying results to other (real-world) situations; and inspiring new research (questions) combining previous findings) the two dimensions of extensibility are essential for the field of mining studies. We need more studies of the same kind to assure our findings are the same and that they generalize beyond the typical small body of systems (a handful to a dozen).

Next, we look into one particular replication study that extended an original software mining studies by adding more systems to be analyzed and by extending its research question.

4.5 Replicating the Study on "Do Time of Day and Developer Experience Affect Commit Bugginess?"

The original study, performed by Eyolfson et al. [20], investigates the correlation between the bugginess of a commit and a series of factors: the time of day of the commit, the day of week of the commit, the experience and commit frequency of the committer. Such a mining study is based on the history of a project extracted from its version control system combined with data from issue tracking. The authors consider as a bug-introducing commit any commit for which there exists another commit explicitly fixing the former at a later point in time. To identify them, the authors first detect all the bug fixing commits using a standard heuristic used in the MSR field: finding the ones that have specific keywords (e.g. "fix", "fixed", etc.) in their commit message. Buggy commits are commits that changed files that were involved in such fixes.

In their investigation, the Eyolfson et al. studied the two projects, the Linux kernel and PostgreSQL, and discovered four major results: (1) about a quarter of the commits in a project history introduce bugs; (2) the time of the day does actually influence the introduction of bugs, as late night commits (between midnight and 4 AM) are significantly buggier and morning commits (between 7 AM and noon) are less buggy; (3) regularly committing developers (daily-committers) and more experienced committers introduce fewer bugs; and (4) the influence of the day of the week on the commit bugginess is project-dependent.

In the replication study of this paper published in [25], Ghezzi et al. verified these four findings by fully replicating the original study. Moreover, they also tested if the findings also hold for three additional OSS projects: Apache HTTP, Subversion, and VLC. They extended the original study by adding more software systems as subjects to the study. And they also extended the study by refining and adding more research questions. The goal of the replication study was to show the potential of a systematic mining platform such as *SOFAS* to draw broader (in number of systems investigated) and deeper (in number of questions addressed) conclusions with little additional effort.

To replicate this study, the following steps had to be performed:

1. Extracting the full version history of the project: This can be accomplished by using a version history extractor.
2. Identifying the bug-introducing and bug-fixing commits (i.e. revisions) from the version history. This can be accomplished by a bug-revision linker, which would find the bug-fixing commits. To accomplish that, the replication study encoded the bug-fixing identification algorithm for Git and Mercurial and provided those in their *SOFAS* platform. Actually, the heuristics was adapted to support a larger vocabulary (*fixes*, *fixed*, *bug(s)* in addition to *fix*).

3. Extracting the commit frequency and experience of the all the developers who introduced bugs (calculated from the bug introducing date). This is achieved by querying the data extracted in the first step with specific (SPARQL) queries, as *SOFAS* works with RDF and ontologies (for data representation) and SPARQL (for querying).
4. Aggregating the buggy commits by time of the day, day of the week, developers experience, and commit frequency. This is also achieved with SPARQL queries.
5. Interpreting the results. *SOFAS* simply supports the extraction and combination of analyses and data. The conclusions still have to be drawn manually by the users of such analyses, depending on their specific needs.

The replication study analyzed the projects in the time frame of July 1–10, 2012. The results were lined up with respect to the original study:

Percentage of Buggy Commits: The replication study confirmed the results of the original study for both Linux and PostgreSQL. Some slightly different values were explained by the different heuristics used to detect bug fixes and the different analysis date (the projects were analyzed a year later than the original study). Moreover, all the other analyzed projects exhibited similar values (22–28%), as shown in Table 2. These results even indicate a trend worth investigating in more detail and with a larger body of projects.

Table 2. Commit characteristics of the analyzed projects - source: [25]

	Commits	Bug-introducing commits	Bug-fixing commits
Linux	268'820	68'010 (25 %)	68'450
PostgreSQL	38'978	9'354 (24 %)	8'410
Apache Http Server	30'701	8'596 (28 %)	7'802
Subversion	47'724	12'408 (26 %)	10'605
VLC	47'355	10'418 (22 %)	10'608

Influence of Time of the Day on Commit Bugginess: The replication study confirmed the results of the original study for both original projects Linux and PostgreSQL. Moreover, the analysis of the additional projects substantiates the finding of late night commits (midnight until 4 AM) versus morning and afternoon commits. However, the replication study showed that these 'windows' of below average bugginess greatly vary across projects. Furthermore, the individual commit bugginess of projects follows different patterns which do not allow any further generalization on the influence of the time of the day on the commit bugginess.

Influence of Developer on Commit Bugginess: The replication study confirms the original results that bugginess decreases with greater author experience for all the projects analyzed. In all projects, a drop in commit bugginess is evident as the time a developer has spent on a project increases. In four of the projects such drops happen between 32 and 40 months of experience, while for the remaining one, PostgreSQL, such a drop takes place at 104 months of experience.

Influence of Day of the Week on Commit Bugginess: The replication study confirms also that the day of week can have some influence on the commit bugginess. However, the added projects and their commit bugginess present quite different patterns. Apache HTTP server and Subversion tend to have two commit bugginess 'phases': a higher than average one from Tuesday to Friday and a lower than average from Saturday to Monday. The bug introduction in VLC is almost the opposite, as it is lower in the middle of the week (Wednesday to Friday). The analysis of these additional projects shows that the finding of the original project that commits on different days of week have about the same bugginess is not generalizable. Moreover, it also shows that the results of a previous study by Sliwersky *et al.* [110], which showed that Friday was the day with the most buggy commits (based on the analysis of Mozilla and Eclipse), cannot be generalized.

4.6   A Plea for Conclusion Stability

Given the need for replication to achieve mining goals and the potential support of analysis platforms, we need to scale and extend studies, and come up with benchmarks based on a multitude of projects analyzed. To advance the field of software mining studies and enable better conclusion stability across studies, at least two things have to be provided:

Infrastructures and Mining Platforms. Analysts should be able to run software mining studies on a large corpus of software systems with only little effort. It is essential to guide them through the process of designing and carrying out empirically sound studies based on good patterns for software data analysis and point them to potential pitfalls based on anti-patterns. Replicability of the studies is key and should be fostered by an adequately formal description of data, data-processing, study design, and study results.

Benchmarking. Software forges store vast amounts of artifacts and data related to the software process. This information can potentially serve as a baseline to assess whether a given software system follows a "healthy" evolution path or whether its underlying development process needs adjustment.

5   Conclusion and Outlook

Mining software repositories is a research area that gained a lot of attention over the last decade. In particular with the open and free access to software archives, such as version control systems, issue trackers, or various other kinds of data about a software project, mining version history has shown great potential for advancing the state-of-the-art in software engineering. Many studies have been published so far, with quite varying benefit to the field. It is, therefore, important to take a fresh look onto the field and discuss the goals, approaches, artifacts, and replicability of these mining studies.

We revisited a decade of software mining studies and highlighted mining goals, study replicability, and trends in mined artifacts. Since the artifacts used for mining software repositories are highly diverse, we visualized changes in artifacts, and thereby indicated some future trends. We also discussed how the replicability of studies is influenced by the evolution of the artifacts.

Our systematic literature review of the research *topics and methods* en vogue in the last two years showed that the main goals to mine software repositories are mostly productivity goals, such as the identification of change impacts, as well as making the development more effective. Other goals are to support quality assurance, for instance by finding and predicting bugs, or the detection of code clones and the calculation of test effort. Management-relevant goals, such as the estimation of change effort, the understanding of human factors, or the understanding of processes, are pursued as well, but by a much smaller number of studies.

Additionally, after investigating the *reusability* of studies, we found that still very few studies are replicable due to the lack of replication information including data and tools. Only 40 % of the studies provided their datasets for reuse, for only about 20 % of the studies the tools are available. Only 2 % of the studies mentioned that data could not be provided due to legal issues. However, if data is available and accessible (e.g. in OSS repositories), mining platforms such as *SOFAS* or the like can replicate a substantial amount of studies (currently up to 60 %) by providing automation support for the analysis and mining.

Software data repositories, such as PROMISE, Krugle, or Open Hub provide the possibility to apply analyses of the data they already preprocessed. However, this does not solve the problem of replicability. Mining platforms do address this problem by supporting the systematic and repeatable analysis of software projects. Still, for conclusion stability, many more systems have to be analyzed and studies have to be replicated on a large scale to enable deep conclusions and benchmarking of systems.

To analyze the mining trends, we investigated 297 papers of the past eleven years of the MSR conference lexically to analyze the *artifacts* used for mining. We found that the popularity of different version control systems changed quite substantially over the years. For the first experiments merely CVS was used. In 2009, the mining of the version control systems Jazz, SVN and git was predominant. From 2009 onwards also GitHub and Mercurial are used for mining. Emails and messages are investigated since 2006 and social media gained popularity since 2011.

We investigated the terms that appeared the first time in the last three years to make an educated guess which artifacts will get more popular in the near *future*. We identified three main topics that could gain popularity in future:

green mining, mobile software engineering, as well as human aspects in software engineering and social mining. Artifacts for green mining could be, for instance, CPU or I/O traces. Artifacts for mobile software engineering may include data from Web IDEs and for human aspects, for instance, psycho-physiological measurements may be conducted, using eye trackers while coding.

As software-project data continues to grow fast, the plethora of mining studies will grow along with the potential to gain more and better insights into aspects of (more) productive software development. However, a clear focus will have to be on conclusion stability of these studies, provided by systematic experiments and studies combined with their proper replicability.

Acknowledgements. This work was partially funded by the German Federal Ministry of Education and Research (BMBF) within the Software Campus projects *KaVE* and *Eko*, both grant no. 01IS12054. The views and opinions expressed in this article are those of the authors and do not necessarily reflect the official policy or position of the funding agency.

References

1. Aggarwal, K., Hindle, A., Stroulia, E.: Co-evolution of project documentation and popularity within github. In: Proceedings of the 11th Working Conference on Mining Software Repositories, MSR 2014, pp. 360–363. ACM, New York (2014)
2. Alipour, A., Hindle, A., Stroulia, E.: A contextual approach towards more accurate duplicate bug report detection. In: Proceedings of the 10th Working Conference on Mining Software Repositories, MSR 2013, pp. 183–192. IEEE Press, Piscataway (2013)
3. Anderson, J., Salem, S., Do, H.: Improving the effectiveness of test suite through mining historical data. In: Proceedings of the 11th Working Conference on Mining Software Repositories, MSR 2014, pp. 142–151. ACM, New York (2014)
4. Bajaj, K., Pattabiraman, K., Mesbah, A.: Mining questions asked by web developers. In: Proceedings of the 11th Working Conference on Mining Software Repositories, MSR 2014, pp. 112–121. ACM, New York (2014)
5. Baldassari, B., Preux, P.: Understanding software evolution: the maisqual ant data set. In: Proceedings of the 11th Working Conference on Mining Software Repositories, MSR 2014, pp. 424–427. ACM, New York (2014)
6. Beller, M., Bacchelli, A., Zaidman, A., Juergens, E.: Modern code reviews in open-source projects: which problems do they fix? In: Proceedings of the 11th Working Conference on Mining Software Repositories, MSR 2014, pp. 202–211. ACM, New York (2014)
7. Bevan, J., Whitehead Jr., E.J., Kim, S., Godfrey, M.: Facilitating software evolution research with kenyon. In: Proceedings of the 10th European Software Engineering Conference Held Jointly with 13th ACM SIGSOFT International Symposium on Foundations of Software Engineering, ESEC/FSE-13, pp. 177–186. ACM, New York (2005)
8. Bird, C., Bachmann, A., Aune, E., Duffy, J., Bernstein, A., Filkov, V., Devanbu, P.: Fair and balanced?: bias in bug-fix datasets. In: Proceedings of the 7th Joint Meeting of the European Software Engineering Conference and the ACM SIGSOFT Symposium on The Foundations of Software Engineering, ESEC/FSE 2009, pp. 121–130. ACM, New York (2009)

9. Bloemen, R., Amrit, C., Kuhlmann, S., Matamoros, G.O.: Gentoo package dependencies over time. In: Proceedings of the 11th Working Conference on Mining Software Repositories, MSR 2014, pp. 404–407. ACM, New York (2014)

10. Bruch, M., Monperrus, M., Mezini, M.: Learning from examples to improve code completion systems. In: Proceedings of the the the 7th Joint Meeting of the European Software Engineering Conference and the ACM SIGSOFT Symposium on The Foundations of Software Engineering, ESEC/FSE 2009, pp. 213–222. ACM, New York (2009)

11. Brunet, J., Murphy, G.C., Terra, R., Figueiredo, J., Serey, D.: Do developers discuss design? In: Proceedings of the 11th Working Conference on Mining Software Repositories, MSR 2014, pp. 340–343. ACM, New York (2014)

12. Campbell, J.C., Hindle, A., Amaral, J.N.: Syntax errors just aren't natural: improving error reporting with language models. In: Proceedings of the 11th Working Conference on Mining Software Repositories, MSR 2014, pp. 252–261. ACM, New York (2014)

13. Chen, N., Lin, J., Hoi, S.C.H., Xiao, X., Zhang, B.: Ar-miner: mining informative reviews for developers from mobile app marketplace. In: Proceedings of the 36th International Conference on Software Engineering, ICSE 2014, pp. 767–778. ACM, New York (2014)

14. Chen, T-H., Nagappan, M., Shihab, E., Hassan, A.E.: An empirical study of dormant bugs. In: Proceedings of the 11th Working Conference on Mining Software Repositories, MSR 2014, pp. 82–91. ACM, New York (2014)

15. Davril, J-M., Delfosse, E., Hariri, N., Acher, M., Cleland-Huang, J., Heymans, P.: Feature model extraction from large collections of informal product descriptions. In: Proceedings of the 2013 9th Joint Meeting on Foundations of Software Engineering, ESEC/FSE 2013, pp. 290–300. ACM, New York (2013)

16. Demeyer, S., Murgia, A., Wyckmans, K., Lamkanfi, A.: Happy birthday! a trend analysis on past msr papers. In: Proceedings of the 10th Working Conference on Mining Software Repositories, MSR 2013, pp. 353–362. IEEE Press, Piscataway (2013)

17. Dyer, R., Rajan, H., Nguyen, H.A., Nguyen, T.N.: Mining billions of ast nodes to study actual and potential usage of java language features. In: Proceedings of the 36th International Conference on Software Engineering, ICSE 2014, pp. 779–790. ACM, New York (2014)

18. Ekanayake, J., Tappolet, J., Gall, H.C., Bernstein, A.: Time variance and defect prediction in software projects. Empirical Softw. Eng. **17**(4–5), 348–389 (2012)

19. Joorabchi, M.E., Mirzaaghaei, M., Mesbah, A.: Works for me! characterizing non-reproducible bug reports. In: Proceedings of the 11th Working Conference on Mining Software Repositories, MSR 2014, pp. 62–71. ACM, New York (2014)

20. Eyolfson, J., Tan, L., Lam, P.: Do time of day and developer experience affect commit bugginess? In: Proceedings of the 8th Working Conference on Mining Software Repositories, MSR 2011, pp. 153–162. ACM, New York (2011)

21. Farah, G., Tejada, J.S., Correal, D.: Openhub: a scalable architecture for the analysis of software quality attributes. In: Proceedings of the 11th Working Conference on Mining Software Repositories, MSR 2014, pp. 420–423. ACM, New York (2014)

22. Femmer, H., Ganesan, D., Lindvall, M., McComas, D.: Detecting inconsistencies in wrappers: a case study. In: Proceedings of the 2013 International Conference on Software Engineering, ICSE 2013, pp. 1022–1031. IEEE Press, Piscataway (2013)

23. Fujiwara, K., Hata, H., Makihara, E., Fujihara, Y., Nakayama, N., Iida, H., Matsumoto, K.: Kataribe: a hosting service of historage repositories. In: Proceedings of the 11th Working Conference on Mining Software Repositories, MSR 2014, pp. 380–383. ACM, New York (2014)
24. Fukushima, T., Kamei, Y., McIntosh, S., Yamashita, K., Ubayashi, N.: An empirical study of just-in-time defect prediction using cross-project models. In: Proceedings of the 11th Working Conference on Mining Software Repositories, MSR 2014, pp. 172–181. ACM, New York (2014)
25. Ghezzi, G., Gall, H.: Replicating mining studies with SOFAS. In: 10th Working Conference on Mining Software Repositories. IEEE Computer Society, Washington (2013)
26. Ghezzi, G., Gall, H.C.: SOFAS: a lightweight architecture for software analysis as a service. In: Working IEEE/IFIP Conference on Software Architecture (WICSA: 20–24 June 2011). IEEE Computer Society, Boulder (2011)
27. Ghezzi, G., Gall, H.C.: A framework for semi-automated software evolution analysis composition. Int. J. Autom. Softw. Eng. **20**(3), 463–496 (2013)
28. Giger, E., D'Ambros, M., Pinzger, M., Gall, H.C.: Method-level bug prediction. In: Proceedings of the ACM-IEEE International Symposium on Empirical Software Engineering and Measurement, ESEM 2012, pp. 171–180. ACM, New York (2012)
29. Gobeille, R.: The fossology project. In: Proceedings of the 2008 International Working Conference on Mining Software Repositories, MSR 2008 (Co-located with ICSE), May 10–11, 2008, pp. 47–50, Leipzig, Germany (2008)
30. González-Barahona, J.M., Robles, G.: On the reproducibility of empirical software engineering studies based on data retrieved from development repositories. Empirical Softw. Eng. **17**(1–2), 75–89 (2012)
31. Gousios, G., Spinellis, D.: A platform for software engineering research. In: Proceedings of the 6th International Working Conference on Mining Software Repositories, MSR 2009 (Co-located with ICSE), May 16–17, 2009, pp. 31–40, Vancouver, BC, Canada (2009)
32. Gousios, G., Vasilescu, B., Serebrenik, A., Zaidman, A.: Lean ghtorrent: github data on demand. In: Proceedings of the 11th Working Conference on Mining Software Repositories, MSR 2014, pp. 384–387. ACM, New York (2014)
33. Gousios, G., Zaidman, A.: A dataset for pull-based development research. In: Proceedings of the 11th Working Conference on Mining Software Repositories, MSR 2014, pp. 368–371. ACM, New York (2014)
34. Guo, L., Lawall, J., Muller, G.: Oops! where did that code snippet come from? In: Proceedings of the 11th Working Conference on Mining Software Repositories, MSR 2014, pp. 52–61. ACM, New York (2014)
35. Gupta, M., Sureka, A., Padmanabhuni, S.: Process mining multiple repositories for software defect resolution from control and organizational perspective. In: Proceedings of the 11th Working Conference on Mining Software Repositories, MSR 2014, pp. 122–131. ACM, New York (2014)
36. Guzman, E., Azócar, D., Li, Y.: Sentiment analysis of commit comments in github: an empirical study. In: Proceedings of the 11th Working Conference on Mining Software Repositories, MSR 2014, pp. 352–355. ACM, New York (2014)
37. Guzman, E., Bruegge, B.: Towards emotional awareness in software development teams. In Proceedings of the 2013 9th Joint Meeting on Foundations of Software Engineering, ESEC/FSE 2013, pp. 671–674. ACM, New York (2013)

38. Hanam, Q., Tan, L., Holmes, R., Lam, P.: Finding patterns in static analysis alerts: improving actionable alert ranking. In: Proceedings of the 11th Working Conference on Mining Software Repositories, MSR 2014, pp. 152–161. ACM, New York (2014)

39. Heffner, C.L.: AllPsych: Research Methods, Chapter 1.11 Replication. http://allpsych.com/researchmethods/replication.html

40. Heinemann, L., Bauer, V., Herrmannsdoerfer, M., Hummel, B.: Identifier-based context-dependent api method recommendation. In: CSMR 2012, pp. 31–40 (2012)

41. Herzig, K., Just, S., Zeller, A.: It's not a bug, it's a feature: how misclassification impacts bug prediction. In: Proceedings of the 2013 International Conference on Software Engineering, ICSE 2013, pp. 392–401. IEEE Press, Piscataway (2013)

42. Hindle, A.: Green mining: a methodology of relating software change to power consumption. In: 2012 9th IEEE Working Conference on Mining Software Repositories (MSR), pp. 78–87, June 2012

43. Hindle, A., Wilson, A., Rasmussen, K., Barlow, E.J., Campbell, J.C., Romansky, S.: Greenminer: a hardware based mining software repositories software energy consumption framework. In: Proceedings of the 11th Working Conference on Mining Software Repositories, MSR 2014, pp. 12–21. ACM, New York (2014)

44. Holmes, R., Murphy, G.C.: Using structural context to recommend source code examples. In: Proceedings of the 27th International Conference on Software Engineering, ICSE 2005, pp. 117–125. ACM, New York (2005)

45. Huang, C., Kamei, Y., Yamashita, K., Ubayashi, N.: Using alloy to support feature-based dsl construction for mining software repositories. In: Proceedings of the 17th International Software Product Line Conference Co-located Workshops, SPLC 2013 Workshops, pp. 86–89. ACM, New York (2013)

46. Inozemtseva, L., Holmes, R.: Coverage is not strongly correlated with test suite effectiveness. In: Proceedings of the 36th International Conference on Software Engineering, ICSE 2014, pp. 435–445. ACM, New York (2014)

47. Jing, X.-Y., Ying, S., Zhang, Z.-W., Wu, S.-S., Liu, J.: Dictionary learning based software defect prediction. In: Proceedings of the 36th International Conference on Software Engineering, ICSE 2014, pp. 414–423. ACM, New York (2014)

48. Johnson, B., Song, Y., Murphy-Hill, E., Bowdidge, R.: Why don't software developers use static analysis tools to find bugs? In: Proceedings of the 2013 International Conference on Software Engineering, ICSE 2013, pp. 672–681. IEEE Press, Piscataway (2013)

49. Kagdi, H., Collard, M.L., Maletic, J.I.: A survey and taxonomy of approaches for mining software repositories in the context of software evolution. J. Softw. Maintenance Evol. **19**, 77–131 (2007)

50. Kalliamvakou, E., Gousios, G., Blincoe, K., Singer, L., German, D.M., Damian, D.: The promises and perils of mining github. In: Proceedings of the 11th Working Conference on Mining Software Repositories, MSR 2014, pp. 92–101. ACM, New York (2014)

51. Kechagia, M., Spinellis, D.: Undocumented and unchecked: exceptions that spell trouble. In: Proceedings of the 11th Working Conference on Mining Software Repositories, MSR 2014, pp. 312–315. ACM, New York (2014)

52. Keivanloo. I.: Online sharing and integration of results from mining software repositories. In: 2012 34th International Conference on Software Engineering (ICSE), pp. 1644–1646, June 2012

53. Keivanloo, I., Forbes, C., Hmood, A., Erfani, M., Neal, C., Peristerakis, G., Rilling, J.: A linked data platform for mining software repositories. In: 2012 9th IEEE Working Conference on Mining Software Repositories (MSR), pp. 32–35, June 2012

54. Keung, J., Kocaguneli, E., Menzies, T.: Finding conclusion stability for selecting the best effort predictor in software effort estimation. Autom. Softw. Engg. **20**(4), 543–567 (2013)

55. Kevic, K., Fritz, T.: A dictionary to translate change tasks to source code. In: Proceedings of the 11th Working Conference on Mining Software Repositories, MSR 2014, pp. 320–323. ACM, New York (2014)

56. Kiefer, C., Bernstein, A., Tappolet, J.: Mining software repositories with isparol and a software evolution ontology. In: Proceedings of the Fourth International Workshop on Mining Software Repositories, MSR 2007, p. 10. IEEE Computer Society, Washington (2007)

57. Klein, N., Corley, C.S., Kraft, N.A.: New features for duplicate bug detection. In: Proceedings of the 11th Working Conference on Mining Software Repositories, MSR 2014, pp. 324–327. ACM, New York (2014)

58. Kononenko, O., Baysal, O., Holmes, R., Godfrey, M.W.: Mining modern repositories with elasticsearch. In: Proceedings of the 11th Working Conference on Mining Software Repositories, MSR 2014, pp. 328–331. ACM, New York (2014)

59. Krutz, D.E., Le, W.: A code clone oracle. In: Proceedings of the 11th Working Conference on Mining Software Repositories, MSR 2014, pp. 388–391. ACM, New York (2014)

60. Lazar, A., Ritchey, S., Sharif, B.: Generating duplicate bug datasets. In: Proceedings of the 11th Working Conference on Mining Software Repositories, MSR 2014, pp. 392–395. ACM, New York (2014)

61. Lazar, A., Ritchey, S., Sharif, B.: Improving the accuracy of duplicate bug report detection using textual similarity measures. In: Proceedings of the 11th Working Conference on Mining Software Repositories, MSR 2014, pp. 308–311. ACM, New York (2014)

62. Lemos, O.A.L., de Paula, A.C., Zanichelli, F.C., Lopes, C.V.: Thesaurus-based automatic query expansion for interface-driven code search. In: Proceedings of the 11th Working Conference on Mining Software Repositories, MSR 2014, pp. 212–221. ACM, New York (2014)

63. Lewis, C., Lin, Z., Sadowski, C., Zhu, X., Ou, R., Whitehead Jr., E.J.: Does bug prediction support human developers? findings from a google case study. In: Proceedings of the 2013 International Conference on Software Engineering, ICSE 2013, pp. 372–381. IEEE Press, Piscataway (2013)

64. Linares-Vásquez, M., Bavota, G., Bernal-Cárdenas, C., Penta, M.D., Oliveto, R., Poshyvanyk, D.: Api change and fault proneness: a threat to the success of android apps. In: Proceedings of the 2013 9th Joint Meeting on Foundations of Software Engineering, ESEC/FSE 2013, pp. 477–487. ACM, New York (2013)

65. Linares-Vásquez, M., Holtzhauer, A., Bernal-Cárdenas, C., Poshyvanyk, D.: Revisiting android reuse studies in the context of code obfuscation and library usages. In: Proceedings of the 11th Working Conference on Mining Software Repositories, MSR 2014, pp. 242–251. ACM, New York (2014)

66. Matragkas, N., Williams, J.R., Kolovos, D.S., Paige, R.F.: Analysing the 'biodiversity' of open source ecosystems: the github case. In: Proceedings of the 11th Working Conference on Mining Software Repositories, MSR 2014, pp. 356–359. ACM, New York (2014)

67. McIntosh, S., Kamei, Y., Adams, B., Hassan, A.E.: The impact of code review coverage and code review participation on software quality: a case study of the qt, vtk, and itk projects. In: Proceedings of the 11th Working Conference on Mining Software Repositories, MSR 2014, pp. 192–201. ACM, New York (2014)

68. Menzies, T., Jalali, O., Hihn, J., Baker, D., Lum, K.: Stable rankings for different effort models. Autom. Softw. Eng. **17**(4), 409–437 (2010)

69. Menzies, T., Zimmermann, T.: Software analytics: so what? IEEE Softw. **30**(4), 31–37 (2013)

70. Merten, T., Mager, B., Bürsner, S., Paech, B.: Classifying unstructured data into natural language text and technical information. In: Proceedings of the 11th Working Conference on Mining Software Repositories, MSR 2014, pp. 300–303. ACM, New York (2014)

71. Minku, L.L., Yao, X.: How to make best use of cross-company data in software effort estimation? In: Proceedings of the 36th International Conference on Software Engineering, ICSE 2014, pp. 446–456. ACM, New York (2014)

72. Mitropoulos, D., Karakoidas, V., Louridas, P., Gousios, G., Spinellis, D.: The bug catalog of the maven ecosystem. In: Proceedings of the 11th Working Conference on Mining Software Repositories, MSR 2014, pp. 372–375. ACM, New York (2014)

73. Mockus, A.: Amassing and indexing a large sample of version control systems: towards the census of public source code history. In: Proceedings of the 2009 6th IEEE International Working Conference on Mining Software Repositories, MSR 2009, pp. 11–20. IEEE Computer Society, Washington (2009)

74. Mockus, A.: Is mining software repositories data science? (keynote). In: Proceedings of the 11th Working Conference on Mining Software Repositories, MSR 2014, pp. 1–1. ACM, New York (2014)

75. Mondal, M., Roy, C.K., Schneider, K.A.: Prediction and ranking of co-change candidates for clones. In: Proceedings of the 11th Working Conference on Mining Software Repositories, MSR 2014, pp. 32–41. ACM, New York (2014)

76. Murakami, H., Higo, Y., Kusumoto, S.: A dataset of clone references with gaps. In: Proceedings of the 11th Working Conference on Mining Software Repositories, MSR 2014, pp. 412–415. ACM, New York (2014)

77. Murgia, A., Tourani, P., Adams, B., Ortu, M.: Do developers feel emotions? an exploratory analysis of emotions in software artifacts. In: Proceedings of the 11th Working Conference on Mining Software Repositories, MSR 2014, pp. 262–271. ACM, New York (2014)

78. Nagappan, M., Zimmermann, T., Bird, C.: Diversity in software engineering research. In: Proceedings of the 2013 9th Joint Meeting on Foundations of Software Engineering, ESEC/FSE 2013, pp. 466–476. ACM, New York (2013)

79. Nam, J., Pan, S.J., Kim, S.: Transfer defect learning. In: Proceedings of the 2013 International Conference on Software Engineering, ICSE 2013, pp. 382–391. IEEE Press, Piscataway (2013)

80. Negara, S., Codoban, M., Dig, D., Johnson, R.E.: Mining fine-grained code changes to detect unknown change patterns. In: Proceedings of the 36th International Conference on Software Engineering, ICSE 2014, pp. 803–813. ACM, New York (2014)

81. Nguyen, H.V., Nguyen, H.A., Nguyen, A.T., Nguyen, T.N.: Mining interprocedural, data-oriented usage patterns in javascript web applications. In: Proceedings of the 36th International Conference on Software Engineering, ICSE 2014, pp. 791–802. ACM, New York (2014)

82. Nguyen, T.H.D., Nagappan, M., Hassan, A.E., Nasser, M., Flora, P.: An industrial case study of automatically identifying performance regression-causes. In: Proceedings of the 11th Working Conference on Mining Software Repositories, MSR 2014, pp. 232–241. ACM, New York (2014)

83. Nguyen, T.T., Nguyen, H.A., Pham, N.H., Al-Kofahi, J.M., Nguyen, T.N.: Graph-based mining of multiple object usage patterns. In: Proceedings of the the the 7th Joint Meeting of the European Software Engineering Conference and the ACM SIGSOFT Symposium on the Foundations of Software Engineering, ESEC/FSE 2009, pp. 383–392. ACM, New York (2009)

84. Nussbaum, L., Zacchiroli, S.: The ultimate debian database: consolidating bazaar metadata for quality assurance and data mining. In: 2010 7th IEEE Working Conference on Mining Software Repositories (MSR), pp. 52–61, May 2010

85. Ossher, J., Bajracharya, S.K., Lopes, C.V.: Automated dependency resolution for open source software. In: Proceedings of the 7th International Working Conference on Mining Software Repositories, MSR 2010 (Co-located with ICSE), Cape Town, South Africa, 2–3 May, pp. 130–140 (2010)

86. Padhye, R., Mani, S., Sinha, V.S.: A study of external community contribution to open-source projects on github. In: Proceedings of the 11th Working Conference on Mining Software Repositories, MSR 2014, pp. 332–335. ACM, New York (2014)

87. Passos, L., Czarnecki, K.: A dataset of feature additions and feature removals from the linux kernel. In: Proceedings of the 11th Working Conference on Mining Software Repositories, MSR 2014, pp. 376–379. ACM, New York (2014)

88. Pinto, G., Castor, F., Liu, Y.D.: Mining questions about software energy consumption. In: Proceedings of the 11th Working Conference on Mining Software Repositories, MSR 2014, pp. 22–31. ACM, New York (2014)

89. Pletea, D., Vasilescu, B., Serebrenik, A.: Security and emotion: sentiment analysis of security discussions on github. In: Proceedings of the 11th Working Conference on Mining Software Repositories, MSR 2014, pp. 348–351. ACM, New York (2014)

90. Ponzanelli, L., Bavota, G., Penta, M.D., Oliveto, R., Lanza, M.: Mining stackoverflow to turn the ide into a self-confident programming prompter. In: Proceedings of the 11th Working Conference on Mining Software Repositories, MSR 2014, pp. 102–111. ACM, New York (2014)

91. Porter, M.F.: An algorithm for suffix stripping. Program Electron. Libr. Inf. Syst. **14**(3), 130–137 (1980)

92. Proksch, S., Amann, S., Mezini, M.: Towards standardized evaluation of developer-assistance tools. In: Proceedings of the 4th International Workshop on Recommendation Systems for Software Engineering, RSSE 2014, pp. 14–18. ACM, New York (2014)

93. Qiu, D., Li, B., Su, Z.: An empirical analysis of the co-evolution of schema and code in database applications. In: Proceedings of the 2013 9th Joint Meeting on Foundations of Software Engineering, ESEC/FSE 2013, pp. 125–135. ACM, New York (2013)

94. Rahman, F., Khatri, S., Barr, E.T., Devanbu, P.: Comparing static bug finders and statistical prediction. In: Proceedings of the 36th International Conference on Software Engineering, ICSE, pp. 424–434. ACM, New York (2014)

95. Rahman, F., Posnett, D., Herraiz, I., Devanbu, P.: Sample size vs. bias in defect prediction. In: Proceedings of the 2013 9th Joint Meeting on Foundations of Software Engineering, ESEC/FSE 2013, pp. 147–157. ACM, New York (2013)

96. Rahman, M.S., Aryani, A., Roy, C.K., Perin, F.: On the relationships between domain-based coupling and code clones: an exploratory study. In: Proceedings of the 2013 International Conference on Software Engineering, ICSE 2013, pp. 1265–1268. IEEE Press, Piscataway (2013)

97. Rahman, M.M., Roy, C.K.: An insight into the pull requests of github. In: Proceedings of the 11th Working Conference on Mining Software Repositories, MSR 2014, pp. 364–367. ACM, New York (2014)

98. Åkerblom, B., Stendahl, J., Tumlin, M., Wrigstad, T.: Tracing dynamic features in python programs. In: Proceedings of the 11th Working Conference on Mining Software Repositories, MSR 2014, pp. 292–295. ACM, New York (2014)

99. Robillard, M.P., Walker, R.J., Zimmermann, T.: Recommendation systems for software engineering. IEEE Softw. $27(4)$, 80–86 (2010)

100. Robles, G.,. González-Barahona, J.M., Cervigón, C., Capiluppi, A., Izquierdo-Cortázar, D.: Estimating development effort in free/open source software projects by mining software repositories: a case study of openstack. In: Proceedings of the 11th Working Conference on Mining Software Repositories, MSR 2014, pp. 222–231. ACM, New York (2014)

101. Saha, R.K., Saha, A.K., Perry, D.E.: Toward understanding the causes of unanswered questions in software information sites: a case study of stack overflow. In: Proceedings of the 2013 9th Joint Meeting on Foundations of Software Engineering, ESEC/FSE 2013, pp. 663–666. ACM, New York (2013)

102. Saini, V., Sajnani, H., Ossher, J., Lopes, C.V.: A dataset for maven artifacts and bug patterns found in them. In: Proceedings of the 11th Working Conference on Mining Software Repositories, MSR 2014, pp. 416–419. ACM, New York (2014)

103. Shirabad, J.S., Menzies, T.J.: The PROMISE Repository of Software Engineering Databases. School of Information Technology and Engineering, University of Ottawa, Canada (2005)

104. Schur, M., Roth, A., Zeller, A.: Mining behavior models from enterprise web applications. In: Proceedings of the 2013 9th Joint Meeting on Foundations of Software Engineering, ESEC/FSE 2013, pp. 422–432. ACM, New York (2013)

105. Shearer, C.: The crisp-dm model: the new blueprint for data mining. Data Warehouse. **5**, 13–22 (2000)

106. Sheoran, J., Blincoe, K., Kalliamvakou, E., Damian, D., Ell, J.: Understanding "watchers" on github. In: Proceedings of the 11th Working Conference on Mining Software Repositories, MSR 2014, pp. 336–339. ACM, New York (2014)

107. Shepperd, M., Kadoda, G.: Comparing software prediction techniques using simulation. IEEE Trans. Softw. Eng. $27(11)$, 1014–1022 (2001)

108. Shi, A., Gyori, A., Gligoric, M., Zaytsev, A., Marinov, D.: Balancing trade-offs in test-suite reduction. In: Proceedings of the 22nd ACM SIGSOFT International Symposium on Foundations of Software Engineering, FSE 2014, pp. 246–256. ACM, New York (2014)

109. Shull, F.J., Carver, J.C., Vegas, S., Juristo, N.: The role of replications in empirical software engineering. Empirical Softw. Eng. $13(2)$, 211–218 (2008)

110. Sliwerski, J., Zimmermann, T., Zeller, A.: When do changes induce fixes? In: Proceedings of the 2005 International Workshop on Mining Software Repositories, MSR (2005)

111. Spacco, J., Strecker, J., Hovemeyer, D., Pugh, W.: Software repository mining with marmoset: an automated programming project snapshot and testing system. In: Proceedings of the 2005 International Workshop on Mining Software Repositories, MSR 2005, pp. 1–5. ACM, New York (2005)

112. Srinivasan, K., Fisher, D.: Machine learning approaches to estimating software development effort. Trans. Softw. Eng. **21**(2), 126–137 (1995)

113. Steidl, D., Hummel, B., Juergens, E.: Incremental origin analysis of source code files. In: Proceedings of the 11th Working Conference on Mining Software Repositories, MSR 2014, pp. 42–51. ACM, New York (2014)

114. Steinmacher, I., Wiese, I.S., Conte, T., Gerosa, M.A., Redmiles, D.: The hard life of open source software project newcomers. In: Proceedings of the 7th International Workshop on Cooperative and Human Aspects of Software Engineering, CHASE 2014, pp. 72–78. ACM, New York (2014)

115. Subramanian, S., Inozemtseva, L., Holmes, R.: Live api documentation. In: Proceedings of the 36th International Conference on Software Engineering, ICSE 2014, pp. 643–652. ACM, New York (2014)

116. Tiarks, R., Maalej, W.: How does a typical tutorial for mobile development look like? In: Proceedings of the 11th Working Conference on Mining Software Repositories, MSR 2014, pp. 272–281. ACM, New York (2014)

117. Tulsian, V., Kanade, A., Kumar, R., Lal, A., Nori, A.V.: Mux: algorithm selection for software model checkers. In: Mining Software Repositories (MSR). ACM, May 2014

118. Tymchuk, Y., Mocci, A., Lanza, M.: Collaboration in open-source projects: myth or reality? In: Proceedings of the 11th Working Conference on Mining Software Repositories, MSR 2014, pp. 304–307. ACM, New York (2014)

119. Garcia, H.V., Shihab, E.: Characterizing and predicting blocking bugs in open source projects. In: Proceedings of the 11th Working Conference on Mining Software Repositories, MSR 2014, pp. 72–81. ACM, New York (2014)

120. Voinea, L., Telea, A.: Mining software repositories with cvsgrab. In: Proceedings of the 2006 International Workshop on Mining Software Repositories, MSR 2006, pp. 167–168. ACM, New York (2006)

121. Williams, J.R., Ruscio, D.D., Matragkas, N., Rocco, J.D., Kolovos, D.S.: Models of oss project meta-information: a dataset of three forges. In: Proceedings of the 11th Working Conference on Mining Software Repositories, MSR 2014, pp. 408–411. ACM, New York (2014)

122. Würsch, M., Ghezzi, G., Hert, M., Reif, G., Gall, H.: Seon: a pyramid of ontologies for software evolution and its applications. Computing **94**(11), 857–885 (2012)

123. Würsch, M., Ghezzi, G., Reif, G., Gall, H.C.: Supporting developers with natural language queries. In: Proceedings of the 32nd International Conference on Software Engineering. ACM, May 2010

124. Würsch, M., Giger, E., Gall, H.: Evaluating a query framework for software evolution data. ACM Trans. Softw. Eng. Method. **22**(4), 38–38 (2013)

125. Yamashita, K.: Modular construction of an analysis tool for mining software repositories. In: Proceedings of the 12th Annual International Conference Companion on Aspect-oriented Software Development, AOSD 2013 Companion, pp. 37–38. ACM, New York (2013)

126. Yamashita, K., McIntosh, S., Kamei, Y., Ubayashi, N.: Magnet or sticky? an oss project-by-project typology. In: Proceedings of the 11th Working Conference on Mining Software Repositories, MSR 2014, pp. 344–347. ACM, New York (2014)

127. Zaidman, A., Van Rompaey, B., van Deursen, A., Demeyer, S.: Studying the co-evolution of production and test code in open source and industrial developer test processes through repository mining. Empirical Softw. Eng. **16**(3), 325–364 (2011)

128. Zanetti, M.S., Scholtes, I., Tessone, C.J., Schweitzer, F.: Categorizing bugs with social networks: a case study on four open source software communities. In: Proceedings of the 2013 International Conference on Software Engineering, ICSE 2013, pp. 1032–1041. IEEE Press, Piscataway (2013)
129. Zanjani, M.B., Swartzendruber, G., Kagdi, H.: Impact analysis of change requests on source code based on interaction and commit histories. In: Proceedings of the 11th Working Conference on Mining Software Repositories, MSR 2014, pp. 162–171. ACM, New York (2014)
130. Zhang, C., Hindle, A.: A green miner's dataset: mining the impact of software change on energy consumption. In: Proceedings of the 11th Working Conference on Mining Software Repositories, MSR 2014, pp. 400–403. ACM, New York (2014)
131. Zhang, F., Mockus, A., Keivanloo, I., Zou, Y.: Towards building a universal defect prediction model. In: Proceedings of the 11th Working Conference on Mining Software Repositories, MSR 2014, pp. 182–191. ACM, New York (2014)
132. Zhang, H., Gong, L., Versteeg, S.: Predicting bug-fixing time: an empirical study of commercial software projects. In: Proceedings of the 2013 International Conference on Software Engineering, ICSE 2013, pp. 1042–1051. IEEE Press, Piscataway (2013)

Theory of Programs

Bertrand Meyer[(✉)]

ETH Zurich, Zurich, Switzerland
bertrand.meyer@inf.ethz.ch

"Computer science" (informatics) is really *program* science since a computer, by itself too general a machine to be of practical interest, yields useful machines through programs that people write for it. While the theoretical study of programs fills volumes, few people realize that a handful of concepts from elementary set theory suffice to establish a clear and practical basis.

Among the results:

- To describe a specification or a program, it suffices to define one relation and one set.
- To describe the concepts of programming, concurrent as well as sequential, three elementary operations on sets and relations suffice: union, composition and restriction.
- These techniques suffice to derive the axioms of classic papers on the "laws of programming" as straightforward consequences.
- To define both program correctness and refinement, the ordinary subset operator "$\subseteq$" suffices.

Paragraphs labeled *"Intuition"* relate the concepts to the experience of readers having done some programming. Readers with knowledge of previous views of theoretical informatics will find comparisons in *"Comment"* paragraphs. Section 5 provides more discussion.

1 Programs

A program is a simple mathematical object: a *constrained relation over a set of states*.

Definition: Program, specification, precondition, postcondition.

A **program**, also known as a **specification**, over a state set S, consists of:
- A relation *post*: $S \leftrightarrow S$, the program's **postcondition**.
- A set $Pre \subseteq S$, the program's **precondition**.

Notation: $A \leftrightarrow B$ is the set of binary relations between A and B, that is, $P(A \times B)$. The domain of a relation r is written $\underline{r}$ and its range $\bar{r}$.

Intuition: A program starts from a certain state and produces one of a set of possible states satisfying properties represented by *post*. *Pre* tells us which states are acceptable as initial states.

B. Meyer and M. Nordio (Eds.): LASER 2013-2014, LNCS 8987, pp. 159–189, 2015.
DOI: 10.1007/978-3-319-28406-4_6

In the general case, more than one resulting state can meet the expectation expressed by *post*. Correspondingly, *post* is a relation rather than just a function.

The definition covers continuously running programs, such as those embedded in devices, since they are just repetitions of individual state transformations. Particular choices for S and for acceptable *post* and *Pre* determine particular styles of programming, such as the following.

Definition: Deterministic, functional, imperative, object-oriented, object, procedural.

A program p is:

- **Deterministic** if $post_p$ is a function, and **non-deterministic** otherwise.
- **Functional** if every subset C of S is disjoint from $post_p$ (C), and **imperative** otherwise.
- **Object-oriented** if S is of the form $0..n \rightarrow O$ for an integer n and a set O of "**objects**", and **procedural** otherwise.

Notation: For a relation r in $A \leftrightarrow B$ and subsets X and Y of A and B respectively, $r(X)$ denotes the image of X, and $r^{-1}(Y)$ the reverse image of Y, by r. The relation is a "function" (short for "possibly partial function") if $r(\{x\})$, for any element x of A, has at most one element. If it always has one, r is "total". $A \rightarrow B$ is the subset of $A \leftrightarrow B$ containing total functions only. An integer interval is written $m..n$. Section 4.2 will present a more elaborate structure for S in which the above characterizations apply to the "store" part.

S_p, Pre_p and $post_p$ are the state set, precondition and postcondition of a program p. In addition, discussions of an indexed set of programs p_i will use S_i, Pre_i and $post_i$ for the i-th program.

The principal concepts of programming, studied in the rest of this presentation, are independent of such choices of style and of the properties of S.

Definition: Feasibility.

A program p is **feasible** if $Pre_p \subseteq \underline{post_p}$.

Intuition: Pre_p tells us when we *may* apply the program, and $post_p$ what kind of result it *must* then give us. A program/specification is safe for us to use if it meets its obligation whenever we meet ours. Feasibility expresses this property: for any input state satisfying Pre_p, at least one output state satisfies $post_p$.

Comment: It would be possible in principle, and would makes theoretical discussions easier, to avoid the introduction of feasibility as a separate condition: define the concept of program by *post* only, and just *define Pre* as $\underline{post}$; then every program is feasible. Such a model, however, does not adequately reflect the practice of programming. Often we get a general relation (such as $\mathbf{Result}^2 \cong input$), clearly defined but not realizable for every possible input state; we must find an input domain (such as $input \geq 0$) on which it is possible to satisfy the postcondition. Hence the need for "program" as the general concept and "feasible program" as a desirable special case.

Definition: Program equality.

Two programs are **equal** if they have the same *Pre* and the same *post / Pre*.

Notation: For a relation r and subsets X and Y of its source and target sets, r / X and $r \setminus Y$ are r restricted to domain X (meaning $r \cap (X \times S)$) and corestricted to codomain Y (meaning $r \cap (S \times Y)$). Two straightforward properties (restriction and corestriction theorems) are that $\underline{r/X \subseteq X}$ and $\overline{r \setminus Y} \subseteq Y$.

Intuition: The results of a program only matter when it is applied to input states satisfying the precondition. Equality as defined is, strictly speaking, only an equivalence relation, but it coincides with ordinary equality (same precondition, same postcondition) on *feasible* programs and makes refinement — introduced next — an order relation rather than just a preorder.

Comment: While it is customary to distinguish between programs and specifications, all definitions of the purported difference are vague, for example that a specification describes the "what" and a program the "how". The reason for the vagueness is that the difference does not exist. It is impossible to assign a given artifact solely to one of the two categories. An assignment instruction is implementation to the application programmer and specification to the compiler writer. (See also Sect. 3.) Any useful notion has to be *relative*: artifact 1 "specifies" artifact 2.

Definition: Refines, specifies, abstracts.

A program/specification p_2 **refines** another, p_1, and p_1 **specifies** (or **abstracts**) p_2, if:			
P1	S_2	$\supseteq S_1$	-- Extension
P2	Pre_2	$\supseteq Pre_1$	-- Weakening
P3	$post_2$	$\underset{Pre_1}{\subseteq} post_1$	-- Strengthening

Notation: $r \underset{X}{\subseteq} r'$ X means $(r / X) \subseteq r'$; in other words, whenever r maps an element of X to a result, r' maps it to the same result. The same conventions applies to other operators on relations, as in $r \underset{X}{=} r'$. Note the names (extension, weakening, strengthening) associated with the three conditions of the definition.

Intuition: A refinement of p gives more detail than p, but still satisfies all properties of p relevant to users of p. So it must cover all of p's states, accept all the input states p accepts and, for these states, only yield results that p could also yield. It may have more states, a more tolerant precondition, and yield only some of the results that p could yield (reduce non-determinism).

Comment: In practice we might want a refined program to work on a different set of states. In that case S_1 would *map* to a subset of S_2, rather than *being* that subset (P1). Generalizing the notion of refinement in this spirit is possible, but does not seem worth the trouble.

Theorem: Refinement Theorem.

P4	Refinement is an order relation.

Proof: Since $\supseteq$ is an order relation, reflexivity, antisymmetry and transitivity hold for the program's state set and precondition parts. For the postcondition part, reflexivity is trivial; antisymmetry follows from P3 since $post_1 \underset{Pre_1}{\subseteq} post_2$ and $post_2 \underset{Pre_2}{\subseteq} post_1$ imply that $post_1$ and $post_2$ coincide on Pre_1 (identical to Pre_2 because of P2), which is what we need for the definition of program equality; for transitivity, if $Y \supseteq X$ then $r_3 \underset{Y}{\subseteq} r_2 \underset{X}{\subseteq} r_1$ and imply $r_3 \underset{X}{\subseteq} r_1$.

Notation: The refinement theorem justifies writing "p_2 refines p_1" as $p_2 \subseteq p_1$. This is an example of a general convention: extending to programs an operator § on relations, so that $p_2 \S p_1$ means $post_2 \S post_1$, with a suitable condition on the preconditions. More examples appear below.

Definition: Implementation.

An **implementation** of p is a feasible refinement of p.

Intuition: Not every refinement of a specification is feasible. For example the infeasible program having the empty relation as its postcondition and S as its precondition refines every specification over S. Hence the importance of finding feasible refinements, also known as implementations. This concept still does not provide a distinction between programs and specifications.

Theorem: Implementation Theorem.

P5   A specification/program having an implementation is feasible.

Intuition: The statement — if a specification has a feasible refinement, it is itself feasible — seems obvious in light of the words it uses, but in fact requires a proof.

Proof: Let p be the specification and i the implementation; we must prove that $Pre_p \subseteq \underline{post_p}$. Weakening tells us that $Pre_p \subseteq pre_i$, and feasibility of i that $Pre_i \subseteq \underline{post_i}$. Hence property A: $Pre_p \subseteq \underline{post_i}$. Strengthening tells us that $post_i \underset{Pre_p}{\subseteq} post_p$, hence property B: $\underline{post_i} \cap Pre_p \subseteq \underline{post_p}$. From A and B we deduce that $Pre_p \subseteq \underline{post_p}$.

2   Operations on Specifications and Programs

The fundamental operations of elementary set theory yield fundamental operations on specifications and programs:

- Union gives choice (intersection, for its part, does not have a directly useful application).
- Restriction gives conditionals.
- Composition of relations gives sequence ("compound" or "block" in programming languages).

- Composition combined with union for symmetry gives concurrency (parallelism).
- Composition of a relation with itself a variable number of times (power) gives loops.

The following definitions cover all these programming constructs and some others. Only the first three (those of Sect. 2.1) refer directly to the basic concepts defined so far; all the rest follow as combinations of these three.

2.1 Basic Constructs

Definition: Choice, Composition, Restriction.

Name	Notation	Mathematical definition		Programming intuition
		Postcondition	**Precondition**	
Choice (or: union)	$p_1 \cup p_2$ (Dijkstra: $p_1 [] p_2$)	$post_1 \cup post_2$	$Pre_1 \cup Pre_2$	Performs like p_1 or like p_2
Composition (or: sequence, compound, block)	$p_1 ; p_2$	$(post_1 \setminus Pre_2) ; post_2$	$Pre_1 \cap post_1^{-1}(Pre_2)$	Performs first like p_1 then like p_2
Restriction (guarded command)	$C{:}p$ (Dijkstra: $C \rightarrow p$)	$post_p / C$	Pre_p	Performs like p on C

Notation: In the "postcondition" column, the semicolon ";" denotes composition of functions or relations, in the order of application, so that $(r; s)(X)$ is $s(r(X))$. (Mathematical texts often use $s \circ r$ for $r; s$.) "Dijkstra" means the notation of [3].

Comment: The first two operators transpose well-known mathematical operations, union in the first case and composition in the second, to programs. They consequently retain their symbols, "$\cup$" and ";". No confusion results since it is always clear whether the operands are sets (including relations) or programs.

Comment: In the definition of program composition, it might seem sufficient to use $post_1 ; post_2$ for the postcondition (rather than $(post_1 \setminus Pre_2) ; post_2$); but that approach is incorrect because $post_1$ could pass on to $post_2$ some elements that do not satisfy Pre_2. An example (with S a set of integers) is $p_1 = <\{[1, 1], [1, 2]\}, \{1\}>$ and $p_2 = <\{[1, 1], [2, 2]\}, \{1\}>$; then $post_1 ; post_2$ is $\{[1, 1], [1, 2]\}$, but results from applying $post_2$ to 2, not part of its precondition. At first sight the precondition $Pre_1 \cap post_1^{-1}(Pre_2)$ appears to guard against this risk, but it does not: this precondition guarantees that p_1 yields *at least one element* satisfying Pre_2, but does not stop p_1 from also yielding *other* results that do not satisfy Pre_2. (Underlying this discussion is a mathematical property of the image operator: $r(r^{-1}(C)) \supseteq C$, a superset property only, not an equality.) We will see that invariant preservation (Sect. 2.7) also requires the corestriction to Pre_2. (Instead of corestriction we may use restriction: $(post_1 \setminus Pre_2); post_2$ is equal to $post_1; (post_2 / Pre_2)$.)

Notation: For a known set of states S, <*post, Pre*> is the program of postcondition *post* and precondition *Pre*.

Theorem:

P6   For feasible operands and arbitrary conditions, the above operators yield feasible programs.

Proof: The definition of feasibility is $Pre_p \subseteq \overline{post_p}$. For choice, we note that for relations r_1 and r_2 $\overline{r_1 \cup r_2} = \overline{r_1} \cup \overline{r_2}$; for composition, that $\overline{r_1; r_2} = \overline{r_1} \cap (r_1^{-1}(\overline{r_2}))$ (for $r_1 ; r_2$ to be applicable to an element x, r_1 must be applicable to x and yield from x at least one element to which r_2 is applicable); for restriction, that $\overline{r/C} = \underline{r} \cap C$.

Theorems: Properties of the basic operators directly reflect those of their mathematical counterparts. Choice, like union of sets, is commutative; composition of programs, like composition of relations, is not. Choice and composition are associative, so we may apply them without parentheses to any number of operands, as in $p_1; p_2; \ldots; p_n$. In addition:

P7	$C_1: (C_2: p)$	$= C_2: (C_1: p)$	-- Restriction is commutative. In fact:
P8	$C_1: (C_2: p)$	$= (C_1 \cap C_2): p$	
P9	$C: (p_1 \cup p_2)$	$= (C: p_1) \cup (C: p_2)$	-- Restriction distributes over choice.
P10	$C: (p_1 ; p_2)$	$= (C: p_1) ; p_2$	-- Composition absorbs restriction.
P11	$q ; (p_1 \cup p_2)$	$= (q ; p_1) \cup (q ; p_2)$	-- Composition distributes left...
P12	$(p_1 \cup p_2) ; q$	$= (p_1 ; q) \cup (p_2 ; q)$	-- ... and right over choice.

(Choice, however, does not distribute over composition.) The proofs are straightforward but must cover both postcondition and precondition.

The following programs are of interest, all of them feasible, the first two total: *Skip*, the identity over S, with postcondition $\lambda x: S \mid \{x\}$ (always applicable, changes nothing); *Havoc*, with postcondition $S \times S$ (always applicable, but we may not assume anything about the result); and *Halt*, defined as <$\emptyset, \emptyset$> (empty relation as postcondition and, for feasibility, empty set as precondition).

Notation: generalized lambda notation serves to define relations in $A \leftrightarrow B$, using either $\lambda x: A \mid Y$ where Y is a subset of B (as here for *Skip*), or $\lambda x_1: A; x_2: B \mid p (x_1, x_2)$ where p is a two-variable predicate. A program/specification is **total** if its precondition is S.

Theorems:

P13	$(p\ ;Skip)$	$=(Skip\ ;p)$	$=p$
P14	$(p \cup Halt)$	$=(Halt \cup p)$	$=p$ -- Does not hold in the demonic theory.
P15	$(Halt\ ;p)$	$=(p\ ;Halt)$	$=Halt$
P16	$(p \cup Havoc)$	$=(Havoc \cup p)$	$=Havoc$
P17	$(p\ ;Havoc)$	$=(Pre_p:Havoc)$	
P18	p	$\subseteq (C:p)$	-- (Reminder: $\subseteq$ on programs is refinement.)
P19	If $D \subseteq C$, then $(C:p) \subseteq (D:p)$.		-- Order reversal (precondition weakening).
P20	If $q \subseteq p$, then $(C:q) \subseteq (C:p)$.		-- Refinement safety, see below.
P21	If $q_1 \subseteq p_1$ and $q_2 \subseteq p_2$, then $(q_1 \cup q_2) \subseteq (p_1 \cup p2)$ and $(q_1\ ;q_2) \subseteq (p_1\ ;p_2)$.		
P22	$p \subseteq (Pre_p:Havoc)$ for any p.		
P23	$p \subseteq Havoc$ for any total p.		
P24	$p \subseteq Halt$ if and only if $p = Halt$		-- *Halt* is refined only by itself...
P25	$Halt \subseteq p$ if and only if $p = Halt$		-- ... and refines only itself.

Comment (Varieties of Non-determinism): p_1 does not generally refine $p_1 \cup p_2$ because of the precondition $Pre_1 \cup Pre_2$. "Internal choice", which has the same postcondition as choice but the precondition $Pre_1 \cap Pre_2$, satisfies refinement but not distributivity from composition, P11. (Consider $q = <\{[0, 1], [0, 2]\}, \{0\}>$, $p_1 = <\{[1, 0]\}, \{1\}>$, $p_2 = < \{[2, 0]\}, \{2\}>$: under internal choice the precondition is empty for the left side of P11 and $\{1\}$ for the right side).

Another terminology is that choice is "angelic" and internal choice can be "demonic". The theory of programs has a demonic sister, obtained by choosing internal choice for all the operator definitions that rely on choice. The discussion will point out places where the difference matters.

Notation: "$\cup$" for choice is a new example (after "$\subseteq$" for refinement) of extending set operators to programs. The following application of this idea is also useful:

Name	Notation	Postcondition	Precondition	Programming intuition
Corestriction	$p \backslash C$	$post_p \backslash C$	$Pre_p \cap post_p^{-1}(C)$	p, applied only when results satisfy C

(There is no need for a restriction notation p/C since we already have $C:p$.) The first of the following properties shows that corestriction can be defined from restriction and composition.

Theorems:

P26	$(p \backslash C)$	$=(p\ ;(C:Skip))$	
P27	$(p_1 \cup p_2) \backslash C$	$=(p_1 \backslash C) \cup (p_2 \backslash C)$	-- Compare with P9.
P28	$(p \backslash C)$	$\subseteq C$	-- Refinement. Compare with P18.
P29	If $D \subseteq C$, then $(p \backslash D)$	$\subseteq (p \backslash C)$	-- Compare with P19.

The restriction and corestriction theorems apply to programs: $C : p \subseteq C$ and $\overline{p \backslash C} \subseteq C$.

Notation: In the same spirit, the range and domain notations apply to programs: $\underline{p}$ is a synonym for Pre_p; and (more importantly) $\bar{p}$ is a synonym for $post_p$ $(\underline{p})$, the set of values that p can actually yield.

Properties P20 and P21 extend to all well-behaved operators in the following sense.

Definition: Refinement safety.

> An operator § on programs is **refinement-safe** if $q_1 \subseteq p_1$ and $q_2 \subseteq p_2$ implies $(q_1 \S q_2) \subseteq (p_1 \S p_2)$.

Counter-Examples: Intersection of programs, defined as intersecting both postconditions and preconditions, is not refinement-safe: with a set of integers for S, $\{0\}$ for all preconditions, and postconditions $\{[0, 0], [0, 1]\}$ for p_1 and p_2, $\{[0,0]\}$ for q_1 and $\{[0,1]\}$ for q_2, the conditions of the definition are met, but $q_1 \cap q_2$, with an empty postcondition, does not refine $p_1 \cap p_2$, which is just p_1. Another counter-example is program difference (set difference of postconditions, intersection of preconditions). The theory of programs, however, eschews such operators:

Theorem:

> P30   All the operators on programs introduced in this article are refinement-safe.

In a corresponding sense, the program properties "functional" and "object-oriented" are refinement-safe (but not their contraries, "imperative" and "procedural").

2.2   Atomic Concurrency

Composition, while associative, is not commutative: when we combine existing programs or specifications, it forces us to decide in which order we want them to perform. If you find this obligation irksome, you need concurrency. Concurrent combination (in its "atomic" form) is sequential composition made symmetric through association with its quintessentially commutative colleague, choice.

Definition: Concurrency.

Name	Notation	Definition	Programming intuition
Atomic concurrency	$p_1 \| p_2$	$(p_1 ; p_2) \cup (p_2 ; p_1)$	Performs once like each of p_1 and p_2

Theorems: Concurrency is commutative, associative and refinement-safe. In addition:

P31	$p_1 \parallel (p_2 \cup p_3)$	$= (p_1 \parallel p_2) \cup (p_1 \parallel p_3)$	-- Concurrency distributes over choice, left...
P32	$(p_1 \cup p_2) \parallel p_3$	$= (p_1 \parallel p_3) \cup (p_2 \parallel p_3)$	-- ... and right.
P33	$C: (p_1 \parallel p_2)$	$= (C: p_1) \parallel (C: p_2)$	-- Restriction distributes over concurrency...
P34	$(p_1 \parallel p_2) \setminus C$	$= (p_1 \setminus C) \parallel (p_2 \setminus C)$	-- ... and so does corestriction.
P35	$(p_1 ; p_2)$	$\subseteq (p_1 \parallel p_2)$	-- Sequential composition refines concurrency...
P36	$(p_2 ; p_1)$	$\subseteq (p_1 \parallel p_2)$	-- ... in any order.

Concurrency generally does not refine composition, but in one particular case it does.

Definition: Commuting programs.

> Two specifications/programs commute if $(p_1 ; p_2) = (p_2 ; p_1)$.

Example and Counter-Example: If S is the set of functions *PERSON* $\rightarrow$ *Z*, recording people's bank account balances, consider an infinite set of programs, defined for any person p and any integer n: the postcondition of *deposit*$_{p,n}$ expresses that the output differs from the input only by having the balance of p increased by n, and similarly for *withdraw*$_{p,n}$. All these programs commute with each other. They do not commute, however, with the program *reset*$_p$ setting p's balance to zero.

Theorem:

> P37   If p_1 and p_2 commute, then $(p_1 \parallel p_2) = (p_1 ; p_2)$.

(Not just refinement, but equality. Immediate generalization to more than two programs.)

Intuition: Commuting programs are a boon for concurrent computation, since they open up many possible realizations for "computing" program results (finding values satisfying *post$_p$*) on actual "computers" (the physical devices that ensure postconditions). Assume for example a large number of *deposit* and *withdraw* operations with various clients and amounts. If the specification is that at the end of the trading day the balance of each should be correct (initial, plus accumulated deposits, minus accumulated withdrawals), any assignment of the operations among any number of computers in any order is suitable. In such cases concurrency is an optimization mechanism.

Comment: Commuting is not refinement-safe: with $\{0, 1\}$ as preconditions, the programs of postconditions $\{[0, 0], [1, 1]\}$ (i.e. *Skip*) and $\{[0, 0], [1, 0]\}$ both refine $p = \{[0, 0], [1, 0], [1, 1]\}$, which commutes with itself, but do not commute since composing them in both orders respectively gives 1 and 0 for 1. Abstraction (the inverse of refinement) also does not preserve commuting: *Skip* and p do not commute even though *Skip* commutes with itself and refines both. On the other hand:

Theorem:

> **P38** For deterministic programs with identical preconditions, refinement and abstraction preserve commuting.

2.3 Non-atomic Concurrency

The atomic concurrency operator has a fixed level of granularity, defined by its operands: if they are themselves complex programs built out of simpler components, it will not interleave these components. For example let *on* be "switch on the light", *off* "switch it off" and p "say whether the light is on". Assuming that in the initial state the light is on, $(on;\ off)\ \|\ p$ will always say no, regardless of which of the operands of "$\|$" goes first, since $(on;\ off)$ is equal to *Skip*.

The practice of concurrency often calls for finer-grain control on concurrency. Here you might want p to execute at the beginning, in the middle (between *on* and *off*), or at the end. Such flexibility causes much of the difficulty of concurrent programming, since it opens up the possibility of "data races" (inconsistent orderings of operations, in some executions only); but a general theory of programming must provide a model for it, given here by a ternary operator.

Name	Notation	Definition	Programming intuition
Non-atomic concurrency	$(p_1, p_2)\ \|\ q$	$((p_1\ \|\ q)\ ;\ p_2)\ \cup$ $(p_1\ ;\ (p_2\ \|\ q))$	Performs once like each operand, with p_1 before p_2

Notation: the only new symbol is the comma, used at a place where the semicolon of composition could also appear. The reuse of "$\|$" is only for convenience: the "Notation" entry describes a new three-operand operator. Its "Definition" entry relies on the previously defined atomic concurrency operator "$\|$". No confusion arises since the non-atomic operator only occurs in conjunction with the comma.

Comment: We do need a specific operator, because proposing a distributive-style law involving standard composition ";" would raise inconsistencies. For example, $(on;\ off)\ \|$ p cannot give any other result than *Skip* $\|\ p$; if you want to allow interleaving, you should specify a finer level of granularity, as in $(on,\ off)\ \|\ p$. In the first case the atomic unit of concurrency on the left side is $(on;\ off)$; in the second case there are two atomic units, *on* and *off*.

Non-atomic concurrency is associative on its first two operands p_1 and p_2, so you may use commas to separate any number of program operands of non-atomic concurrency. (Reduced to one operand, as in $(p_1)\ \|\ q$, atomic and non-atomic "$\|$" coincide, as they should for consistency.) You may also put q first, writing $q\ \|\ (p_1, p_2)$. In other words, the notation lets you use a comma, to specify a finer granularity of interleaving, where you might otherwise use a semicolon.

Theorems:

P39	$(p_1, p_2) \parallel q$	$= (q; p_1; p_2) \cup (p_1; q; p_2) \cup (p_1; p_2; q)$	
P40	$(p_1; p_2) \parallel q$	$\subseteq (p_1, p_2) \parallel q$	-- Coarser-grained refines finer-grained.
P41	$p_1; (p_2 \parallel q)$	$\subseteq (p_1, p_2) \parallel q$	-- First "law of exchange" of [8].
P42	$(p \parallel q_1); q_2$	$\subseteq p \parallel (q_1, q_2)$	-- Second "law of exchange" of [8].

Proof of P41: The left side is $(p_1; p_2; q) \cup (p_1; q; p_2)$, which from P39 (itself a direct consequence of the definition) is a subset of the right side; similarly for P42. Both of these properties appear in [8] as fundamental axioms of concurrency, but here they are simple theorems.

It is straightforward to symmetrize the non-atomic concurrency notation to $(p_1, p_2) \parallel (q_1, q_2)$, yielding the generalized law of exchange from [8]: $(p_1 \parallel q_1); (p_2 \parallel q_2) \subseteq (p_1, p_2) \parallel (q_1, q_2)$.

2.4   Conditionals

Definition: Conditionals.

Name	Notation	Definition	Programming intuition
Guarded conditional	if C_1: p_1 [] C_2: p_2 end	$(C_1: p_1) \cup (C_2: p_2)$	Performs like p_1 on C_1, like p_2 on C_2
If-then-else	if C then p_1 else p_2 end	$(C: p_1) \cup (C': p_2)$	Performs like p_1 on C, like p_2 elsewhere

Notation: C', for a subset C of S, is its complement: $S - C$. The usual programming notation is "**not** C" (see Sect. 2.5 below). The guarded conditional is in fact not new since **if** p_1 [] p_2 **end** was introduced in Sect. 2.1 as a synonym for $p_1 \cup p_2$, but it highlights the important case of p_1 and p_1 being restrictions.

Theorems: The guarded conditional is commutative; the corresponding property for if-then else is that (**if** C **then** p_1 **else** p_2 **end**) = (**if** C' **then** p_2 **else** p_1 **end**). Both operators are associative; as a consequence they can be applied to more than two operands (if-then-else uses **elseif** for the second to next-to-last branches, as in **if** C_1 **then** p_1 **elseif** C_2 **then** p_2 **else** p_3 **end**), and to just one: for the guarded conditional, **if** C: p **end** is the same as C: p; for if-then-else, by convention, **if** C **then** p **end** is an abbreviation for **if** C **then** p **else** *Skip* **end**.

Theorems: Both forms are distributive over choice and concurrency, but not over composition. The guarded conditional is commutative, but not if-then-else. In addition (direct consequences of earlier theorems, particularly P19 and P21):

P43	If $D_1 \subseteq C_1$ and $D_2 \subseteq C_2$, then (**if** D_1: p [] D_2: q **end**)	$\subseteq$	(**if** C_1: p [] C_2: q **end**).
P44	If $q_1 \subseteq p_1$ and $q_2 \subseteq p_2$, then (**if** C: q_1 [] C: q_2 **end**)	$\subseteq$	(**if** C: p_1 [] C: p_2 **end**).
P45	If $q_1 \subseteq p_1$ and $q_2 \subseteq p_2$, then (**if** C **then** q_1 **else** q_2 **end**)	$\subseteq$	(**if** C **then** p_1 **else** p_2 **end**).
P46	(C: p)	$=$	(**if** C: p **end**)
P47	(**if** C_1: p_1 [] C_2: p_2 **end**)	$\subseteq$	C_1: p_1 -- A conditional refines any of its branches
P48	(D: (**if** C_1: p [] C_2: q **end**))	$=$	(**if** ($D \cap C_1$): p [] ($D \cap C_2$): q **end**) -- Distributivity.
P49	(**if** C **then** p_1 **else** p_2 **end**)	$=$	(**if** C: p_1 [] C': p_2 **end**)
P50	(**if** C **then** p_1 **else** p_2 **end**)	$=$	(**if** C' **then** p_2 **else** p_1 **end**)

Proof: For P48, see P8 and P9. As seen next, "$\cap$" in these rules can also be written "**and**".

2.5   Conditions

Two special conditions are useful for building programs. *True* is another name for S, and *False* another name for the empty set. They should not be confused with the similarly named constants of propositional calculus: *True* and *False* are, like all conditions, sets (subsets of S). In fact the theory of programs relies on set theory rather than directly on logic, although it is easy to define boolean-like operators on conditions: **and** and **or** as other names for "$\cap$" and "$\cup$", **not** as another name for complement (in P50 we may write C' as **not** C), **implies** or "$\Rightarrow$" as other names for "$\subseteq$", and so on. Here, in addition to P19, are some properties involving operations on conditionals.

Theorems:

P51	(*True*: p)	$=$	p -- And correspondingly for conditionals.
P52	(*False*: p)	$=$	*Halt*
P53	$p \setminus True$	$=$	p -- Here "$\setminus$" is corestriction on programs.
P54	$p \setminus False$	$=$	*Halt*
P55	(**if** *True* **then** p_1 **else** p_2 **end**)	$=$	p_1
P56	(**if** *False* **then** p_1 **else** p_2 **end**)	$=$	p_2 -- And similarly for guarded conditionals.
P57	**and, or, not, implies** distribute over choice, restriction and conditionals.		

Proof: For P54, note that the postcondition of $p \setminus False$ is $post_p \cap (S \times False)$, that is, an empty relation (since *False* is the empty set).

2.6   Loop

Definition: Repetition constructs.

Name	Notation	Definition	Programming intuition
Fixed repetition	p^i for any natural integer i	$p^0 = \underline{p}: Skip$ $p^{i+1} = (p \,;\, p^i)$	p repeated i times
Arbitrary repetition	**loop p end** (or p^*)	$\displaystyle\bigcup_{i \geq 0} p^i$	p repeated any number of times
"While loop"	**from a until C loop b end** (or a; **while not C loop b end**)	$a \,;\, (\textbf{loop } C' \colon b \textbf{ end}) \setminus C$ or equivalently: $a \,;\, (\displaystyle\bigcup_{i \geq 0} (C' \colon b)^i \setminus C)$	a, then p repeated until C holds

Notation: in the second definition of the while loop, it does not matter how we parenthesize the "\"; see P27. Since composition is associative, the inductive expression for fixed repetition can also be written $(p^i; p)$.

Intuition: **loop p end** is the program that performs like p repeated some finite (but unknown) number of times. Cyclic programs, such as those on embedded devices, follow this pattern. The rest of the present discussion concentrates on the **from a until C loop b end** loop, which starts like a then performs like b, the loop's "body", as many times as needed (possibly zero) until reaching a state satisfying C. In slightly different terms: for the loop to yield a result from a given input state x, that result must be the first element of C reached by successive executions of b after a. All the previous states are not in C, so they are in C', meaning that what we are iterating is not the whole b but just $C'\colon b$.

From distributivity follows another expression of the loop:

Theorem: Loop Lemma.

> **P58**   The loop $l =$ **from a until C loop b end** can be written $\displaystyle\bigcup_{i \geq 0} q_i$, where q_i is $a \,;\, (C'\colon b)^i \setminus C)$.
> As a consequence, $\overline{l} = \cup\, \overline{q_i}$.

Notation reminder: $\bar{p}$, a subset of $\overline{post_p}$, is the set of values that p can produce.

Intuition: q_i represents a restricted version of the loop, which yields a result (satisfying C) after exactly i iterations. The loop is the union of all such partial versions of it.

Comment: Unlike previous constructs, the loop does not automatically get feasibility from the feasibility of its operands: it is possible for a, b and all q_i to be feasible, while l is not. (A trivial example is **from** $Skip$ **until** $False$ **loop** $Skip$ **end**.) A loop is feasible if and only if for every suitable state s there exists an integer i (typically not the same for different s) such that a; $(C'\colon b)^i (\{s\})$ contains an element in C; in other words, that $q_i (\{s\})$ is not empty.

The feasibility condition for loops relies on the notion of invariant.

2.7   Invariants

Definition: Invariant.

> A condition I is an **invariant** of a program/specification p if $post_p \, (\underline{p} \cap I) \subseteq I$.

Intuition: An invariant is called that way because if it holds before application of p it will hold afterwards. More precisely, for the initial condition we need not the whole of I but just $\underline{p} \cap I$, since results of p only matter when it starts from the precondition. The following two theorems ensue directly from the definition.

Theorems:

> P59   Any I disjoint from $\underline{p}$ is an invariant of p.
> P60   If I is an invariant of p, so is J if $J \subseteq I$.
> P61   If I and J are invariants of p, so are $I \cup J$ and $I \cap J$.

Comment: Properties involving intersection are usually not as strong as those involving union, because $r \, (I \cap J)$ is only a subset of $r \, (I) \cap r \, (J)$, rather than equal to it as with "$\cup$"; but P61 has both operators on an equal footing.

Theorem: Invariant Refinement Theorem.

> P62   If I is an invariant of p_1 and $p_2 \subseteq p_1$, then I is an invariant of $p_2 \, / \, Pre_1$.

Comment: In practice, the precondition often stays the same under refinement, but in the general case p_2 might have a broader precondition; there is no guarantee that the original invariant will hold for the new states, hence the restriction to Pre_1.

Definition: Invariant-preserving operator.

> An operator on programs is **invariant-preserving** if any invariant of all its program operands is also an invariant of the operator's result.

Example: Program composition is invariant-preserving.

Proof: Assume I is an invariant of both p_1 and p_2. The definition of program composition (Sect. 2.1) gives $(post_1 \setminus Pre_2)$; $post_2$ as the postcondition of $q = (p_1 \, ; p_2)$. From 26 and properties of image $((r_1; r_2) \, (A) = r_2 \, (r_1 \, (A)))$ and restriction $((C: r) \, (A) = r \, (C \cap A))$, it follows that $post_q(q \cap I) = post_2(Pre_2 \cap Res_1)$ where $Res_1 = post_1(q \cap I)$. Since I is an invariant of p_1, $Res_1 \subseteq I$; since it is also an invariant of p_2, then, $post_2 \, (Pre_2 \cap Res_1) \subseteq I$.

Comment: The discussion after the definition of program composition in Sect. 2.1 noted that taking just $post_1$; $post_2$ as postcondition for p_1; p_2 would not yield a feasible result: we need the corestriction to Pre_2. This property is also essential for invariant preservation: without it we would be applying $post_2$ not to $Pre_2 \cap Res_1$ but just to Res_1, on which $post_2$ does not preserve the invariant.

This result about composition is only a particular case of the following general property.

Theorem: General Invariant Theorem.

> **P63**   All the program operators defined so far are invariant-preserving.

Proof: The result for all the basic operators (choice, sequence, restriction) follows from the set-theoretical properties of relational image, including the following in addition to those used in the preceding proof: $r\ (C \cup D) = r\ (C) \cup r\ (D)$; $r\ (C \cap D) \subseteq r\ (C) \cap r\ (D)$; $r\ (C) \setminus D \subseteq r\ (C)$. The subsequent operators (concurrency, conditional) are defined from the basic ones and retain their invariant preservation.

Every element of the infinite unions that define loops is made out of basic operators and, by induction, is invariant-preserving. Since union maintains this property, the loops themselves possess it. They benefit, however, from a more specific form of the notion of invariant.

Definition: Loop invariant.

> A **loop invariant** of **from** a **until** C **loop** b **end** is a subset of $\bar{a}$ that is an invariant of C': b.

The Invariant Refinement Theorem, P62, implies that a "loop invariant" is an "invariant", in the general sense, of the part of the loop that comes after initialization (a). The following theorem yields a stronger form of the relationship between the two concepts.

Theorem: Loop Correctness Theorem.

> **P64**   If I is a loop invariant of the loop $l =$ (**from** a **until** C **loop** b **end**), then $\bar{l} \subseteq C \cap I$

Intuition: The theorem characterizes the fundamental property of loops [5, 11]: the goal of a loop is to obtain on exit ($\bar{l}$) a combination of the exit condition (C) and a judiciously chosen invariant (I, a weakening of the desired result).

Proof: Since I is an invariant of C': b, it is an invariant of $(C': b)^i$ for any integer i; since I is also a subset of $\bar{a}$, it follows that $\overline{q_i} \subseteq I$ for every i, with q_i as defined in the Loop Lemma, P58. Then, from the second part of the Loop Lemma, $\bar{l} \subseteq I$. In addition, the corestriction theorem tells us that $\overline{q_i} \subseteq C$ as well, again for every i; this property extends to $\bar{l}$.

Comment: Despite its fundamental role, the Loop Correctness Theorem does not fully cover the theory of loops because it says nothing about feasibility. It states that loop results — elements of $\bar{l}$ — possess interesting properties, but not that such elements exist for every legal input state. In fact, a loop yielding no results at all (an empty $\bar{l}$) would satisfy the theorem. In the traditional terminology of theoretical informatics, the theorem is a *"partial correctness"* result, useful only if we can also guarantee *"termination"*. The complementary theorem follows.

Theorem: Loop Feasibility Theorem.

> P65 For feasible a and b, the loop **from** a **until** C **loop** b **end** is feasible if both:
> - $\underline{b} \cup C$ is a loop invariant.
> - $C': post_b$ is well-founded.

Notation: a "well-founded" (or "Noetherian") relation is one that admits no infinite chain.

Proof: Assume $\underline{b} \cup C$ is a loop invariant and $C': post_b$ is well-founded. For any element s of $\underline{a}$, define S_0 as $a\ (\{s\})$ and S_{i+1} as $(C': post_b)\ (S_i)$. Both S_i and $\overline{q}_i$ are subsets of a; $(C': b)^i$; what distinguishes $\overline{q}_i$ is that its elements are also in C. Assume that these two subsets are disjoint for all i. Induction shows that S_i is not empty: since a is feasible, S_0 is not empty; and if S_i is not empty, the invariant property tells us that $S_i \subseteq \underline{b} \cup C$; with S_i disjoint from $\overline{q}_i$ this really means $S_i \subseteq (\underline{b} \cup C')$ which implies, b being feasible, that S_{i+1}, the image of S_i by $C': post_b$, is not empty. But then elements of successive non-empty sets in the infinite sequence S_i are related by $C': post_b$, an impossibility since the relation is well-founded. As a consequence, the disjointness assumption $(S_i \cap \overline{q}_i = \varnothing$ for all $i)$ cannot hold. So for every s there exists an i such that applying $a; (C': b)^i$ — the program iterating the loop i times — to s yields an element of C. That element is in $\overline{q}_i$ and hence in $\bar{l}$, showing that the loop is feasible.

Comment: While the theorem gives a general condition for loop feasibility, it is often not practical to check directly that $C': post_b$, the loop body, is well-founded. A standard technique is to map states to a simpler domain on which it is easier to check that the counterpart of $post_b$ is well-founded, according to the following definition.

Definition: Loop variant.

> A **loop variant** of **from** a **until** C **loop** b **end** is a total function v from S to a set V equipped with a well-founded relation "<", such that $v\ (post_b\ (s)) < v\ (s)$ for any s in C'.

(Strictly speaking, v only needs to be total on $(\cup \overline{q}_i) \cup (C' \cap (\cup \underline{q}_i))$.) The existence of a variant shows that $post_b$ itself is well-founded, fulfilling the second condition of the Loop Feasibility Theorem. The most frequent choice for V is the set of natural integers.

3 Contracted Programs

There is, as noted, no difference of principle between specifications and programs. In practice we are used to different connotations for these terms. Since the distinction is so commonly accepted, let us see if we can find a justification serious enough to earn it a place in the theory of programs.

We already saw that the first attempt, stating that specifications are abstract and programs concrete, does not make the cut, since "level of abstraction" is a relative notion (the example was an assignment instruction, abstract for some and concrete for others). A seemingly more promising intuition is that programs are *executable* while specifications are purely descriptive. But that is also not right, even if we ignore the case frequently made for "executable specification" formalisms and stick to more traditional forms of the concepts. "Executable" cannot mean "directly appropriate for execution on a computer", since in that case the notion would depend on hardware details. It has to mean "expressible in a programming language'. A staple example is that $\textbf{Result}^2 \cong input$ is a specification whereas a particular square root computation, using for example Newton's algorithm, is a program. But such examples also fail, since there are many programming languages today in which you can just write $\textbf{Result}^2 = input$ and let the compiler figure out the implementation.

Just like the distinction between abstract and concrete is relative, the distinction between descriptive and executable shifts with the evolution of language and compiler technology. To find a true difference, we must look elsewhere.

The relevant criterion is correctness. As captured by the notion of feasibility, a specification can be inconsistent (if it tells you that the result must be zero and also that it can be one) or consistent; but it makes no sense to ask whether it is correct. Correct with respect to what? Probably with respect to the customers' desires, or to their actual needs, but these would have to be written down as another, higher-level specification, only pushing the problem further. We do know, however, what it means for a program to be correct: it performs according to a stated specification. Correctness is a relative notion.

Indeed what truly distinguishes a program from a specification, in the common usage of these terms, is neither the level of abstraction nor the possibility of execution, but the existence of *two* programs/specifications in the sense of the present theory, such that one of them is a refinement (as also defined above) of the other. The following notation reflects this analysis.

Definition: Contracted program, specification part, contract, implementation part, correctness.

The notation **require** *Pre* **do** *b* **ensure** *post* **end**, a **contracted program**, asserts that *b* is an implementation of the specification/program $p = \langle post, Pre\rangle$.

Then *p* is the **specification part**, or **contract**, and *b* the **implementation part**. The contracted program is also said to be a **correct program**.

Reminder: An implementation of p is a feasible refinement of p. The refinement theorem, P5, indicates that p is feasible as well. The definition of refinement indicates that the precondition of b is a superset of *Pre* and its postcondition a subset of *post*. (The name b stands for "body".)

Intuition and Comment: The notion of contracted program simply introduces a programming notation for the concept of refinement. Since a program is useless without a precise understanding of what it is supposed to do, program authors should only produce contracted programs. Regrettably, this practice is not yet universal.

The above definition provides a final clarification of what programs in the usual sense of the term (*contracted programs* in the present theory) really are: **a program is a proof obligation**. Writing **require** *Pre* **do** b **ensure** *post* **end** is a way to state that b must refine p, and requires the author, before clicking "Compile", let alone clicking "Run", to click "Verify".

Theorem:

> **P66** If *post* $\subseteq$ *post'*, *Pre'* $\subseteq$ *Pre*, and **require** *Pre* **do** b **ensure** *post* **end** is a contracted program, so is **require** *Pre'* **do** b **ensure** *post'* **end**.

Comment: In this case, since we keep the implementation and go to a new specification, we can only strengthen the precondition and weaken the postcondition.

The following concepts are defined for given *Pre*, *post* and b.

Definitions: Weakest precondition, strongest postcondition.

> $post_b$ / *Pre*, also written b **sp** *Pre*, is the **strongest postcondition** of b for *Pre*.
> $\underline{b} - post_b - post$, also written b **wp** *post*, is the **weakest precondition** of b for *post*.

Intuition: $post_b - post$ is a set difference between two relations, giving us the set of pairs that belong to the first but not to the second. Its domain, $\underline{post_b - post}$, is the set of states for which b produces at least one result that *post* could never produce. Subtracting this domain from $\underline{b}$, the domain of b, gives us the set of states on which b is guaranteed to agree with *post*.

The following property justifies the terms "strongest" and "weakest".

Theorem:

> **P67** If **require** *Pre* **do** b **ensure** *post* **end** is a correct program, then $(b$ **sp** *Pre*$) \subseteq$ *post* and *Pre* $\subseteq (b$ **wp** *post*$)$.

Proof: Let p be $<post, Pre>$. Since b is a refinement of p, $post_b \underset{Pre}{\subseteq} post$ by the definition of refinement, yielding the first property of the theorem. By refinement, *Pre* $\subseteq \underline{b}$;

the just mentioned property $post_b \subseteq_{Pre} post$ implies that $\overline{post_b - post}$ is disjoint from Pre, so $Pre \subseteq \underline{b} - post_b - post$, giving us the second property.

As a corollary, we get a compact definition of program correctness.

Theorems:

P68	**require** Pre **do** b **ensure** $post$ **end** is correct if and only if $Pre \subseteq \underline{b} - post_b - post$.

Theorems:

P69	b **sp** $False$	$= Halt$
P70	b **wp** $Halt$	$= False$
P71	$Halt$ **sp** C	$= Halt$
P72	$Halt$ **wp** p	$= False$
P73	b **sp** $(p \cup q)$	$= (b$ **sp** $p) \cup (b$ **sp** $q)$
P74	b **wp** $(p \cup q)$	$\supseteq (b$ **wp** $p) \cup (b$ **wp** $q)$

(and so on). As an example of why P74 is not an equality, consider postconditions $\{[0, 1], [0, 2]\}$ for b, $\{[0, 1]\}$ for p and $\{[0, 2]\}$ for q, all with precondition $\{0\}$. Then both b **wp** p and b **wp** q are empty (since $b - p$ has postcondition $\{[0, 2]\}$ and $b - q$ has $\{[0, 1]\}$), but b **wp** $(p \cup q)$ is $\{0\}$. This property is related to the comment (after P25) that in the angelic theory p_1 does not generally refine $p_1 \cup p_2$.

Definition: Generalizing refinement to contracted programs.

If $q \subseteq p$ (q refines p), **require** Pre **do** q **ensure** $post$ **end** refines **require** Pre **do** p **ensure** $post$ **end**.

Comment: It is possible to generalize the definition further by having different *specification* parts.

Definition and theorem: Most Abstract Implementation.

P75	For feasible p, **require** $\underline{p}$ **do** p **ensure** $post_p$ **end**, the **most abstract implementation** of p, is a correct program, which every implementation of p refines.

Intuition: The most abstract implementation is the specification used as its own implementation.

4   States and Environments

The exact nature of S, the state set, varies considerably between application domains and the formalisms supporting programming (*programming languages* as defined next in Sect. 5). Some properties, however, are common to most variants.

4.1   Mappings

The state tracks the evolution, during the computation, of certain elements of information relevant to the results. As a consequence, a state almost always includes (as its essential components) one or more mappings between these elements and their current values. "Mapping" is a general term roughly equivalent to "function"; in programming, since the memories of both humans and computers are finite, these functions will also be finite. S, then, includes components of the form $Name \nrightarrow Value$ for appropriate sets of names and values.

Notation: $A \nrightarrow B$ is the set of possibly partial functions, and $A \nrightarrow\!\!\!\!\rightarrow B$ the set of finite functions, from A to B. Inclusions are: $(A \nrightarrow\!\!\!\!\rightarrow B) \subseteq (A \nrightarrow B) \subseteq (A \leftrightarrow B)$ and $(A \rightarrow B) \subseteq (A \nrightarrow B)$.

4.2   Environment and Store

It is common for the state to have two clearly identified components: the environment and the store, also known as the static and dynamic parts. In a simple variant, with a set *Var* (for "variables") of names and a set *Type* representing the types of possible values, the environment is of the form $Var \nrightarrow Type$ and the store of the form $Var \nrightarrow Value$. This division reflects the typical process of executing programs on a computer:

- A first step known as **compilation** creates the environment.
- The actual computation, known as **execution**, takes place in the second step, which builds and transforms the store, constrained by environment built in the first step.

One of the advantages of this approach is that it requires programmers to define types for every variable, making it possible to detect mistakes (such as applying a boolean operation to integer variables) in the first step; in that case the second step does not take place until the programmer has corrected the mistake. Such a process limits the risk of erroneous computation. Another advantage is that it is not necessary to repeat the first step once it has succeeded: subsequent executions of the same program, applied to different input states, can use the result of the compilation.

Definitions: Declaration, instruction.

> A function in $S \twoheadrightarrow S$ is a **declaration** if it leaves the store part unchanged, and an **instruction** if it leaves the environment part unchanged.

Intuition: It is good practice to separate the two kinds of operation; declarations set up the environment; instructions, working in a defined environment, change only the store.

Comment: The characterization of programming styles (functional, object-oriented) in Sect. 1 properly applies to the store component of the state. So do the definitions of *Skip* and *Halt* (Sect. 2.1) if we wish to treat these operations as instructions.

4.3   Notational Principles: Cartesian Product Considered Harmful

The preceding discussion has stopped short of specifying S as the cartesian product $E \times M$ where E is the environment and M (for "memory") the store. It does not even use the common programming-like "record" notation (*environment: E; store: M*) (mathematically denoting a function in *Tag* $\twoheadrightarrow$ U, where *Tag* is the set of names to the left of the colons and U the union of the sets to their right, with the constraint that the function's values for the i-th tag are in the i-th set). The two models are isomorphic and either one would be suitable for a purely mathematical discussion, but for modeling software concepts they are too constraining.

   The reason is that the theory of programs, like the development of programs, calls for more incremental notations, allowing us to extend and adapt existing models. Both cartesian product and the record notation are closed: if you have defined a concept such as "state" through a particular set of components, such as the environment and the store, and later want to add a component, you must rework all previously defined operations (functions or relations) on states. An example of such an operation is a declaration, defined as $\lambda\, e, m\,|\,[d\,(e), m]$ where d is an function on the environment (for example, if e is or includes a mapping in *Var* $\twoheadrightarrow$ *Type*, d yields a new version of the mapping, extended with a new pair such as [n, *INTEGER*]). If you add a third component to the concept of state, this definition, which yields a pair rather than a triple, no longer makes sense.

   Cartesian product is not the only culprit: definition by alternation is just as bad. It is common to use definitions of the form $L \overset{\Delta}{=} J|K$, specifying that an element of L is disjointly either an element of J or an element of K. (Again there is a simple mathematical model, applicable even if J and K are not disjoint: the notation describes pairs in $\{1, 2\} \times (J \cup K)$ such that the second element is in J for 1 and in K for 2, with generalization to any number of alternatives.) This notation suffers from the same drawback: adding an alternate breaks all previous derivations.

In programming, the "object-oriented" method of programming, with its concept of "inheritance", is an effective remedy to these problems. Solutions are also necessary on the theoretical side.

This article does not introduce the details of the appropriate notation but it is useful to see the principal convention, used as the replacement for cartesian product. When a set needs to be defined with a number of components, we give each a name, as in

S   **component**

> *environment*   : *E*
>
> *store* : *M*

This mathematical notation simply asserts the existence of two total functions, *environment* in $S \to E$ and *store* in $S \to M$. Projections are written (for a state *s*) *s. environment* and *s.store*. A function on composite objects defined from functions on their components is of the form

on *S* **update**

> *environment'*   = *d* (*envir onment*)

end

denoting a function in $S \to S$, with the important rule that the function leaves unchanged any component not named, here *store*; the example is just a notation for the function that for any state of components *e* and *m* yields the state of components *d* (*e*) and *m*. At first sight, these notations are equivalent to the cartesian product and record forms, but there is a practical difference: you can include as many "**component**" and "**on**" definitions as you like, even for the same target set *S*, in an incremental fashion. In many cases, the existing specification can remain unchanged; in particular, existing function definitions using **on** do not name the new components, and indeed in general they do not need to change them, so you can just rely on the rule that anything not named is unchanged.

Such definitions are cumulative: mathematically, the resulting specification is the cartesian product of all the **on** ... **component** declarations. (This convention assumes that the network of declarations involves no recursion; it can be extended through fixpoint techniques to support recursive definitions.) A similar convention applies to sets defined by alternation.

In both cases, a simple notation supports "lifting" an operation on a component into an operation on the whole. For example if *d* is an operation on the environment it is convenient to treat it also as an operation on the state, which as in the above **on** ... **component** example leaves all other components unchanged.

This article will not need further details of these techniques, but it is important to know of their existence, since they are useful for the practical development of specifications and programs.

4.4   Kinds of State

While the precondition is a set of states, the postcondition in the general case is a relation over two states, initial and final; a common term is "*two-state assertion*". For example, we may want to specify that the initial state contains a positive number (precondition, a set) and the final state its approximate square root (postcondition, a relation between input and output).

Some postconditions, for example "the output is positive", do not involve the initial state:

Definition: Markovian, one-state.

A postcondition *post* is **Markovian, or one-state,** if $\forall\ s, s_1, s_2 \mid (s_1 \text{ post } s) = (s_2 \text{ post } s)$

Notation: $x\ \mathbf{r}\ y$, for a relation r, expresses that $[x, y] \in r$ (the relation connects the two elements). The equality in the definition is equivalence (equality between two boolean properties).

Intuition: A Markovian postcondition characterizes only the final state, regardless of the input.

Comment: A useful program produces different results for different inputs, and so is generally not Markovian if considered as a whole. But postconditions are often expressed as intersections (conjunctions) of properties, some of which can be Markovian; for example the result's square is close to the input *and* the result is non-negative. The Markovian property can also characterize intermediate steps in the program. This observation extends to the following state properties.

Definition: Trivial, irrelevant, relevant.

For a postcondition *post*, a state s is:
- **Trivial** if $\forall\ s_1 \mid s \text{ post } s_1$.
- **Irrelevant** if $\forall\ s_1, s_2 \mid (s \text{ post } s_1) = (s \text{ post } s_2)$.
- **Relevant** if not irrelevant ($\exists\ s_1, s_2 \mid (s \text{ post } s_1) \neq (s \text{ post } s_2)$).

Intuition: If a state is trivial, a transition to *any* other state will fulfill the postcondition. If it is irrelevant, it plays no role in whether the next state satisfies the postcondition.

Theorem:

P76   A specification *<post, Pre>* is feasible if and only if every state is either trivial or relevant.

Proof: We may assume a non-empty *Pre*. ($\Rightarrow$) Assume the specification is feasible. If a state s in *Pre* is irrelevant and not trivial, s **post** s_1 holds for no s_1. Feasibility implies *Pre* $\subseteq$ *post*, meaning there is an s_1 such that s **post** s_1, yielding a contradiction. ($\Leftarrow$) Assume every state s in *Pre* is either trivial or relevant. If it is trivial, it is in *post*. If it is relevant, then there exist s_1 and s_2 so that either s **post** s_1 or s **post** s_2, so it is also in *post*.

5 Languages and Programming

"Programming" is the act of writing correct programs according to the preceding definitions. Such a program has two parts: the contract represents the goal of the program, as advertised to its users; the implementation represents the operations that will run on the computer. The definition ensures that the implementation matches the contract.

5.1 Programming Languages

If the contract is given, in the form of *Pre* and *post*, programming consists of solving **require** *Pre* **do** *b* **ensure** *post* **end**, viewed as an equation of which *b* is the unknown.

The Most Abstract Implementation, as defined above, yields a trivial solution, often non-deterministic, to the equation: $post_b = post\,/Pre$, $Pre_b = Pre$. The reason why that solution is generally of little use, and programming an interesting endeavor, is the *practical* difference between contract and implementation. For *b* we seek a relation $post_b$ that a material computer can process (not necessarily directly, but through the services of tools such as "compilers"). For the specification, since the goal is to describe the problem, we can rely on a broader set of mathematical mechanisms.

In both cases we need a repertoire of mathematical tools to build programs and specifications.

Definition: Programming language, specification language.

A **programming language** over a state set *S*, also known as a **specification language** over *S*, is a set of feasible programs over *S*. In practice it is given by:.

- A finite set of base programs, obtained from a finite set of relations in $S \leftrightarrow S$ (serving as base postconditions) and a finite set of subsets of *S* (serving as base preconditions).
- A finite set of operators for deriving new correct programs from previously defined ones.

Intuition: A programming language is a set of possible programs. Any useful programming language is infinite, but it is derived from a few basic postconditions and preconditions, and a few operators to combine them. Many of these basic elements, introduced in the earlier sections of this presentation, can be used by programming languages regardless of the application domain:

- *Havoc, Skip* and *Halt* as base programs, with *True* and *False* (*S* and $\varnothing$) as base preconditions.
- The program construction operators of Sect. 2, including the three basic ones (choice, composition and restriction) and those derived from them (concurrency, conditionals, loops).

Beyond these universal elements, a language will offer specific mechanisms for the intended application domain, beginning with a suitable set *S* of states and a suitable set of operations over *S*.

Since specification and implementation are often considered separate activities, it is frequent to find separate specification and programming languages. A better approach is to use a single language; this approach is in fact required if we want to produce *correct* programs (contracted programs), which include both a contract and an implementation. (As noted after the definition of refinement, it is possible to define a variant of the theory in which the state set changes under refinement, but at the price of much added complexity.) Many contemporary approaches to producing reliable software are hampered by this failure to understand the fundamental unity of the programming process: in spite of the obvious differences in levels of abstraction, the problems and solutions, for which this presentation offers a mathematical framework, are the same. (Reference [13] discusses the *seamlessness* of the development process in a software-engineering rather than mathematical context, and [14] develops its application to software requirements.)

Absent such a single framework, not only is it hard to produce correct software; even *expressing* what it means for the program to be correct is a challenge, since the implementation and specification belong to different worlds (such as an ordinary programming language and some specification framework). One must define a mapping between these two worlds, an approach that introduces complexity and introduces its own correctness issues.

With a single S and a single specification and programming language, the language description will identify, among the language's mechanism, the subset suitable for implementation. Then the requirement on program authors is simply to produce a final version **require** *Pre* **do** b **ensure** *post* **end** of the program in which the implementation part b only relies on that subset. Establishing correctness means establishing:

- Refinement: $b \subseteq <post, Pre>$.
- Feasibility: $Pre \subseteq post$ (or alternatively, thanks to the implementation theorem P5, $Pre_b \subseteq post_b$ if the preceding condition holds).

One can express these properties convincingly, and prove them, since all three components, *post*, *Pre* and b, are part of the same mathematical framework, even if the last one restricts itself to a subset of that framework's mechanisms.

5.2   Approaches to Programming

The most common approach to programming today ignores the *Pre* and *post* elements of the definition, concentrating only on building implementations b from a programming language with the hope that in some informal sense they will match the corresponding user needs. We may call this the "hacking approach"; it has little to commend itself if correctness is part of the objectives.

At the other extreme, a "refinement approach" [1, 15, 17] has made its mark in informatics research and led to such development methods as B. If we set out to implement a given contract, the Most Abstract Implementation theorem P75 tells us that we may use the contract itself — specifically, $<post, Pre>$ — as its own first implementation. Refinement as a software development method starts with this first version and repeatedly takes advantage of theorems to choose a "refinement" in the sense of the formal definition, P2 and P3, of the previous implementation until reaching an implementation that belongs to the implementation part of the language.

This approach is elegant but faces some obstacles:

- *Hindsight*: we seldom know the entire specification in advance. This uncertainty is not necessarily a mark of incompetent software engineering: the very process of implementation suggests new elements of specification — "esprit de l'escalier" as discussed in [13].
- *Extendibility*: even if the specification is initially clear, it usually changes as a project progresses and after initial deliveries. If a change affects a property that was used in an early step of the refinement process, it becomes necessary to redo much of the work. (*Invariants*, which play an important role in refinement methods, can help control this change process [2].)
- *Reusability*: A top-down refinement process does not easily take into account implementations previously produced for variants or subsets of the problem. It is desirable for a development process to accommodate a bottom-up component, supporting reuse.

The ideal process should combine the best elements of the "hacking" and "refinement" approaches, retaining the practicality of the first and the rigor of the second. It is not the goal of the present discussion to present such a process, but a general definition helps set the stage.

Definition: Programming.

> **Programming** is the process of devising interesting contract-implementation pairs and discharging the associated proof obligations.

The starting point for any step in the process may indifferently be:

- A contract element, for which we have to devise a satisfactory implementation (top-down).
- Existing implementation elements (bottom-up). Ideally these elements already have full contracts. In practice, they often have no contracts, or incomplete ones; part of the process then involves uncovering the precise intent of the components and writing the contracts.

This approach seems to yield the necessary flexibility while accommodating the need for rigor and proofs. It yields a useful view of programs.

Slogan: Program.

> **Program = Contract + Implementation + Proof obligation**

6   Discussion

This article applies to programming the standard method on which science and engineering rely to solve practical problems in any application domain:

- Develop a mathematical model resulting in equations (in the present case, the feasibility equation $Pre \subseteq \underline{post}$ and the program equation **require** Pre **do** b **ensure** $post$ **end**, where b is the unknown).
- Solve the equation.
- Build the solution in the application domain.

The main argument for the model developed in the preceding sections is the simplicity of its premises: the mathematical baggage is elementary set theory, learned in high school around the age of 15; the construction relies on just three mechanisms from that theory: union, composition and restriction. The approach seems to have the potential to cover all the relevant concepts of programming, although the present article takes only a first dig.

6.1   Axioms or Theorems?

In theoretical informatics the habit has often been different: devising axiomatic theories. The most developed example is the admirable work of Hoare and colleagues [7, 8]. A notable property of these efforts is that they postulate their laws; then "*of course, the mathematician should also design a model of the language, to check completeness and consistency of the laws, to provide a framework for the specifications of programs, and for proofs of correctness*" [7]. The justification for this method — postulate your ideal laws, the model will follow — is that it has, in Russell's words cited in [9], "*the advantages of theft over honest toil*".

However good the wisecrack, this is not how normal mathematics works. Unless your last name is Euclid or Peano, or your first name Alfred or Bertrand (and even in this last case, only if you have a hereditary peerage), few people will pay attention to axioms you assert on them as if walking down from Mount Sinai. Imagine a world where every mathematical concept were defined axiomatically; in trigonometry, sine and cosine would be postulated as functions satisfying certain properties — the sum of their squares is 1, the derivative of the former is the latter, and so on; and similarly for every important notion. People would quickly tire of having to make incessant leaps of faith.

We expect instead, when presented with new results, to see them *derived*, in the form of definitions and theorems, from what we already know. True, it is often a mark of elegance, for the presenter of a theory and of the laws that it satisfies, to prove that it is the simplest possible construction satisfying these laws; but it is a mark of politeness to perform this feat only as a bonus step, coming after an explanation relying only on material already familiar to the reader.

Stretching Russell's aphorism, we may note that even if Balzac's observation ("*The secret of great fortunes without apparent cause is a forgotten crime*") may explain the *origin* of some hereditary peerages, just as axioms explain the foundations of mathematics, in practice most hereditary peers find it less bothersome to obtain the objects of their daily desires through "honest toil", or at least honest means, than by stealing.

These observations do not rule out occasional reliance on the axiomatic method in the introduction of theories. Aphorisms aside, however, it is hard to justify asserting properties as postulates when they can be proved as theorems. When a manageable mathematical derivation from known concepts exists, it should be the first choice.

As the presentation of the theory of programs has attempted to show, such exactly is the situation with programming. Programs are just relations over sets. An informal and non-exhaustive review of the axioms of classic articles such as [7] and its extension to concurrency [8] (not considering properties specific to individual calculi), as well as [6, 10], suggests that most of the properties they introduce can be derived, often straightforwardly, from the framework of this article; many indeed appear above as theorems.

Many authors seem to have a suspicion, conscious or not, of the set-theoretical basis of programming; but most — an important exception is Hehner with his "predicative programming" [6] — resist the obvious solution of explicitly building the theory on that basis. They prefer to throw in axioms, even if these axioms mimic the elementary properties of set operators. A dizzying example is the seminal "Laws of Programming" article [7] (together with the more recent [8]), whose authors axiomatically introduce operators with names such as "$\cup$" for non-deterministic choice and "$\subseteq$" for refinement. They never suggest that these could actually *be* the standard mathematical operators bearing the same names; but they cover several pages of *Communications of the ACM* with such fascinating "axioms" as $P \cup (Q \cup R) = (P \cup Q) \cup R$. One wonders whether the thought ever arose that if it associates like union, commutes like union, distributes like union, and typographically uses the exact symbol of union, perhaps it is union.

6.2   Keeping Simple Things Simple

Because informatics already struggles to describe inherently complex phenomena, we should not introduce complexity of our own making. Programming theory does not always keep the complexity of the descriptions commensurate with the complexity of the described. Another seminal paper of great elegance [10] introduces the "natural semantics" of the if-then-else conditional thus:

$$\frac{\rho \,|- (E_2 \Rightarrow \alpha)}{\rho \,|- (\textbf{if } \textit{True} \textbf{ then } E_2 \textbf{ else } E_3 \textbf{ end}) \Rightarrow \alpha} Z$$

with a similar rule for the *False* case. In words: if in the environment ρ the expression E_2 evaluates to α, then in ρ the expression **if** *True* **then** E_2 **else** E_3 **end** also does. The companion rule tells us that if E_3 evaluates to β the expression with *False* instead of *True* evaluates to β.

In reality, if-then-else is a very simple concept. It expresses that one may solve a problem by partitioning the domain into two parts and using a different solution in each. Euler would undoubtedly have explained it to his 15-year-old princess pupil [4] by a little illustration:

and she would have understood on the spot. (A pedagogical presentation of the theory of programs' concepts should indeed use Euler-Venn diagrams throughout, although this article has shunned them under the presumption that its putative audience does not need pictures.)

Instead, the above "natural" semantics refers to advanced concepts of mathematical logic and notions such as the "environment" (ρ), which are a distraction from the idea of a conditional instruction. These observations do not put into question the value of [10] and other classic semantic articles, which were conceived as research advances, not tutorials. But they highlight the benefit, as a domain gets understood better, of seeking simplicity and trimming down the set of prerequisite concepts to the indispensable.

6.3   De-emphasizing the Program Text

One source of complication in theories of programming is reverence for the program text.

Almost every discussion of programming — where "almost" is just to be on the safe side — starts by defining a programming language. (Denotational or operational semantics often starts with *two* languages, one to express programs and the other to express their meanings.)

This attitude seems to be a leftover from the early days when parsing was the difficult problem. Programmers and theorists were awe-struck when Backus, Bauer, Hopper and others showed that instead of coding with zeros and ones it was possible to use a human-readable notation and have it translated automatically. The program text became the alpha and omega of programming. But it is only an artifact. A computer is a mathematical machine for computing pairs in relations. All the rest is decoration.

Programming is no more about programs than electricity is about plugs.

Parsing is the original computer science problem and even though it has long lost its theoretical difficulty it remains our unconscious template for all others. Semantic specification, for example, often looks like a smarter kind of parsing, also starting from program texts and deriving its properties — just more interesting properties. Denotational semantics, in particular, defines "meaning functions" operating on program texts. Electrical engineers, if they worked that way, would start from plugs, dutifully noting how different Swiss, French and Italian plugs are from each other. In reality, of course, what counts is the electrical current — the same in all three countries, with their interconnected networks — and specifically the relevant equations.

In programming too a more productive approach — the application to semantics of the idea of *unparsing*, the reverse of parsing — is to start from an analysis of what we need mathematically: what kinds of postconditions and preconditions give rise to useful specifications and realistic implementations. From this analysis we construct programming notations, not the other way around. For example we do not start from if-then-else as a given construct of interest, but identify the union of two relations as a relevant concept. We consequently derive suitable notations to express it, each adapted to different mathematical situations: if the relations' domains are provably disjoint, **if** C **then** p **else** q **end**; otherwise, the guarded conditional **if** $C: p$ [] $D: q$ **end**.

Far from lessening the value of the traditional objects of interest in informatics, such as programs and programming languages, this reversal of perspective makes them even more interesting, turning them from arbitrary products of taste and circumstance into rationally justified modes of expression for useful mathematical concepts.

6.4   The Basic Duality

The presentation of the theory has highlighted a characteristic property of programming: the natural need for two distinct methods to assess what a program can do and whether it will actually get to do it. This separation is hardly a revelation: in theoretical discussions of programming it recurs under many guises, such as partial correctness versus termination, safety versus liveness, loop invariants versus loop variants. The present discussion provides more evidence of its inevitability. Note the two loop theorems (Loop Correctness, P64, and Loop Feasibility, P65) and the separate definitions of "program" and "feasible program". Even the attempt to define "correct programs" in a single formula, P68, requires two operands reflecting the two sides of the question. In [3] Dijkstra also attempted to cover loops through a single rule, but in practice one must still separately use an invariant and a variant. Partly blessing, partly curse, the duality seems to be an inescapable part of informatics, reflecting some built-in limits of human reason.

7   Perspectives

The thesis of this article is that it is possible to found all of programming on a small set of concepts from elementary set theory. The discussion has shown the basic applications, but is only a start. (Also note that the theorems have not been mechanically checked.) Future tasks include:

- Reconstructing entire programming languages on that basis.
- Using the theory to build a "Formal Language Innovation Platform" (FLIP) for experimenting with programming language mechanisms.
- Developing it towards specific approaches to programming, particularly object-oriented.
- Assessing whether the approach can produce effective program verification tools.
- Assessing whether it can help teach programming, including at the elementary level.

Acknowledgments. The authors invoked explicitly or not in Sect. 6 (Hoare and coauthors, Kahn, Dijkstra, Scott/Strachey/Plotkin and other pioneers of denotational semantics), complemented by Abrial for his work on Z and B and by Mills and Gries, deserve deep acknowledgments for pioneering the formal approach to programs and programming. Back's and Morgan's seminal work on refinement (following Wirth's) is another fundamental inspiration. Hehner's work on Predicative Programming is a comprehensive theory of programming based on binary relations, corresponding to the postconditions of the present work. (I am also indebted to him for a particularly careful reading of the first draft.) Also influential have been informal comments by David Parnas on the merits of different assertion styles. A note by Shaoying Liu [16], criticizing a purported deficiency in classical refinement approaches (the risk of refining into an unfeasible program), suggested the need for a proper notion of feasibility.

I am grateful to Daniel de Carvalho and Colin Adams for corrections on the first draft.

References

1. Back, refinement papers
2. Michael Butler: Personal communication
3. Dijkstra: *A Discipline of Programming*
4. Euler: Lettres à une Princesse d'Allemagne sur divers Sujets de Physique et de Philosophie, pp. 1760–1762
5. Furia, Meyer, Velder: *Computing Surveys* invariant article
6. Hehner: *Predicative Programming*
7. Hoare: Original paper on Laws of Programming
8. Hoare, van Staden: Newer article
9. Hoare, van Staden: Slides accompanying [8]
10. Kahn: *Natural Semantics*
11. Meyer: IFIP 1980 paper
12. Meyer: ETL
13. Meyer: OOSC
14. Meyer: *Multirequirements*
15. Morgan: *Programming from Specifications*
16. Shaoying Liu: paper and slides from the 2014 Futatsugi Festschrift
17. Wirth: Stepwise refinement

Author Index

Printed in the United States
By Bookmasters